The **Smart Woman's Guide** to Midlife Horses

Finding Meaning, Magic and Mastery in the Second Half of Life

MELINDA FOLSE

FOREWORD BY KOELLE SIMPSON

INTRODUCTION BY CLINTON ANDERSON

TRAFALGAR SQUARE
North Pomfret, Vermont

First published in 2011 by
Trafalgar Square Books
North Pomfret, Vermont 05053

Printed in China

Library of Congress Cataloging-in-Publication Data
Folse, Melinda.
  The smart woman's guide to midlife horses : finding meaning, magic, and mastery in the second half of life / Melinda Folse.
    p. cm.
  Includes index.
  ISBN 978-1-57076-466-0
1. Middle-aged women–Psychology. 2. Middle-aged women–Attitudes. 3. Horsemen and horsewomen–Psychology. 4. Horses–Psychological aspects. I. Title.
  HQ1059.4.K35 2011
  646.70082–dc22
                                  2011009860

Book design by Carrie Fradkin
Cover design by RM Didier
Front cover photo by Karen Patterson
Back cover photo by Darrell Dodds
Typefaces: ITC Bauhaus, Front Page

10 9 8 7 6 5 4 3 2 1

Dedication

To midlife horses and all they bring to our lives—and to all the women who dust off their dreams to make a bold and carefree gallop into the second half of life.

"Life is made of moments, small pieces of glittering mica in a long stretch of grey cement. It would be wonderful if they came to us unsummoned, but particularly in lives as busy as the ones most of us lead now, that won't happen. We have to teach ourselves how to live, really live . . . to love the journey, not the destination."

–Anna Quindlen, *A Short Guide to a Happy Life*

Contents

Foreword by Koelle Simpson ix

Author's Note x

Acknowledgments xi

Introduction by Clinton Anderson xiii

1 Are you a "woman of a certain age"?   1

One sure way to know we've reached the "intermission" in our life is an undeniable urge to overlay our childhood dreams with our present reality—and then project forward and wonder if we're ever going to be able to make those dreams come true.

2 Why horses? Why now?   11

The mystical and magical connection between humans and horses is well documented and woven through civilizations, cultures, and generations. But perhaps the most pronounced and profound examples of this connection are the relationships that develop between women and horses.

3 Take the reins   35

Making the decision to reignite an old passion—in this case, adding horses to the middle of your life—can either be much more complicated or much simpler than you think. It all depends on the decisions you make, and how you make them. Here are a few things to consider, a few options to ponder, and a few tips for processing this half-ton decision.

4 Leg up!   55

Competitors know that "getting a horse legged up" means getting him in physical condition to do what he is being asked to do without risking injury. For the returning rider or the middle-aged woman riding horses for the first time, this is equally important—and for the same reasons. So before you can get serious about a horse, you need to get serious about your fitness.

5 Find your happy trail 79

Maybe you still have your childhood jumping saddle stashed away under a pile of your kids' outgrown clothing. Maybe you've always pictured yourself out in Big Sky Country, galloping across an open field on the back of a horse. Maybe you want horses in your life, but can't ride for any number of reasons. Maybe you have no idea. What will your happy midlife trail look like? In this chapter we'll take a look at some horse-related activities and disciplines that could be your next step on this bold and exciting journey of self-discovery.

6 Finding the magic 109

Now that you've made the life-altering decision to follow your dream, and you're beginning to have an idea of what your horse experience might look like, what's next? Most people don't realize the many options that exist for today's horse enthusiast. Here are a few tips on determining which midlife horse experience is the best fit for you, your riding needs, your lifestyle, and your budget.

7 Good horsekeeping 135

While entire volumes can be—and are—written on how to properly care for a horse, here are a few key areas to consider, along with important questions to ask the experts as you remodel your life to include a horse.

8 Healthy as a horse 167

Horse health is a subject as full of controversy as any you'll find in the equine world. From those who consider horses delicate creatures in need of constant care and coddling to the crusty old cowboy at the other end of the spectrum, knowledge and technology offer many options as we seek solid middle ground for the very best care we can provide.

9 Let's get tacky 205

Without guidance, stepping into the worldwide tack shop can be an overwhelming, confusing, and downright dizzying experience. But, if like me, your eyes glaze over and your brain locks up when too much advice starts flowing, here's just enough basic information to help you get tacky enough to ride while keeping you safe and your horse comfortable.

10 Getting there   *227*

Whether you board or keep your horse at home, whether you trail ride or compete, the day will come when you'll face the big "truck-and-trailer" quandary. With shows any number of miles away and veterinary hospitals sometimes across town (and country-side), there's a certain peace-of-mind that comes with having a rig of your own parked out back. Even when that's not the case, you still need to be able to get your horse ON a trailer from time to time. Here's what you need to "get there" safely.

11 Picking up the correct lead   *239*

When it comes to matters of the horse, is everyone you talk to a know-it-all? Are you confused by conflicting advice? Have you ever felt worse instead of better after a riding lesson? In the pages ahead, successful midlife horse owners share why it's crucial to align with the training information and approach that makes sense to you, and find riding buddies and teachers that have your best interests at heart.

12 Plateaus and ruts—and FEAR...Oh My!   *269*

When we start out on this midlife journey, we might imagine it's all exhilarating gallops on grassy fields and sandy beaches, but the reality is, having horses in your life is just as likely to challenge you at times as it is to fulfill you in ways you desperately need. It's easy to get stuck, and there's a good chance that something, somewhere along the way may scare you back OUT of the saddle. Here are a few useful tools for conquering the fears that having horses may bring to light.

13 From the horse's mouth   *287*

Trouble with a horse, the great horsemen of our time will tell you, almost always comes down to some kind of breakdown in communication—and more often than not, the breakdown is on our end. Here are some surprising insights on taking your horsemanship to a whole new level by learning to listen to your horse.

14 Full circles and half-passes   *303*

Sometimes the midlife horse journey is a jagged path to success, where progress just doesn't always follow a straight line. In fact, sometimes it looks a little bit like going backward. And sideways. And occasionally, in circles. But if you examine these experiences closely, chances are good you'll find the lesson you came looking for, disguised as a horse problem that you must solve to continue your journey. Bless these things—they're your pot of gold at the end of a long, colorful rainbow.

Resources & Selected Bibliography   *311*
Index   *318*

"Interacting with [horses] on their own terms encourages a fluidity of human thought, emotion, and behavior that sedentary twenty-first-century life makes difficult. Horses also model the strengths of what are often referred to as 'feminine values': cooperation over competition, relationship over territory, responsiveness over strategy, emotion and intuition over logic, process over goal, and the creative approach to life that these qualities engender."

–Linda Kohanov, *Riding Between the Worlds*

foreword

By Koelle Simpson

As a Master Life Coach trained by Martha Beck—Life Coach, O, The Oprah Magazine columnist, and best-selling author—and student of the world renowned "horse whisperer" Monty Roberts, I've learned firsthand about the incredible impact horses can have on helping women reconnect with their true spirit.

After many years, apprenticeships, and training, I am now what you might call an "Equus Coach." I share this work around the globe, and help others to discover the empowering lessons that horses are teaching us every day about how to lead more joyful lives.

It is not uncommon for a participant in one of my workshops to feel the velvety muzzle of a horse gently nuzzling her shoulder and all at once begin to tear up. In an instant, this four-legged teacher calls upon her to remember the pure joy that comes from melting with nature into the present moment.

Melinda Folse speaks to those women whose hearts yearn for this reconnection at a time when life seems to have run its own course and childhood dreams of playing with horses are only a vague memory. She not only helps you to rekindle the possibility of bringing a little equine energy into your life, but Folse also takes you on a gentle journey of small steps to help your childhood passion become a reality.

Once you have discovered it is "never too late," Folse takes the time to thoroughly guide you through the sometimes confusing and overwhelming horse industry. She helps you steer clear of the unnecessary stress that can accompany the horse world and keeps you on a realistic course with your desire to recharge your soul.

The Smart Woman's Guide to Midlife Horses is down-to-earth, witty, and filled with practical wisdom. It is a must-read for midlife women who yearn to reignite their inner childhood dream: to dance in life alongside or aboard an equine companion.

Koelle Simpson
Life Coach & Horse Whisperer
www.KoelleInc.com

Author's Note

When I went to work for Australian horse trainer and clinician Clinton Anderson, it followed about two years of studying his Method and practicing it with my own horses. Then, as the writer who helped Clinton develop and put his book *Lessons Well Learned* and many other materials into print, I developed an even greater appreciation for the road-tested wisdom Clinton brings to helping horses and humans learn to get along.

This book, which sprang quite naturally out of my firsthand observations of this work and its particular effectiveness with women like me, might well have been titled "Downunder Horsemanship, From the Inside Out." So, if it seems like I'm playing favorites in the pages ahead, I am. As just one of many middle-aged women now trying to go from "horse lover" to "horsewoman," I so appreciate the foundation Downunder Horsemanship provides that, regardless of new knowledge I've acquired, Clinton's Method continues to permeate my thinking and writing when it comes to dealing with horses.

As I continue my own horsemanship journey, I'm always glad for the time I've invested in the foundation Clinton's program offers—and for my own "lessons well learned."

Oh, and one more thing. That "Smart Woman" in the title of this book? I think you'll see in the coming pages that it *definitely* isn't me we're talking about! But hopefully, if you can use my missteps as your guideposts in your own midlife horse journey, that Smart Woman could be YOU!

Happy trails!

Melinda Folse

Acknowledgments

I could never count all the two- and four-legged beings who helped me with the creation of this book; to everyone I talked to, bugged with questions, and followed around with camera and notebook, I extend my deepest gratitude for your generosity, patience, and kindness. In addition to this "blanket" of thanks, I also extend special acknowledgement to:

Sam Horn, creative consultant, for her enthusiastic help in developing this concept and showing me its potential; Clinton Anderson and the Down-under Horsemanship team for letting me ride along and experience the thrill of watching people learn to live their horsemanship dreams; Deborah McCormick, PhD, for her special insights on the many connections between horses and humans—and how this especially relates to midlife women.

The fine team at Trafalgar Square Books—from the delightful-to-work-with Martha Cook, to the talented and patient editor/designer Rebecca Didier, and to the admirably restrained Caroline Robbins (for not killing me when this project took on a life—and girth—that surprised us all). I, and the many women who will hopefully find this book helpful, thank you for believing in this project and seeing it through in such an exciting way.

The Fort Worth Horseshoe Club where the idea for this book actually originated on morning rides with Teresa and Margie. I wish for everyone on this midlife horse journey such a community of friendship, support, and camaraderie. Special thanks go to Carole, Jill, Margie, Sheryl, Jane (both of them!), Janeil, Linda, Kathy, Sherri, Betty, Linden, and countless others there who contributed their thoughts, ideas, observations, and experiences to the development of this book. Deep appreciation also to Tommy Blackmon, Fort Worth Horseshoe Club manager, for our many conversations that led to further exploration and development of this book's horsekeeping content.

Barbara Epps and the Old People's Riding Club chapter based at McClendon Community College's Highlander Ranch in Waco, Texas, and to the staff, therapists, and clients of R.E.A.C.H. Therapeutic Riding Center in McGregor, Texas; Kathy Taylor, founder of HerdWise, in Weatherford, Texas, for letting me watch her sessions and witness the truth as only horses can tell it.

A crackerjack team of readers and content evaluators at all three levels of horsemanship (beginning, intermediate, and advanced), representing both English and Western riding disciplines: Gail, Emily, Kathy, Barbara, Carole, Kristen, and Pam.

Technical expertise gained in live interviews with Buck Neil, DVM; Juliette Getty, PhD (Getty Equine Nutrition); Michael and Margaret Korda; Dr. Deb Bennett (Equine Studies Institute); Purdue University Animal Science Department; Emily Kutz (Sport Horse Massage); Adreinne Richwine, DC; Dave Genadek, Master Saddle Maker (About the Horse); and Ron McDaniel (McDaniel Saddlery). In addition to these live interviews, I appreciate all who contributed their knowledge on the more technical subjects (they're listed in the Resources, p. 311) for giving us all plenty of "places to dig."

In addition to the patient, generous, amazing, and entertaining teaching abilities of Clinton Anderson, I express my sincere thanks to Ian Francis, Everett Mrakava, Denise Barrows, Liz Graves, Greg Dial—and countless others who contributed to this book without even knowing it through their writing, DVDs, and live presentations (please see their names, products, and materials listed in the Resources). This is intended to be a guidebook of sorts—a cross-referencing of ideas and information that helped me—designed to help you seek and find your own answers.

I also must take a moment to acknowledge my family—and express my appreciation for their patient support of my lifelong horsecraziness: Mom and Dad, who taught me how to love without condition, how to keep my feet on the ground (even with my head in the clouds), and how to find the courage to dig in my heels when I need to, regardless of how big the thing is on the other end of the line; Kristen and Ali, my beautiful daughters who bless my life every day with laughter, love, and continual amazement; and David, my love, my friend, and my own personal cheerleader. Thank you all for believing in me even when I forget to believe in myself.

And to Susan Williams, who, after making that first midlife horse introduction, has provided me with a steady supply of friendship, laughter, "questionable" instruction, and just enough badgering to keep me going when I wanted to give up. I owe her. Big time. And by the way, Susan, that horse you sold me does too buck and spook, and he's ALL attitude—but now that I know he's just a "mirror," I suppose it's obvious that he's also just right. And at least you also brought me to Rio, my kinder, gentler, more playful reflection. Thanks to you, these two guys have infused my midlife journey with new excitement, fresh challenges, and the rediscovery of a long-lost dream.

Introduction

By Clinton Anderson

The American Horse Council Foundation tells us that of the more than 9.2 million horses in the United States today, 75 percent are owned by women over the age of forty. This statistic doesn't surprise me at all; in fact, I see it reflected at every tour stop and every clinic I teach across the nation. For me, there is nothing more professionally gratifying than to see the look on these women's faces when they overcome a personal obstacle with their horses.

Women at this time of life are looking for many different things in their relationships with their horses. I make my living giving them tools to help them find whatever they are looking for with their horses—and to stay safe in the process. What bothers me most in observing the sometimes turbulent relationship between midlife women and their horses is how often I see women who have chosen the wrong horse, women who are getting pushed around by their horses, and women who are afraid to do the very things that will bring them the happiness and satisfaction they are looking for.

In gathering this broad range of information into one book for you, Melinda Folse has touched on many of the issues these women face when dealing with horses at this time of life. And, while choosing horses as your midlife adventure can be one of the best things you can do for yourself, it can also be one of the most challenging things—mentally, physically, and emotionally—you have ever done. To meet these challenges safely and effectively, you need to be able to find good information, and then make informed decisions in the face of many different options.

After working with her on my most recent book, *Lessons Well Learned*, I can tell you that that not only is this a subject very close to Melinda's heart, but it also taps into her professional passion for presenting solid, usable information in a very readable way. I can also assure you that she has dug to the very bottom of these issues (and probably drove each person she interviewed half crazy with about a million questions) to bring you the very best information she could find on these topics—and then to help you raise your own questions as she points you in the direction of some first rate resources for learning more.

When it comes to horses, learning is constant, and no matter how much you know, there is always more we all can learn. So happy reading, mates, and if I can ever help you on your midlife horsemanship journey, Melinda has made sure you know where to find me!

Clinton Anderson
Trainer, Clinician, and Founder of Downunder Horsemanship®
www.downunderhorsemanship.com

"Time doesn't change a person — it just helps you get a better handle on who you are"

—Dara Torres, five-time Olympian and author of *Age Is Just a Number*

Are you a "woman of a certain age"?

One sure way to know we've reached the "intermission" in our life is an undeniable urge to overlay our childhood dreams with our present reality—and then project forward and wonder if we're ever going to be able to make those dreams come true.

SOMETIME DURING THE SUMMER of my forty-fifth year, I found myself standing before a pen of horses for sale. I wasn't there for myself. My father, with whom I have shared a life-long love of horses and a desire to someday have "a house with a barn," had finally achieved his dream. Some-one had given him a horse, and now he needed another horse to keep the "free one" company. So actually, it was my father's horse that needed a horse. Dad's invitation to "go look at a horse" had been too good to resist. (I also thought there might be barbeque involved.) As Dad and the agent discussed the relative merits of the horses before us, I watched an adjacent pen of geldings milling around, and I felt the old familiar tug of longing. But this time it was accompanied by a new sensation—a profound sadness I had never felt before. Now, make no mistake. I had dealt with sadness. Adult life had already knocked me to my knees with several soul-rattling disappointments. This came from another place entirely, and seemingly out of nowhere, tears welled up.

In her book, *Finding Your Own North Star* (Crown Publishers, 2001), Martha Beck tells us that when observing or remembering something brings unexpected tears to your eyes, your emotions are telling you that you need the type of experience you're observing or remembering. For me, the answer was obvious. I was 45 years old and not living at all the life I had once imagined for myself. Not that my life was bad, mind you. It was actually very good—filled to overflowing with blessings too numerous to count.

But something was missing. As so many women do at this time in life, I realized that the path I was on was leading farther and farther away from my heart's oldest desire—to ride and own horses. Drawing from a passage in Dante's *Divine Comedy*, penned in the middle ages (and by a man, no less), Martha Beck quotes: "right in the middle of my life, I realized I wasn't where I wanted to be . . .and I don't know how I ended up so off course."

In the course of the soul-searching that followed, and in the time it took to develop this book, I hit upon several insights and observations that make Dante's historic observation seem normal, relevant, and in an odd way, hopeful rather than tragic. I feel they provide the perfect impetus for making the most of this pivotal time and developing a strategy for recapturing the essential being you were at 15, and remaining true to her dreams as you enter the second half of your life.

"Seasons change, but all of them are spectacular"

In *Simple Abundance: A Daybook of Comfort and Joy* (Grand Central Publishing, 2009), Sarah Ban Breathnach remarks on the quaint—if unintentional—accuracy of the famous French description of middle-aged women as "women of a certain age." Ban Brethnach makes the point that this is, in fact, the age at which we become *more certain of ourselves* as our "authenticity" emerges. "I think it's vital," she writes, "for us to change the concept of feminine aging from 'invisible' to 'vibrant.'"

That day when I went horse shopping with my dad, I realized that instead of feeling more vibrant, I was just plain exhausted. I knew my malaise had something to do with being so far off the course I thought my life would take, but I didn't have a clue what to do about it. I felt so disconnected from my childhood dreams I could barely remember what they were, much less figure out how to attain them.

In her book *The Age of Miracles: Embracing the New Midlife* (Hay House, 2008), Marianne Williamson explores the idea that midlife gives us the unparalleled opportunity to find new depth to our life and dreams. By setting our intention on "aging within our joy," she contends, we can make our midlife years (and beyond) something to celebrate and cherish. It occurred to me as I read Williamson's book that the key to living with this kind of "joyful intent" lies in being able to zero-in on our personal dreams—for some it might be art, for others music or working with children. Still others may need to take off for places unknown on a big, loud Harley. My heart's desire has always centered around horses—and the numbers show that I'm not alone in this infatuation.

The good news for me was that my dad's newly acquired "horse life" offered me an apparently much-needed place of re-entry, but how exactly could I act on this opportunity without completely obliterating the precarious balance that was my already over-packed, over-committed, over-complicated existence? What good is it to know what will make you happy if you can't make room for it in your life?

What do you really, *really* want?

This may sound like a simple question, but it sometimes takes a little introspection to figure out. We often must first identify the feeling of having what we most definitely *do not* want before we can identify the feeling of all the things we *do* want. Latching on to these two feelings (Martha Beck's book, which I mentioned on p. 2, details exercises designed to help us identify these feelings in a very visceral way), we attune our hearts to the voice of our "essential self." From this we can measure everything that comes our way as that which *is* and that which *is not* aligned with what we really, *really* want.

When you listen to what your feelings are really telling you, then you can begin to weed out the "true possibilities" from the "truly out of reach." For example, I love to watch reining competition, so unsurprisingly, I dallied with the fantasy of becoming a top reiner in my fifties. But this dream required time, travel, top-notch facilities, perfect arena footing, extremely well-bred and well-trained horses, superior riding ability, and oh yes, a bottomless budget. When I imagined the stress of constant travel, the anxiety of competition, the lonely ache I get when I'm away from my family, the immense amount of time it would take to learn the sport and practice with a trainer, and the related expenses that would mean giving up other things I enjoy in my everyday life, it made my stomach hurt. That was my essential self saying, "No!"

But when I thought about just getting a horse of my own and learning to ride through a rollback, loping those big easy, then small, collected circles, and maybe even doing a flying lead change or two, my heart beat a little faster and I could just feel the exhilaration of moving like that with a horse—a resounding, "Yes!" from my essential self.

▦ How do you get *there*, from where you are right now?

Once you discover what you really, *really* want (what Martha Beck describes as "the canary in the coal mine of your soul, singing away

EXERCISE

Four Questions to Help You Identify What You Really, **Really** Want

1   What am I feeling?
2   Why am I feeling this way?
3   What will it take to make me feel better about this?
4   What is the most effective way to get that?

From *Finding Your Own North Star* by Martha Beck (Three Rivers Press, 2002).

EXERCISE

Locate Your "Joy"

1   Write a short quick description of the situation that best completes each of following statements:

The last time I:

‣   laughed until I couldn't catch my breath.

‣   lost track of time while working on something.

‣   woke up excited about a brand new idea.

‣   cried tears of joy.

‣   made someone laugh or smile without meaning to.

2   Looking at your answers, do you see an activity, event, or experience that appears more than once? If so, this could be your "joy." What are three things you can do this week to work even a moment of this activity into your life?

3   This time next week, make a date with yourself to sit and start a journal describing these moments quickly, in the fullest detail possible, along with any feelings or emotions that are present before, during, or after these experiences.

4   Repeat this process weekly.

5   Determine additional actions you can take to get more of your "joy" in your life.

under tons of bedrock"), what should you do about it? The consistent wisdom of the experts is, above all else, to heed the urgency of this call. Begin *now*. "At midlife, we see the endgame," Marianne Williamson writes in *The Age of Miracles*. "No more time for meandering detours, relationships that don't serve, situations that aren't authentic. No more time for any of the psychic roadblocks between you and the joy meant to be yours."

It's time, midlife sisters, to recapture our runaway horse dreams and bring them back to the main road of our life's journey. Where do you start? "Once you've figured out what brings you genuine joy," Williamson advises, "begin filling your life with as much of it as possible." Just as we constantly hear fitness experts encouraging us to work exercise into our daily life and routine by taking the stairs instead of the elevator, parking farther away from the door of the grocery store, tightening our abs while we brush our teeth, and clenching our butt cheeks while pausing the car at stoplights, we can find dozens of small ways to add a little bit of "horse" into the various spaces in our days, for example:

>) Join an online community or singles group dedicated to people of a "horsey" turn of mind, and visit it regularly.

>) Subscribe to a horse magazine dedicated to your favorite horse sport, and carve out 15 minutes a day to enjoy it.

>) Pull over next to that horse farm you drive by on your way to work, lean against the fence for five minutes, watch the yearlings capering, and just *breathe*.

The funny thing is that once you wedge that "joy foot" in the door, it usually finds a way to wiggle the rest of the way into your life. So the first step from *here* to *there*, it appears, is following Martha Beck's two noteworthy rules:

Rule #1: If it brings you joy, do it.

Rule #2: No, really. If it brings you joy, do it.

Of course, it must be noted that, even when you find a way to add horses to your life—whether for the first time ever or for the first time in a long time—there is still a sense of balance that must be maintained. Sometimes this is a matter of trial and error, but always it is a matter of staying tuned in to the voice of your essential self. (Remember the stomach ache I got when I imagined trying to become a serious reiner?) There is a chance that you'll be swept away by the joy of it all, and before you know it, your life really could be out of control. (I talk more about this in chapter 3—pp. 40–51.) The key to making all this work at midlife, unlike when you're young and energy and time seems to have no limits, is remembering to keep listening to that voice within you and following its wisdom to find—and maintain—the right balance.

▥ **What do you *think*?**

Upon considerable reflection I agree with Marianne Williamson's opinion that many, if not most, of our typical thoughts about midlife and middle age are outdated and no longer fit who we are as twenty-first-century human beings. "If we want to create something new for ourselves," she writes," we have to recognize how limiting traditional thoughts about age are—and then let them go."

Although you may not realize it, such thoughts as "My best riding years are behind me," or "I missed my chance to ride with so-and-so," or "My life led me away from horses," can be damaging to your ability to make them part of your reality *now*. Because our experiences reflect our thoughts, the way to *doing* better at this time of life—or at any time of life, for that matter—is *thinking* better. Here are some guidelines for evaluating the "quality" of your thoughts:

> ❭ Are you starting to define yourself more by *what you aren't any-more*, rather than *what you are*?

⟩ Are you choosing the path of least resistance?

⟩ Are you satisfied with being part of the "lost generation," or do you want to be part of "the generation that lost a decade or two while finding themselves"?

⟩ Is midlife going to be a cruise to the *end of your life*, or a cruise to the *meaning in your life*?

The key to having horses at midlife is changing the way you *think* about having horses at midlife:

⟩ Instead of, "I wish I had been a working student for so-and-so when I had the chance," think "I will audit a clinic with so-and-so early next summer."

⟩ Instead of, "I should have pursued riding when I was young and athletic," think "Learning to ride in middle age will be a concussion-free way to tone my body and keep me fit."

⟩ Instead of, "I should have bought my own horse before I had kids," think "It will be so much fun to teach the girls how to help me with barn chores."

Telling yourself that the time to have enjoyed horses is in your past is so often the "path of least resistance"...dare to choose a different trail, and the challenges will be far exceeded by your eventual rewards.

Getting a handle on who we are

When five-time Olympic swimmer Dara Torres staged her third professional comeback to compete at age 41 in the 2008 Olympic Games in Beijing, she became the oldest female Olympic swimmer ever. Torres said she didn't feel old, but rather, "happily middle-aged," adding, "Besides, the water doesn't know how old you are." (Horses don't know how old you are either. Or if they do, they're not talking about it!)

When I read this in *Age Is Just a Number: Achieve Your Dreams at Any Stage in Life* (Crown Archetype, 2009), the book Torres wrote with Elizabeth Weil just after becoming the winner of more Olympic medals than in any swimmer in history, I smiled. Dara did all women proud. But that's not why she did it. In fact, she says she's confused and humbled to find herself the poster child for women pursuing midlife hopes and dreams. "I started swimming again for myself," she writes. "I kept going because I wanted to—it made me happy and gave meaning to my life. It helped me remember the joy."

Torres was determined to push past the self-limiting beliefs people hold about age and sought to learn for herself what she could expect her body to be able to do. She discovered a performance model created by a Yale University Economist named Ray Fair that predicted performance at specific age markers with a table he called "The Fair Model." Fair reported that the deterioration rate was insignificant in middle age, and that he wondered whether society has been too pessimistic about the potential athletic performance of older individuals who stay healthy and fit.

Torres also relates a story about running through Central Park, wondering if she was indeed too old for a comeback...then she was passed by a woman in her seventies!

Nevertheless, as Torres honestly notes in her book, the reunion with one's passion isn't always immediately blissful. "For the first few laps I felt sluggish and winded, unconnected to the water I used to love," she writes, "In five minutes, however, I felt happy to be back in the pool, to feel that old sense of connection, to soak up the quiet peace—even the smell of the chlorine was a relief."

Reading that passage brought to mind that awkward disconnection I felt the few times I'd been on a horse's back in recent years, and how, moments later when the old familiar connection returned, I was filled with an exhilaration as inexplicable as it is unforgettable.

Speaking as an older professional athlete, with wisdom that applies particularly well to riding and owning horses midlife, Torres asserts that "if you want to make it work, you can; you just have to be smarter about your preparation and more efficient." That's really what this book is about—being smarter, more prepared, and making having horses work well enough, most of the time, so that we get to keep on doing it.

Finding your dream, or returning to it, later in life can reveal very different benefits than what you may have considered important in your youth. Torres talks about how swimming "teaches you to rein in your thoughts and come back to the present so you can focus on the small details." Dealing with horses calls for this same kind of in-the-moment presence, and is precisely what creates the rich layers in life that we so deeply crave, and that have likely been missing during years of meeting the constant needs of others, as well as the numerous distractions in a busy woman's life.

2

Why horses? Why now?

The mystical and magical connection between humans and horses is well documented and woven through civilizations, cultures, and generations. But perhaps the most pronounced and profound examples of this connection are the relationships that develop between women and horses.

LIKE SO MANY WOMEN, BY THE TIME I spent that afternoon "looking at a horse" with my dad, I had spent the past two decades riding the life roller-coaster. Although there were plenty of ups to balance the downs—and I knew I had much to be grateful for—a sense of malaise was settling over me, and a strange uneasiness was taking root in my soul. How had my life gotten so far away from what I once dreamed it would be? What happened to my dream of a little house with a barn and a few horses just outside my back door? Even though I was technically in charge of a lot of things in my life, I had no idea where my independence and power had gone.

"A lot of women, especially at this time of life, have lost touch with who they are on the inside," say the "Doctors McCormick," co-authors of *Horse Sense and the Human Heart* (HCI, 1997) and *Horses and the Mystical Path* (New World Library, 2004). Reconnecting with *any* lost dream can help regain that missing sense of "self," or your "inner lead mare." They theorize that many women feel drawn to horses at midlife because the very nature of horses demands that we locate this "inner lead mare" and summon a full arsenal of self-preservation skills, as well, which also may have gotten lost in the midlife shuffle. "To command the attention, respect, and willing response of a horse," the McCormicks write, "you have to communicate from that core strength of your 'inner lead mare.'"

Where's *your* "inner lead mare?"

Horses see you for exactly who you are *on the inside*. In order to communicate with them, you have to be "real" and honest. Because this kind of authenticity is what many women are searching for at midlife, many of them find it in working with horses. "As you encounter the primordial forces of the cosmos within the horse," writes McCormick, "you gain a keen sense of direction, composure, and inner strength, teaching you to elevate your desires and increase your capacity to love."

I experienced this concept firsthand during a week-long "Equine Experience" retreat at Hacienda Tres Aguilas, near San Antonio, Texas. Here, the three "Doctors McCormick"—Deborah (director and trainer), her mother, Adele von Rust McCormick, PhD (director), and her father, the late Tom McCormick, MD (consultant and training coach)—have done more than 35 years of pioneering work integrating traditional psychotherapy with horses and using it with their psychiatric patients.

However, as I discovered (and am still discovering), this magical and mystical transformative process is not something that happens in a week—and at first, it can be just plain ugly.

"Move the horse without touching or speaking to her," Deborah McCormick instructed me during the demonstration of an exercise on the next-to-last day of the Equine Experience Retreat. At that point I had no idea how to "move a horse from the inside." The day before, an aging Peruvian Horse named Maximo had demonstrated for the group how he could use his buddy sourness to play my overactive nurturing instinct like a cheap fiddle. Then, as I later tried to lead him "with authority," he plain-old ignored my pace and used each turn as opportunity to graze, oblivious to my yanks on the lead rope. "Max sees that you have no boundaries," McCormick explained to me and to the group. The message resonated with issues I had dealt with time and again in my life, without resolution.

Now here we were again, this time with a mare. "Go ahead," McCormick coaxed, "just walk toward her in a way that tells her to move that shoulder out of your path." This time we were working with a young mare who observed all of us as if she was fully aware of her role as "teacher." (I once had a college professor who surveyed her new incoming class with the same expression.) And how do you move a horse without speaking or touching her? The concept seemed ridiculous.

McCormick waited. My fellow retreat participants waited. So I took a deep breath and gathered up my "inner whatever," and staring intently at that front shoulder, I walked as forcefully as I knew how toward the mare. She didn't budge. She didn't even look my way. If she had thought of it, I think she would have yawned. Everyone laughed.

"Let me show you what I mean," McCormick said. She moved deliberately toward the mare. The mare's head went up and she moved two steps sideways. Something about the mare's reaction silenced all of us. It was obvious that the horse felt the change in energy coming from McCormick. I didn't know how to get it, but I recognized the second I saw it that whatever moved that mare back was *exactly* what was missing in my life.

"When you've lost touch with your core being, you've lost touch with what I call your 'inner lead mare mentality and attitude,'" McCormick explained. Rebuilding this inner strength gives you the opportunity to create impact. "It gives you the power from within to move the world in a nonlocal way," she said. "This is not about aggression, but about inner authority—knowing for certain *who you are* and *what you want* and accepting nothing less."

"Given half a chance, horses quite naturally draw out and reinforce the authentic self," says Linda Kohanov, author of *Riding Between the Worlds* (New World Library, 2007). "It's like they have been waiting for thousands of years to catch us offguard to help us remember who we really are—in part, I suppose, so they can finally be appreciated for who *they* really are."

EXERCISE

Lead Mare Lesson

This exercises requires that you already have established a "horsey" refuge of some sort—a boarding or lesson stable, or a friend's barn.

1   Set aside a chunk of quiet time to watch a herd of horses (more than two). Sit quietly nearby, observing their behavior as they move around their pasture. Watch how the lead mare moves the others from place to place. Take your journal and describe each interaction.

2   Now try to reenact these interactions with a horse, preferably one you don't know well—a school horse at the barn or a friend's. Summon your "inner lead mare" and focus on a specific part of the horse, such as the shoulder or hindquarters. Try to move that part of the horse without speaking to him or touching him. Write down what happens.

3   Continue the exercise, but change the part of the horse you try to move.

EXERCISE

Awaken Your Horse Sense

1   Take your journal and go sit with a horse—in his stall or near his paddock or pasture. Don't touch or speak to the horse, but instead just write down anything that crosses your mind. No matter how random or seemingly unrelated, write your thoughts and feelings.

This exercise, first engineered by author Linda Kohanov, does the following:

▸ Sharpens your sensory awareness

▸ Gives you a glimpse of your ambient feelings, emotional resonance, non-verbal thoughts

▸ Builds a sense of trust between your mind and body

▸ Acquaints you with your critical inner voices that can block the flow of information

"Mirror, mirror"...how can a horse see in me what I can't?

In the study of psychology, *mirroring* is a behavior when one person reflects another person's body movements, breathing, and attitude while engaged in social interaction. Experts tend to agree that horses posses an innate ability to resonate with human emotions—the horse simply "reads" and "mirrors back to you" your own feelings and emotional state. (I, of course, wonder exactly what my midlife horses are mirroring in me—and more importantly, what I should do about it!)

In *Riding Between the Worlds* Kohanov classifies this kind of equine-inspired wisdom as "embodied spirituality—fully present in this world while deeply connected with the soul's divine origins." This mirroring, she explains in the many layers of her enlightening book, "is devoid of ambition or ulterior motive" and allows riding to become "an adventure in self-discovery more honest than many purely human works of art."

Like me, Kohanov struggled to understand and articulate for others what this "discovery" means, and what to do with this understanding once we have it. So she gathered the research and wisdom of the likes of Karla McLaren (social science researcher and author of *The Language of Emotions*—www.karlamclaren.com); Peter Levine, PhD (Research Director at Tufts University, author of *Waking the Tiger*, and expert in trauma resolution—www.peterlevine.ws); Elaine Aron, PhD (author of *The Highly Sensitive Person*—www.hsperson.com); and Kathleen Ingram (life coach, consultant, holistic counselor, equine assisted therapist—www.sacredplaceofpossibility.com), and came up with the following human characteristics commonly mirrored in horses.

) Fear
) Depression
) Sadness
) Frustration
) Vulnerability
) Anger

When we recognize that a horse's behavior is quite often a mirror of our emotional state, and when we pinpoint exactly what that reflection is trying to show us (Kohanov gives us some help in this area in *Riding Between the Worlds*), then we can get to work changing our inner emotional landscape. "Transformation," Kohanov writes, "is a natural process that flows without forcing, as simple as a pony ride, as powerful as a hurricane, as gentle and miraculous as wings unfolding in the soft shadows of a misty Kentucky pasture."

Beautiful imagery, isn't it, for something that can initially start out so ugly? As author and poet Anaïs Nin once said, "And the day came when the risk to remain tight in a bud was more painful than the risk it took to blossom." And to sum up this spirit of awakening to our inner turmoil via the drumming hoofbeats of the horses in our life, Sue Monk Kidd writes in *When the Heart Waits* (HarperOne, 2006): "Is it possible,

I ask myself, that I'm being summoned from some deep and holy place within? And being asked to enter a passage in Spiritual Life—the journey from false self to true self?"

▥ Resolution and "moving on"

In reference to Asian philosophy that views life experiences as a continuous spiral in which the same lessons keep coming back to us until we learn them, author Marianne Williamson says that midlife is our chance to rewrite old scripts and get on top of these lessons once and for all. With horses as teachers and facilitators in this process, you can identify these lessons, as I did with help from Deborah McCormick and the herd at Hacienda Tres Aguilas, for a unique and tangible opportunity to deal with and finally resolve issues "on the inside" that may have been dogging you for decades.

The important thing, McCormick emphasizes, is not to try to hide who you are or how you're feeling from a horse (despite the old "never let them see your fear" cowboy adage, usually followed by a hearty "you've just gotta let 'em know who's boss"). "Horses appreciate honesty above all," McCormick says. "Relying on your authenticity and who you are inside are your best tools for dealing successfully with horses."

This wisdom harkens all the way back to Xenophon, an ancient Greek horse trainer and cavalry officer who was one of the first advocates of "sympathetic horsemanship," and is often cited as being the original "horse whisperer." His detailed book, *On Horsemanship*, on the training and management of horses, written about 350 BC, is one of the oldest books on horsemanship in the Western world (presumably written before the invention of the saddle!), yet is still considered by many, especially in the world of dressage, to be quite relevant today.

One lesson we take from Xenophon is that horses are pure souls with the unique ability to mirror human emotion. Once you see this reflection, if you're brave and willing to learn, the horse can help you find your way through emotional baggage to the authenticity and "lead mare" inner strength for which you crave.

Kelly of Tyler, Texas, thought her midlife horse dreams had finally come true when she and her husband decided to invest in the picture-perfect training and temperament promised by a Clinton Anderson Signature Horse (a horse hand-picked by world-famous horse trainer Clinton Anderson and his staff, and trained through advanced maneuvers using his Downunder Horsemanship Method). At first, everything was a blissful honeymoon. Then a few problems began to crop up—Reno began behaving erratically, and he frequently wouldn't respond to Kelly's instructions and cues.

Kelly took Reno back to Anderson's ranch to repair a few holes in her technique, and this helped a great deal. Then the bucking and resistance began again, and Kelly was about to give up, despairing that she had "ruined" this perfect horse, when an experienced horsewoman friend of hers, after observing Kelly's interactions with Reno one day, made a casual remark about Kelly's anger. Kelly at first insisted she wasn't angry, merely frustrated, but when she began to dig a little deeper into her own psyche, she realized that she did have a few things to resolve. "It was the most amazing thing," she told me. "Once I dealt with my personal 'stuff,' Reno changed back into the sweet, kind, willing horse he was when I first got him. I had always heard that horses are mirrors, and Reno proved it in a way I'll never forget!"

Horses as healers

When I think of my life, I always think of this old country song lyric that goes something like, "Feed what needs feedin', mend what needs mendin', hold what needs holdin'"—taking care of people and living up to my responsibilities is what I do. It's who I am.

But one day as I was hand-grazing my midlife horse Rio, the profound truth of this whole horse experience arrived: *Horses* feed what needs feedin', mend what needs mendin', and hold what needs holdin'—in *us*. They do this in a way other humans simply cannot. If we let them, horses provide a source of healing, transformation, connection, and service attuned to our true life's work—you could say, our soul's "calling." "There's something about the outside of a horse that's good for the inside of a man," Sir Winston Churchill is well known for saying. I guess that goes double for women.

By ignoring the opportunity horses are waiting to provide, we remain on the human hamster wheel, and neglect the very thing in life that allows us to "let down on the inside" and "know where our feet are." Whether it's self-discovery, healing, and transformation of old wounds and limitations, service to others, or saving some little corner of the world, horses are our "Bridge to Terabithia," the source for making a difference in our own world and in the lives of others. The midlife horse experience can evolve into a much bolder expression of who we are, and the result is a whole new world opens its doors to us.

The very nature of horses uniquely equips them as healers. They are insightful and intuitive on physical, mental, emotional, and spiritual levels. "Horses have a special way of pulling us through transitions in our life," Deborah McCormick observes. Let's face it, midlife is a time of transition for most women. Death, divorce, children leaving home, deteriorating health, and physical changes that wreak havoc on the hormones and chip away at our body can leave us feeling a little—if not completely—rudderless. Horses can help redirect us with a sense of equilibrium that comes only from the natural world. "We are all part of nature," McCormick says. "When we've been thrown off course by life and we don't know how to get back to who we really are on the inside, horses, if we let them, will show us the way."

Survey Your Relationship Patterns

1   List the names of all the individuals with whom you have had significant relationships over your lifetime. After each name, note as many of the qualities and issues you can think of that appeared, occasionally or often, in that relationship. Do you see any consistent aspects and patterns?

2   Once you start to connect the dots from relationship to relationship (that is, note recurring themes), you may see a particular issue that has blocked or interfered with the ability of a relationship to mature or continue at all. Once you discover these "personal demons," you may even see how your relationship choices lead you, time and again, to the exact same conclusion! Common recurring themes include:

▸ Fear

▸ Anger

▸ Insecurity

▸ Jealousy

▸ Lack of boundaries

▸ Need for Control

▸ Neediness

Emotions or behaviors that keep popping up in different relationships are signs of personal inauthenticity, and a horse will not only sense this and "mirror" it back to you, he will also provide the means to finally conquer the demon and move on with your life.

Horses tend to evoke human healing on many levels—far beyond emotional and mental, all the way to the physical. As one therapist sums up, "Horses always know exactly what you need, and they'll give it to you whether you want it or not." The healing magic of making a special connection with a horse, and what the process of making this connection reveals, is a journey that, at our life's halfway point, can make all the difference.

Horses are now part of many types of human therapies, from physical to mental and emotional practices. Programs, certifications, and qualifications have sprung up around the theory of horses as healers—some good, some less so, but all, I believe, well intentioned. The miracles consistently brought about in these programs are well documented, bringing to light how it is in the nature of horses to heal humans if given half the chance.

On its website (www.narha.org), the North American Riding for the Handicapped Association (NARHA) explains equine-assisted activities and therapies (EAAT) as providing immense rewards to hundreds of thousands of individuals with (and without) special needs. As they say, "A physical, cognitive, or emotional special need does not limit a person from interacting with horses." EAAT includes a number of healing branches in which you can become involved:

> **Therapeutic riding,** which is geared to meet specific riding and/ or social objectives, and to teach riding skills that build toward independence.

> **Hippotherapy** is performed by licensed therapists and employs the movement of the horse as a tool to improve posture, balance, and movement, as well as fine and gross motor responses.

> **Non-mounted equine-assisted activities** are designed to build confidence and personal interaction skills through a series of exercises on the ground.

On the pages that follow, we'll see how two women found a source of joy, a place of peace, and even a new beginning as they work with horses in their healing capacities.

When Lisa, a police officer in Fort Worth, Texas, was shot in the line of duty and confined to a wheelchair, she thought she'd never be able to return to her childhood love of working with horses. An invitation to horse trainer Clinton Anderson's Stephenville, Texas, ranch to see if she could learn to work with horses from her motorized wheelchair, helped Lisa discover a whole new sense of connection and healing.

"When you're riding on a horse's back, that's fun and one kind of feeling," Lisa relates, "but when you're sitting on a horse's back, you're not looking into his eyes. When you connect with a horse at eye level, there's just nothing like it in this world."

While her one-on-one lessons with Clinton Anderson and his horse Diez was not physically healing per se (she is still in that wheelchair), Lisa says she experienced a feeling of freedom and exhilaration that felt like flying. "That horse saw me for who I am, beyond this chair, beyond my situation, and physical limitations," she said. "He saw me on the inside and set me free in a way I will never forget."

Lisa began weekly therapeutic riding sessions, and even though she was paralyzed from the waist down and often had difficulty even holding herself up in her wheelchair, she found that time on a horse was improving her balance and control. "At first when I got there I looked for one of those saddles with a 'back' on it," she remembers. "They said, 'Oh, we don't have those here. It'll be okay.' I knew either it would or

it wouldn't, and the only way to find out for sure was to try."
Then laughing, she adds, "What's the worst thing that could
happen? I'm already in a wheelchair!"

Lisa rode each week on Thursday afternoons, and once
on the horse, she says she felt different...she was free. This
time was precious, and because it also tapped into her life-
long love of horses and her competitive spirit, she began to
push herself a little bit more with each ride.

Noticing Lisa's progress, the directors at her riding facility
asked if she would like to be in the Chisholm Trail Challenge—
an obstacle course for disabled riders in which they compete, with leaders and sidewalkers, as part of the Fort Worth
Stock Show and Rodeo. "I was hoping to do this someday,"
Lisa says, "But I never dreamed it would be the first year!"
She did compete that first year—and won. The trophy buckle
from that triumph is among her most prized possessions.

When the Professional Bull Riding Association (PBR)
decided to make Lisa's riding program their philanthropic
project, they invited rider representatives to do a demonstration before an arena packed with people who had come
to watch the top names in bull riding. Lisa and three other
riders executed their maneuvers in a way that earned the
crowd's riveted attention, and at the end, a standing ovation.
"I never dreamed we'd get a standing 'O,'" she says, beam-
ing. "Imagine this happening to me. What an unbelievable
experience. And it all started with getting on a horse."

Isn't that the way it is, in one way or another, for all of us?

▒ One woman finds her soul's "calling"

For one little girl born with cerebral palsy, just taking a few steps, even with the help of leg braces, was very difficult. After several sessions on a horse, her parents noticed that her hips seemed to be more relaxed and moving more correctly in the steps she was able to take with the braces. After a summer of regular hippotherapy sessions, the little girl took 15 steps *without* her braces or the help of corrective shoes. For a little boy born with severe autism who had never spoken a single word, riding horses brought first a spark to his otherwise expressionless demeanor, and then, just a few short months later, his very first words: "Walk on."

Stories like these abound in the annals of equine-assisted activities and therapies documentation. Stories so miraculous they are almost unbelievable, unless you're there every day to witness it yourself. After living her midlife journey through all its own stages of wonder, struggle, delight, and frustration, Barbara Epps of Waco, Texas, knew she wanted above all, to be part of creating these stories.

Finding the path

First, she volunteered. She went a few times a week to a nearby program and worked as first, a helper, then as a sidewalker. Meanwhile, partly as a way to regain her confidence after a tumble from her own horse that fractured a vertebra, she became certified by the Certified Horsemanship Association (CHA) as a Level One riding instructor. She taught riding at a few summer camps as a volunteer, then as a paid instructor to able-bodied children.

But all the while Barbara knew where she wanted to go next. "About six months after I became an instructor, I realized that not only did I enjoy teaching, but I really had a gift for it," she says. "At the same time I was also volunteering at our local therapeutic riding center. I guess it was the combination of riding instruction for able-bodied children and the amazing gratification of working with special needs children at the center that made me realize what I most wanted to do with my life: Therapeutic riding instruction brought it all together for me—working with horses, being part of the difference this therapy can make for these kids, and my newfound love for teaching."

Taking it higher

Barbara is one of those linear creative people who likes to do things right—and with style. A bigger goal stemmed from her initial dream: She wanted to help grow the small, struggling therapeutic riding center in Waco by using her professional (and recently shelved) advertising, design, and marketing talents to bring it to the attention of those who could make it a viable program. The goal? To reach out to many more people and in many more ways than it was currently able to do. She also knew that to be able to communicate with sponsors and clientele, she needed to become a certified therapeutic riding instructor.

Barbara discovered an organization called Equest (www.equest. org) that offered a six-week NARHA Instructor Certification Course that would teach her what she needed to know to pursue this new horse-related passion professionally. As the first, and still one of the largest therapeutic riding centers in Texas, Equest has been around for nearly 30 years and has served thousands of children and adults with varying disabilities and special needs.

With the blessings of her husband, Ron, Barbara plunked down the $2,700 tuition, and then, from August 20 to October 3, 2009, she became a full-time student in a program that surprised her in its intensity, but not nearly as much as she surprised herself in hers. "I expected in-depth information and high expectations," she said, "but what I didn't expect was how anxious and nervous that would make me. I took it all very, very seriously. I had worked enough in this environment to know that there was so much I wanted to learn—it got to be a race to see how much I could get into my brain in just six weeks!"

A soul's "calling"

Above all, Barbara's source of satisfaction and fulfillment in this second career with horses far exceeds any expectations she might have had. "Nothing can describe the thrill of stepping into that arena as an instructor for the first time," she says, eyes glistening. "I can't even begin to put into words what it means to me to be able to provide this amazing experience to a child with a disability, and to have some small part in improving his or her life. It is a dimension of fulfillment I never could have imagined. I feel so blessed that this door opened to me, and I'm so glad I had the courage and the opportunity to walk through it."

Walk on, Barbara.

Texans REACH Out with Horses

The REACH (Riding Equines to Achieve Confidence and Health) Therapeutic Riding Center near Waco, Texas, states their mission as "Improving the health, increasing the confidence, and promoting the independence of persons with special needs through the use of horses." The center's literature goes on to say, "Helping physically, mentally, or emotionally challenged people reach their potential is what it's all about. Drawing upon both the rhythmic, repetitive motion of the horse and the bond formed between rider and horse, equine-assisted activities can produce life-changing results."

But just a few minutes onsite tells the real story: There is much more at work at REACH. When you see the expressions of the children, the volunteers, the instructors, and the therapists—not to mention the grateful parents looking on—you know immediately that there are a million tiny miracles happening all around you.

Whether these miracles are visible to the naked eye, building quietly within the body or mind of a challenged child, or part of a puzzle that will yield a full picture on its own timetable, it is easy to feel the sacred nature of the place.

And it is no surprise that at the center of it all stands the horse, as always helping humans find their way.

▦ Building better human relationships through horses

The woman began to cry softly as she shared a devastating problem she was having with a family member, her fears and worries tumbling out without warning at a gentle prompt from the therapist. Others in our group stood helpless, aching for this woman, but unsure of what to say or do. A horse that was grazing 30 or 40 yards away suddenly stopped, turned, and walked slowly toward us. The mare stood quietly behind the woman, then inched closer until her lowered head was actually inside our circle.

This single profound moment showed me how a horse could sense human distress, even from a distance. That the mare then moved toward the woman in a gesture of quiet comfort demonstrated the miraculous connection between humans and horses that is the basis for equine-assisted psychotherapy (EAP). I'd seen similar things before with dogs and their owners, but this horse didn't know this woman, and a dozen other strangers surrounded her. I was fascinated and understood immediately what draws people to this work.

When Kathy Taylor, Equine Specialist and President of HerdWise, LLC, an equine-assisted learning (EAL) company she founded in 2009, was first invited to a demonstration of EAP, she had no idea what it was. "I thought it was the *coolest* thing ever," she says, still glowing at the recollection. More than just cool, it was something she knew immediately that she wanted in some way to be involved. However, she wasn't a therapist (and didn't want to go back to school to become one), so Kathy wasn't sure if there was a place for her in this new field of interest.

"I really wanted to go to an EAP training to see what might be out there for me," she remembers, "but I talked myself out of it, telling myself that I was being selfish. While we had the money, we *barely* did, and I felt I should not be spending it on something that just 'might be fun to know.'" Kathy talked to her husband, Tim, about her struggle between going and not going. "I had his blessing," she says, "but not really my own." She decided to forget it. Then came "the nudge" she couldn't deny.

"I was quite content with my decision to stay home," she recalls, "but then I heard a voice inside me say, 'But *I* want you to go.' To me, that was nothing less than the voice of God—and when He talks, I try to listen! So I went to the training, and I've never looked back. It's been an incredible journey, and it's not over yet!"

A longtime follower of the Pat Parelli Natural Horse Training Method, Kathy explains, "Most people think Parelli is strictly a horse training program, but it is actually a *people training* program for horse owners." Kathy says she found EAP/EAL to be a purposeful extension of Parelli's philosophy of "emotional fitness."

"If my horses can help *me* be more mentally and emotionally fit, then they can also help others," she reasoned. Because she was not a licensed psychotherapist, Kathy realized that her role in facilitating the EAP/EAL process was through her knowledge and experience with horses. "I decided I could partner with a licensed therapist during therapy sessions," she says. "The therapist's primary responsibility would be the safety and well-being of the human client, whereas my role would be to provide the same care for the horses."

Once Kathy was certain this was a trail she wanted to explore, she enrolled in the Equine Assisted Growth and Learning Association (EAGALA) certification program (www.eagala.org). At this point in the story I should note that there are several different philosophies that explain how horses help people mentally, emotionally, and physically, and many people hold very strong opinions regarding the validity of each. If *you* are interested in EAP/EAL, I encourage you to do some homework and find the best fit and the right training course for your intentions and abilities. Kathy, for her part, doesn't believe it's the *philosophies* themselves that are so much at odds, as it is the *people* who've subscribed to one or the other, and whose opinions are naturally going to differ on what's best. (Welcome to the horse world.) For other EAP/EAL organizations, see the resources I've provided on p. 311.

Kathy says the horses' mirroring of the very different groups and individuals she now works with never stops amazing her. And, for her, the unique vantage point of seeing the same horses mirror so many different kinds of people makes it all the more inspiring. "The horses are never 'in your face' about it," she adds, "but rather, just come gently forward as if to say, 'We've got some information for you, and you can choose to use it however you want or are able.'"

Kathy believes that everything you do with horses shows up somewhere else in your life; you can find proof of this if you just look for it. When you work on improving yourself in small ways in your work with horses, your "exterior life" will get better, and vice versa. These are minute things, she is quick to explain, and you have to pay attention. To quote Parelli, "Everything is something; nothing is *nothing* to a horse."

Applying EAL in the business world

Although Kathy started out with an emphasis on EAP, which seeks to heal past issues, she has since shifted her focus to EAL, which focuses more on life skills and learning that can be applied to the future. She is fascinated by the ways horses can help people become better leaders and team members. "Equine-assisted learning is recognized around the globe as a valuable tool for business and used by major companies, such as BMW, Disney, and Volkswagen," she says. "Horses have a lot to teach us if we are just willing to open our minds to the possibilities."

Kathy's company, HerdWise, explores EAL concepts with work teams and other groups whose "herd" dynamics are critical to their success. "This has everything to do with emotional intelligence, or EQ—how aware we are of our emotions and how much we are able to control them in a given situation," she explains. It's been shown that EQ has a great deal more to do with a person's long-term personal and professional success than does the IQ (intelligence quotient) that we spend so much time focusing on. Horses are natural teachers of emotional intelligence."

Some of the EAL benefits Kathy has seen in her sessions with business and corporate clients include:

⟩ **Stronger teams** "A herd of horses is an example of excellence in teamwork," Kathy explains. "Although the lead mare may be the primary decision-maker for the herd, she relies on the other members of the herd for the vital information that goes into making that decision. Even the lowest horse in the herd hierarchy has an important role to play in the survival of the whole." Kathy says it is fascinating to watch how a horse herd will actually mirror a human team.

As an EAL session unfolds, facilitators encourage participants to consider the value each member contributes to the success of her team, as reflected by the herd. In asking and answering the questions key to team dynamics (Who is the "lead mare"? Who is the best communicator? What is working for you and what might be hindering your success?), the team gains valuable insight into issues, along with an opportunity to practice alternative solutions to determine the best course of action in the future, and then measure the success of these changes with the help of the herd. "I'm never surprised at what happens in these sessions," Kathy says, "but I am always amazed."

⟩ **A new breed of trust** "Horses are honest creatures that are incapable of acting differently from how they feel," Kathy explains, paraphrasing horseman Mark Rashid. "People, on the other hand, often feel one way but act another. With a horse, the feedback you receive is honest, immediate, and non-judgmental. They are not impressed by fancy cars or clothes or that you were tops in sales for the past three years. They see and respond to the 'inner' you." While Kathy admits this kind of raw assessment is a little unsettling to some, participants tend to find comfort in the knowledge that everyone in a session is getting the same shakedown!

In his bestselling book, *The 5 Dysfunctions of a Team* (Jossey-Bass, 2002), corporate guru Patrick Lencioni's writes, "Trust lies at the heart of a functioning team. Without it, teamwork is all but impossible." What Kathy has noticed in her corporate team-building sessions is that once the herd shows each team member who she is and how she fits into the team, the honesty the horses elicit creates and/or deepens trust amongst colleagues.

) **Enhanced communication** "We humans tend to assume that just because we say something, the people we say it to a) hear us, and b) understand exactly what we mean," Kathy says. "Horses, on the other hand, communicate almost exclusively non-verbally and are experts at reading both the body language and emotions of the others in their herd." As prey animals, this kind of communication was essential for survival (we'll talk more about how horses communicate in chapter 13, p. 287). Kathy asks us to consider that, as studies show, our body language "speaks" to people as much as our verbal observations or directions. It tells others of our emotions and motives, whether we are conscious of it or not. In the business world, this is knowledge that is essential to clear communication.

In HerdWise sessions, participants get a sense of how body language (in themselves and others) reveals:

) Whether team members say what they mean and mean what they say.

) Whether team members are direct in their requests or assume that the person on the receiving end of the communication knows what they mean.

) What happens to the team when there is miscommunication—who takes responsibility, and who doesn't.

By interacting with horses on the ground only, people are challenged in way that helps them unlock answers and solutions to a variety of challenges. "As mirrors of human behavior, horses provide us with unique insights that can lead us then to realize what we need to do to achieve the success and satisfaction we were meant to have in our work and in our life," says Kathy. Calling on the wisdom of horses to help others discover life-changing answers is a trail she is glad she took the time to explore. In it she has found fulfillment in the service to others, which her midlife soul was craving.

"Regardless of who it is I'm working with or what the issues are, this is always a fascinating process," she says. "I feel so blessed to be part of it, and I never get tired of learning more and thinking of new ways to help make EAL available to people who want to learn and grow through the innate healing and motivating power of horses."

Opportunity on four legs

Carol Thigpen has spent much of her adult life riding and showing horses at all levels, amassing a career show record that includes numerous national and world championships. She says that opportunities for learning with horses only deepen with age and experience, but that midlife horsemanship carries with it a different measuring stick—one that she feels is more real and more valid in the long run than any show ring criteria of her accomplished past. "Gone is the need to prove anything to others," she says with a smile. "What we must focus on now is proving something to ourselves. For each of us, this is something different."

Thigpen says that horsemanship at this time of life is, as much as anything else, a spiritual path. Since her first horse in 1974, Thigpen acknowledges that in each horse she has known since—spanning many breeds, including Quarter Horses, Paints, Palominos, and Arabs— she found a teacher...and new lessons to learn. "Horses are pure souls, our truest mirrors, and mirrors of how we relate to others," Thigpen says. "Chances are very good that how you approach and interact with horses is a reflection of how you tend to interact with people." And, quoting the old English proverb, she adds, "Show me your horse, and I'll tell you who you are."

What a Horse Can Teach a CEO

In her article, "Top 5 Ways that Horses Can Bring Teams Together," HerdWise founder Kathy Taylor of Weatherford, Texas, explains how horses make the best CEO advisors/consultants. "Due to their position in the company, CEOs and other top leaders often find it difficult to obtain a candid/sincere assessment of how they are truly performing in the workplace," Kathy writes. "This has been called 'CEO disease'— the boss only hears the good news, even if that's not the whole story."

While it is often difficult to find a human in the workplace willing to tell the emperor he has no clothes on, horses are ideally suited for this task. They are natural followers looking for natural leaders. Status, wealth, achievements, or accolades don't matter to a horse. They respond to what's on the inside of us—and what's "real."

With this in mind, the following actions can provide invaluable insight into your own struggles to grow and improve in the second half of life:

> Getting a horse to ground tie can help you identify, understand, and deal with personal boundaries.

> Picking up a horse's foot can teach you about the importance of trust and support in yourself and others.

> Leading a horse over an obstacle can help you overcome obstacles in your own life.

Thigpen believes horses are uniquely able to address the four parts of true healing—body, mind, spirit, and emotion. "The parallels are everywhere," she says. "Horses help us heal, or help us find the path to the parts of us that need to be healed. We have to learn to stay open and aware, to trust this process, and try very hard to keep our egos in check and stay out of the way."

Much has already been said about how horses mirror our emotional and mental states, but Thigpen shares a convincing story of mirroring the physical state, as well. "I had scoliosis," she says, "and I also had three different show horses that were always short-strided in the right front. I never made any connection between the two things, but when my condition deteriorated to the point where I had to do something about it, I made a startling discovery. After I was treated for my physical problem, all three of my horses suddenly 'got sound'!"

"Horses are the 'be here now' part of my life," says Thigpen. "As much as anything else, midlife horsemanship is a spiritual journey—a special connection to God."

Think you're ready to begin—or rejoin—your horsemanship journey? Ask yourself:

)   *What do I want and need from this experience?*

)   *Where do I want to go?*

)   *What are my strengths and weaknesses?*

)   *What do I know and what do I need to know?*

The answers represent the first lesson in regaining your inner strength, and we'll explore each of them, and more, in the pages ahead.

3

Take the reins

Making the decision to reignite an old passion—in this case, adding horses to the middle of your life—can either be much more complicated or much simpler than you think. It all depends on the decisions you make, and how you make them. Here are a few things to consider, a few options to ponder, and a few tips for processing this half-ton decision.

"HE'S A SWEETHEART, ISN'T HE?" I heard the voice of Susan, the buyer's agent, behind me. "His name is Trace. Want to ride him?"

"No, that's okay," I replied, withdrawing my hand from the gelding's neck.

"He's actually sold to a friend of mine," she continued, putting a halter on him as if I hadn't declined her offer. "She won't mind if you ride him, though. I was actually going to ride him in a little while, anyway. I want to make sure he is worked while they're on vacation. I'll just throw a saddle on him and you can hop on."

Moments later, as I found myself putting my foot in the stirrup, I had a moment of panic. Could I even still ride? It had been 20 years since I last rode a horse, but it really didn't seem that long. As I prepared to mount, Trace's head went straight up. I stopped.

"Oh, it's okay," Susan said, "He always does that. He's just very alert. He won't do anything. No buck, no spook, no attitude." I actually hadn't considered buck, spook, or attitude—until now.

"He looks like a giraffe," said my dad, who had joined us. I laughed and swung myself up onto this horse as if I had just ridden yesterday, noting as I did how it seemed much farther from the ground and took much more effort than it used to. I didn't really like the tension I felt in Trace's body, but, as Susan predicted, he stood perfectly still.

We moved off at a walk. For the first few moments of that first slow lap around the arena, I felt awkward—a little bit wobbly. Then I felt that old familiar connection returning. I relaxed and released a deep sigh, directly from the center of my soul. I smiled as we started moving faster. I had heard the term, "light as a feather," used to describe a horse, but had never experienced it. Suddenly, I knew exactly what that expression meant. When we moved into a lope, I laughed out loud, surprised at the sound of the purest form of joy I had emitted in a very long time.

"He's great," I said as I dismounted, grateful for the ride, and even more grateful he was already sold, because in my ecstatic state I would have bought him on the spot.

"Do you want me to see if my friend is sure she wants him?" Susan asked. "She hasn't paid for him."

Oh, dear. "Sure," I heard myself say. I stepped closer to Trace and rubbed his neck. I felt my dad's eyes on me. "Ride him," I said, answering his silent question.

Dad rode him, around and around. "I still don't like the way he carries his head," he said when he was done, handing the reins back to me. "And he has a pinchy butt."

Dad was used to the short, stocky build of cutting horses. Trace was lighter, leaner, a little short in the back, and high in the withers. And yes, I thought, as I walked around the backside of him, his hips were more angular, kind of coming to a point at the top instead of being rounded and smooth.

I suddenly felt defensive of my new high-headed friend. Dad had never liked a single one of my boyfriends, and had no use for either of my husbands (with good reason, it turned out—I was still fresh out of a second miserable marriage). Now here he was similarly dissing this horse.

"She says you can have him if you want him," Susan said, rejoining us.

I heard myself say, "Okay, I'll take him." Dad looked at me like I'd lost my mind. I knew for sure that I had either lost it or found it. Time would tell which one.

The "jumping-off place"

It goes without saying that this is *not* the smart way to buy a horse. In fact, I realized as Susan unloaded Trace at my parents' house a few days later, the way I went about this life-altering decision was not only rushed, it was plain dangerous. I suppose in my desperation to make a change in my life and not to let horsey opportunity slip away yet again, I acted with uncharacteristic decisiveness that was as foolish as it was courageous. Regardless, I was in with both feet, and I had dragged along a 1,000-pound animal.

As you'll see in the coming chapters, there's a better way to embark on this horse course. We all have to find our own path, but perhaps this book will transform some of my missteps into your warning markers. This is what we affectionately call the "jumping-off place." It's decision time, and most of the decisions related to riding and owning horses are bigger than they look. Take your time, get a lay of the land, ask a lot of questions, and as always, let your heart be your truest guide.

More than likely, by midlife you have made plenty of big decisions. And, like most of us, there are some you're more proud of than others. The decision to take the reins—and take control of your pursuit of your dreams and goals—is no different than any other change of course.

This time, however, with the help of a few experts in the field, you can make the decisions that will serve you best without a lot of time-wasting missteps. (Let's face it, we've let enough time pass us by.) But moving too fast, as I did, carries its own set of challenges. Making sound decisions makes all the difference.

How do you make decisions?

From those who rely solely on "gut," to advocates of the infamous pro/con list, to those who make decisions by consensus, here's news that could rock your world. Suzy Welch, author of the bestselling decision-making treatise, *10-10-10: A LifeTransforming Idea* (Scribner, 2009), explains that many of these common methods of decision-making are somewhat unreliable because they can be skewed by what she calls "neurological bias"—something that feels like "gut" but is actually your brain playing tricks on you based on past experience or observations.

According to Welch's book, following your "gut" on big decisions—or any of the other ways we usually analyze our options—can be misleading, calling into play things like fear, other people's expectations, and beliefs based on others' experiences. "At the end of the day," Welch writes, "many of our choices are so personal and so complicated that by necessity and convention, we are alone with them."

For many of us, it seems, who by this time in our life have made a number of decisions that haunt us, the fear of making the *wrong* decision can be the controlling factor. And, sometimes, even if we've made a decision that doesn't seem to be the best, we cling to it for fear of making things worse.

Welch explains that this reluctance to make a new choice is sometimes the result of what cognitive scientists call "escalating commitment," in which we refuse to acknowledge when something isn't working for fear that we're giving up too soon—or that it might get better. The way out of both scenarios and onto the road to a more authentic life is as simple as asking, "What are all the possible positive and negative consequences of staying in this mess (whatever it happens to be for you) over time?"

Welch's 10-10-10 approach to decision-making is deceptively sim-ple. By calling upon us to consider the impact of any decision 10 min-utes (short-term), 10 months (midterm), and 10 years (long-term) from now, she takes us out of the emotional state instigated by neurologi-cal bias and exposes solutions we may not have otherwise been able to visualize. Although it is certain that no one can know for sure what will happen 10 years from now, it is the act of *imagining* the possible out-comes, both positive and negative, that give us a frame of reference for our expectations and help guide us to what we most desire.

So if we take the example of my decision to buy Trace after one short ride and a spontaneous infatuation borne of, yes, perhaps a "midlife crisis" of sorts, and analyze it using the 10-10-10 technique, we might get something like this:

Should I buy this horse? If I say "Yes," this decision will affect me how?

10 minutes from now: I will still be walking on air, but starting to come down as I cut the deposit check and hand it to the agent.

10 months from now: I don't know anything about this horse, really; he might not get along with my dad's horse; he might not get along with me. I don't know how he trailers or how he goes on the trail. He might have stable vices. He might have a hidden unsoundness. I might not be able to afford special shoeing or special feed or supplements that he requires. He might not be "the one" after all, but knowing my nature, I won't be able to "give up on him," and we'll both be stuck.

10 years from now: Hopefully I'll still be fit and agile enough to get in the saddle, but if not, what else can I do with this horse? What kind of groundwork would he like? In 10 years I'll need to help my daughter pay off her college loans. Will owning a horse allow me to fulfill that commitment?

After going through the 10-10-10 process, I might ask if I can come back in a week and try Trace again, or perhaps arrange to take him on a trial basis while I crunch the numbers, do some planning, and get to know him. Welch believes that 10-10-10 is a powerful decision-making tool because by methodically sorting through possible outcomes at three pivotal time frames (short-, mid-, and long-term), the process forces us to analyze our options in the light of *who we want to become*. "If you seek a new life of clarity and intention," she writes, "10-10-10 spurs us to deliberate, *then* act."

▓ It's time to sweat the small stuff

Besides the decisions that we *realize* are of life-changing magnitude, of possibly even greater threat to our path of authenticity are the little decisions we make every day that, with their 10-10-10 impact ignored, may play an ever greater role is leading us astray from our core values. Since reconnecting with our deeply held values is what "taking the reins" of our life is all about, it is worth a little space here to stop and ask if we have a good understanding of what those really are.

It seems that a key piece of making decisions that are better and truer to the calling of our authentic self would be to create a sharper and more meaningful awareness of what we value most. So before we go any further down the bridle path, let's stop and take a few minutes to get a really clear idea of our most deeply held personal values—our "soul values." By getting in solid touch with these, decisions you make from here on out will be much easier and better aligned with where you want to go and who you want to become.

Making room in your life for a horse

One of the biggest questions most of us face when contemplating a big life change, such as adding all that horses entail to the mix of an already busy existence, is how do we do it without making the craziness we may already

EXERCISE

Find Your Soul Values

The widely available "Proust Questionnaire" was developed by French Memoirist Marcel Proust more than 100 years ago and still rings true today when we're hunting our "soul values."

1   Get out your notebook and answer the following questions expansively (write as much as you can, as fast as you can, for as long as you can before going on to the next one):

   ▸   What is your idea of happiness?

   ▸   What is your idea of misery?

2   Now, take a swing at the questions Suzy Welch added to the Proust Questionnaire in her book *10-10-10*:

   ▸   What would make you cry at your seventieth birthday party?

   ▸   What do you want people to say about you when you're not in the room?

   ▸   What do you love about the way your parents live(ed), and what do you hate?

3   Take a look at your answers and look for themes—these will help you put your finger on your "soul values" and whether having horses in your life is a part of being true to them.

be feeling worse? It can be done, but it takes some mental restructuring and flexibility, a new set of rules, and what experts call "self-management."

▥ Prepare to give up something else

"Horses are not like boats, RVs, or motorcycles," says Equine Massage Therapist and midlife horsewoman Emily Kutz, referring to the other kinds of "big purchases" frequently made in and around midlife. Her path back to horses began when her neighbor's daughter shared stories of her own horseback riding lessons, and once Emily felt her old dream reawaken, she began making changes to her life to accommodate it. "People need to really understand what they're getting into when they commit to bringing a living, breathing being into their life with another set of needs, requirements, and responsibilities."

Contemporary philosopher and best-selling author Alexandra Stoddard hits the nail on the head when she tells us "You're going to have to give up something you already have or possibly, another dream . . . when you say goodbye to the weeds you didn't plant, you make room for the flowers of your choice."

▥ Practice the "art of no"

We are perhaps the last generation to grow up driven by a need to please others at the expense of pleasing ourselves. Now don't blow this out of proportion here. I'm not advocating selfishness, nor am I dogging niceness and "doing for others." But when the inability to say "No" to the requests of others, even to your own detriment, robs you of the ability to live an authentic, fulfilling life, it's time to hit the brakes and find a new way to get your "doing for others" into a healthier perspective. Here are a few tips from the experts to acquire this skill with the ultimate goal of making room in your life for your own heart's desire.

"The reason 'No' is difficult at first," writes Stoddard in her book *Making Choices* (Harper Paperbacks, 1995), "is that many of the demands made on us appear as though they are our responsibility." However, the onus is not really on us, she advises, until we say, "Yes."

Combine this sense of mislaid responsibility with the pace at which most of us are used to living—and the momentary adrenaline rush we have become addicted to when we do manage to be all things to all people—and the idea of slowing down, reflecting on our life, making new choices, and creating time and space to live out our dream may seem completely unrealistic.

"Just say 'No,'" says Stoddard. Start small. Start anywhere. Just start. Say "No" to everything in your life that isn't part of your new master plan built around your deepest personal "soul" values. "Being in a position to say 'No' is a privilege that comes with being a self-sufficient, responsible, mature, well-balanced, independent adult," writes Stoddard. What's more, she tells us, the art of saying "No," which Stoddard calls "the first bullet you'll need in your arsenal in the battle to take back your life," will:

⟩ Help you move away from unrealistic expectations and pressures others put on you.

⟩ Provide you with balance, order, clarity, discipline, restraint, and guidance.

⟩ Be a definitive way for dealing with the contradictions and distractions all around us.

Recognizing the power and importance of this two-letter word is only half the battle. The hard part comes in learning how to use it and still live with yourself, as well as those around you who think you've taken leave of your senses! It should be mentioned that those in your life who love and support you will toggle back and forth a bit in their approval of the "No You." It takes some readjusting on everyone's part as you learn to play life by a new set of rules.

"Bear in mind," advises Cheryl Richardson, author of *Stand Up for Your Life* (Free Press, 2003), "that there is a spiritual principle that operates in life: When you take good care of yourself, it's always in the best interests of the other person as well. [He or she] may be disappointed or angry, but it doesn't make your decision the wrong choice." She adds that when you start to practice what she calls "extreme self care" in which you honor your personal values with your choices and decisions regardless of the expectations of others, "a

Divine force rallies behind you to support your decisions and will actually make your life easier."

Explaining that time, for all of us, is a finite gift of 168 hours a week, 52 weeks a year, Richardson cautions us not to confuse a tough choice with "no choice." The notion of "time management, therefore, is a myth; what we must embrace instead is the discipline of "self-management." So, to clear out an overcrowded life to make room for horses to enter requires us to follow three simple sounding (but challenging at first) instructions:

> **Say "No"**   As we've already discussed, this is the first step toward making time for yourself and for horses.

> **Schedule less**   If a project will take one week, say it will take two. Take an extra 15 minutes before and after appointments so you're not rushing from one thing to the next.

> **Don't be afraid to cancel**   "It's hard to disappoint people," Richardson acknowledges. "Apologize, but stick to your guns. Be gracious, direct, and don't over-explain."

Building Your "No" Muscle

It takes time, determination, and practice to build your "No" muscle. With that in mind, here are a few workout tips from self-help experts:

> Take some time between receiving a request and responding to it to help break the habit of the "Automatic Yes."

> Let friends and family know what you're doing and enlist their help.

> Identify why you're afraid to say "No." (Are you afraid of conflict? Rejection? Missed opportunity? Regret? Guilt?) Sometimes just shining a little light of awareness on your fear puts it into a healthier perspective.

EXERCISE

Start Clearing Your Own Trail

1   To figure out where to start clearing the trail to your horse-filled life, track your time use in your journal for a full week. At the end of the week, group your time entries in the following categories:

▶   Work

▶   Sleep

▶   Home (household tasks and errands)

▶   People (family and friends)

▶   Personal maintenance (bathing, dressing, personal appointments and tasks)

▶   Self (activities that renew you mentally, physically, emotionally, spiritually)

2   Tally the total time spent each week in each category. These numbers reveal where your priorities are right now. Is this a life of balance and joy? What adjustments do you need to make? What do you wish your priorities were?

3   Now reorder your priorities to reflect the "horsey" life you want to lead in terms of how you spend your time. Use this new list as your guide as you start to enforce your new set of priorities by saying "No," scheduling less, and canceling until you reach a balance of time and choice that reflects your personal values and who you want to become in the second half of your life.

Adding time for horses into your busy life is not about cramming yet another thing into your schedule, and then killing yourself to make time for it. Echoing Richardson's advice, Timothy Ferriss, author of the best-seller *The 4-Hour Workweek* (Crown Archetype, 2009), writes that the trick to making space in your life is found in what he calls the "wonder-

Tracking the Causes of Pain and the Harbingers of Joy

1   In your journal, list the things that you know cause you emotional pain or discomfort. Leave plenty of space between entries. Now, writing fast, without thinking or censoring, write about the ways/ situations in which you ignore your own emotional and physical health for the sake of avoiding these feelings.

2   Now, make a list of what makes you feel good, strong, and lifts your spirits. Write about all the ways you would incorporate these things into your regular life if you could.

3   Now, finally, where were you and what were you doing the last time you felt peaceful and relaxed? Describe the entire scenario, detail by detail, as if you're reliving the moment.

What you've written here provides a way to measure requests and demands on your time and your life. This is a process you now need to handle proactively if you plan to ride and own horses.

ful world of elimination." Once you've discovered what it is you want to do more of in your life, you have to figure out what you can eliminate.

▥ Employ Parkinson's Law

The next tool Ferriss offers is even more striking in its simplicity and power. Employing two synergistic approaches for increasing productivity known as "Parkinson's Law" ("A task will swell in [perceived] importance and complexity in relation to the time allotted for its completion"), Ferriss unwittingly gives answer to those of us looking to make enough space in our busy life for something as big as a horse. He says:

1   Limit your tasks to the important to shorten your work time.

2   Shorten your work time to limit your tasks to only the important.

Sound like he's talking in a circle? He is. The process is clear and simple: Block off time for the tasks you need to complete each day and that's it. That's all you have. With a little ironclad self-discipline and a good watch or timer, you'll learn quickly to stay focused and then move on. Can it really be that easy? If you've done the journaling and soul-searching exercises I provided in the pages leading up to this one, you already know which activities can be considered "mission critical" to the life you want to lead and which, therefore, *deserve* your focus. "If you don't identify the mission critical tasks and set aggressive start and end times for their completion, the unimportant becomes the important," Ferriss writes. And isn't that the truth we've all lived up til now?

If you've ever wondered "what happened to your day"; if writing a few emails, picking up groceries for dinner, making two phone calls, and attending a meeting leaves you exhausted; if you've worked hard all week but only crossed off one "mission critical" task from your bottomless to-do list, Ferriss' point applies to you.

▥ Derailed but not demoralized

David Allen is yet another noted expert in the field of time and productivity management. In his book, *Making It All Work* (Penguin, 2009), Allen acknowledges that choosing the path of balance and focused productivity in our volatile, high-speed world is tricky at best. And sometimes (my words, not his), shit happens. For all your careful planning and discipline, something comes along and knocks you right off your carefully laid tracks, and there you are stunned and bewildered, having to begin all over again.

The advantage of building a framework and "laying track," Allen points out, is that when you deal with life's little (or big) surprises, you

Recapture Your Day

Using Ferriss' *4-Hour Work Week* as our guide, here are a few point-specific ways to pare down your to-do list and "recapture" parts of your day to devote to your "mission critical" activities (i.e. HORSES):

1   Create a to-do list each night of what must be accomplished the following day. Don't computerize these lists—write them out on a small notepad or 3- by 5-inch index card.

2   Include no more than two "mission critical" items on your list each day. Look at each one and ask, "If this is all I get done today, will I be satisfied with my day?" and "What will happen if I don't do this today?"

3   Identify the activities that interfere with your focus each day—you know, those things we all fall prey to (e-mail, Internet, television). Be vigilant and bust yourself whenever you drift into these areas and lose focus on the tasks on your daily list.

4   DO NOT MULTITASK. (Do you see the capitalized letters? That's me, yelling at myself.) While it's seductive and a little bit egotistical to think we're smart and talented enough to do more than one thing at a time, recent brain research indicates that multitasking leads only to brain overload and poor results in each activity. And you might as well quit this habit right now, because eventually your horse will stop it for you. Horses are the best cure in the world for multitasking.

5   Shorten deadlines to force your immediate, concentrated action and prevent procrastination. Your reward? High productivity and more time for the things you *want* to do. Would that be pure bliss or what?

6   Stop asking for opinions; instead, propose solutions. This saves hours over the course of a few months in the "What do you want for dinner?"..."I don't know what sounds good to you?" category, alone. When you propose a solution, you incite decisive action.

have pathways and trail markers to help you get back to where you were and take the actions necessary to reorient yourself and restart. Here are a few of Allen's track-laying tips that I think can be adapted to fit most any life and set of priorities, and will prove most useful when trying make time for horses:

1   Create a system for handling the information coming into your life: A simple set of exact processes or routines that eliminate the need for thought.

2   Place physical "inbaskets" at key locations in your home, office, and car for holding information to be processed at a later time. Designate an hour a day for going through it and attending to those tasks "on deck."

3   Set a reminder mechanism on your calendar—online versions include audible alarms, flags, and message boxes. If you live by a wall or pocket calendar, organize a system to remind yourself of deadlines and appointments in hard copy. Colored "flags" or post-its can work well for this.

4   Collect any random thoughts ideas, goals, or plans in a spiral note-book for your perusal at a later date. You're less likely to waste time dwelling on them *now* if you promise them attention at in the future.

5   Create a dedicated workstation at home, at the office, and even in the car if you're in it a lot, to give yourself a place for thinking, planning, and making decisions about future actions.

6   Schedule two hours at the beginning or end of each week for a "weekly review" to regroup, refresh, refocus, and make any changes to any part of the system that's not working as it should be.

Creating time, space, and opportunity where you think there's none

If you've searched your soul and decided that although this horse thing is really something you want to pursue at this time in your life, you really and truly don't have the time, or money, or ability to commit to it, perhaps you should think again.

> **Take one lesson a week.** Or, just one lesson a month. This isn't as much about gaining ground as a rider as it is about just getting on a horse on a regular basis and "keeping the dream alive."

> **Make a "horse date" with yourself once a week.** Or, once a month. You can do this in addition to your monthly lesson, or in place of it, if you can't afford a trainer at this time. Use your "date" to watch a training DVD, read a horse book or magazine, or attend an online webinar. Become a student of the horse, as Dr. Deborah McCormick advocates.

> **Go to the show!** Depending on where you live, there is probably some kind of horse event within driving distance. Just Google your favorite breed name or discipline, along with your location, and fill up your calendar! Admission is often free or minimal, and it's a great way to tap into the horse community even if you don't show, own a horse, or even ride. If you love the sight, sound, and yes the smell of horses, it can be quite a welcome mental break to just go, watch, listen, and learn. It is also an opportunity to stroll down barn aisles, meet owners and breeders, and maybe even pet a few noses (watch out for teeth).

> **Physically unable to ride?** Join one of the many horse-related online communities now available, check out an equine encounter retreat, and find imaginative ways to be around horses and horsemanship, either in reality or in the virtual realm. You don't have to see the world from the back of your horse to enjoy exploration in his company. Disciplines such as driving, trick training, liberty work, and agility offer many options for fun without geting in a saddle.

Moving forward

Now that you have a firm grip on your decision-making process, your core values, and specific tools for recapturing time to devote to that which really matters, we can move step by step through some common issues experienced at all levels of horsemanship, hear the stories of those who've been there (and are still there today), and ask a few experts to weigh in with ideas, information and guidance for making the next leg of this important journey everything you want it to be—and more!

Horsewoman Carole Thigpen offers a final word of guidance regarding making decisions and taking charge of your life, and especially, parlaying these decisions to eventual horse ownership. "You have to make a choice," she says. "Am I going to take action on this information or not? Is there something I need to modify or change? Is there something I need to learn first? What are some baby steps I can take with this action as the eventual goal? You don't always have to do it all at once. There are almost always baby steps."

A REAL-LIFE, MIDLIFE HORSE STORY   *GAIL*

During a childhood and youth growing up in the middle of Virginia's horse and cattle country, Gail says she was "horse crazy, like most young girls." She read about horses constantly and asked for a horse every Christmas. As luck would have it, the new family who moved into the farmhouse nextdoor brought her an opportunity beyond her wildest dreams.

The new neighbors all rode, including two daughters. Their mother volunteered to host Pony Club events at the farm and soon became a District Commissioner for the organization. The family was kind enough to offer Gail a retired show pony to ride if she wanted to be involved in Pony Club, and Gail took them up on it, spending many gloriously happy hours acquiring a broad foundation in horsemanship.

Her youth was filled with Friday afternoon riding lessons, trail riding for hours with friends or alone, and, sometimes, foxhunting with some of the local hunt clubs. Each hunt had a distinct personality, Gail explains. Some were more formal, some more youth-friendly, and some quite challenging over rougher terrain.

Gail's first horse was a Thoroughbred named Richard—a "big forward-moving, strapping horse." Her father, impressed with the horse's looks and demeanor, insisted on buying Richard for her (her father didn't ride). Gail was never completely sure she could handle Richard, was never able to relax on him, and as a result, rarely hunted on him.

Her father meant well, but Gail's early horse ownership taught her a very important lesson: "*You*, the *rider*, must be comfortable with the horse you get. It only matters what others think about a horse when they are trying to talk you *out* of buying a particular horse. *You* are the one who has to live with the horse, usually for a long time."

During and after college, Gail worked at various Thoroughbred training facilities, here and abroad, "galloping" young horses. She returned home to Virginia to finish up school, and eventually, the lure of a career in the travel industry took hold. She cut back on riding, then stopped altogether as corporate life ruled.

Fast-forward a few decades of real life. Gail and her husband were living in Texas. She still worked in travel when first her father, then her mother passed away. Like so many of us during pivotal times, Gail needed to find meaning in a new phase of life. She wanted to do something just for herself—something no one else, including her husband, was part of... something that took her back to who she *used* to be. Her thoughts, of course, turned to horses.

When she spied an advertisement for a local event, Gail rounded up a couple friends and went to watch. She ended up serving as a jump judge for the cross-country phase because there weren't enough volunteers, and the ball began to roll. She took a few lessons, talked to a lot of people, and before she knew it, she was looking for a horse.

Because of her history with racehorses, Gail was interested in off-the-track Thoroughbreds (OTTBs). She was perusing the LOPE (LoneStar Outreach to Place Ex-Racers) Web site when she found Jamaica Bet, a retired Thoroughbred with a bowed tendon. She says she liked the sweet look on his face and knew how to care for and rehabilitate bowed tendons (and for the kind of riding she was planning to do, she knew it wouldn't be a problem).

Even though several knowledgeable people tried to talk Gail out of buying Jamaica Bet, the vet check concurred with her opinion on the tendon, and $1,000 later, Gail had herself a horse. "We got along well from the start," Gail says of her relationship with Jamaica. "He's an affectionate and social horse, and nothing much bothers him. He's been around, is well-traveled, and at seven years old, is over the three-year-old 'stupids.'"

So Gail found, in Jamaica Bet, exactly what she was looking for. Just enough challenge to provide stimulation and distraction from life's cares ("You have to be alert when working around *any* horse," she says, "which gets your mind off of tension-causing issues!"), and just enough calm to soothe her soul ("It calms me to go out and work with him," she says. "I trust him and I think he trusts me.")

4

Leg up!

Competitors know that "getting a horse legged up" means getting him in physical condition to do what he is being asked to do without risking injury. For the returning rider or the middle-aged woman riding horses for the first time, this is equally important—and for the same reasons. So before you can get serious about a horse, you need to get serious about your fitness.

I HAVE TO ADMIT THAT IN THE FIRST few weeks of midlife horse ownership, I felt a certain amount of smug satisfaction in the soreness of my muscles. Each twinge was a delightful reminder to me that I wasn't going "gently into that good night," as Dylan Thomas had cautioned. I was doing something wonderful for myself, and my new set of aches and pains were proof of my self-liberation from the midlife doldrums.

Still, when a two-hour trail ride turned into eight (we got lost), and I wasn't sure I would be able to walk straight ever again...and when the weakness in my upper body caused me to repeatedly clobber my horse with his saddle rather than lifting it gently and gracefully up onto his back...and when getting on and off my horse more than a couple of times in one afternoon was a real struggle, I realized I was in desperate need of some conditioning exercises specifically geared to this new set of physical challenges.

But shoehorning the horse into my life and schedule was tough enough. How in the world would I find time to exercise, too? As a former athlete, I had a basic understanding of what I needed to do: aerobics for stamina and recovery (and maybe even to lose the "pudge" that added obvious drag during my mounting efforts); and strength training for my upper body (so I'd be better able to lift saddles, bales of hay, and sacks of feed) as well as my lower body (squeezing with my calves could be less of a strain and slightly more muscle control would help me "hang on with my legs" when my horse spooked sideways).

I realized the need for core strength for better balance, sitting straighter in the saddle, and "sitting on my pockets." Improving my flexibility would help me move "with the horse," and conscious relaxation techniques were needed to give me the ability to relax some muscles while using others, and to use breathing to release areas of unwanted tension.

Calculating the time it would take to work all this conditioning into my schedule, I realized that unless I got smarter about it, working out would be a full-time job—and probably leave me too tired to get on my horse for weeks, if not months! Maintaining this new level of conditioning would continue to take what little free time I had hoped to devote to enjoying my horse. This set me off on a new quest to overhaul the way I thought about getting fit, and how I went about it, too.

Addressing the physical demands of horsemanship

It's about midlife when many of us realize that our center of gravity has shifted, physical conditioning doesn't come as quickly or stay as easily as it did in decades past, and it's very likely that we don't "bounce" as well as we used to, either. Contemplating a return to horsemanship requires a physical assessment to determine the shape you're in and what you might need to do to get your fitness level in tune. "The rider's body is like a balancing pole to the horse," writes Sylvia Loch in Richenda van Laun's book, *Flexibility and Fitness for Riders* (J.A. Allen, 2000). "A loose, flaccid body gives little support; similarly, a tight one restricts movement."

So not only do we have to be strong enough to control the horse and provide good solid leadership with clear effective cues and direction, we have to be flexible and relaxed enough to move with the horse and to stay out of his way as he tries to do whatever we're asking him to do. On top of that, we have to have enough endurance to stay effective during long or challenging rides, then have enough left over to untack and cool out the horse, tote water buckets, muck stalls, and move around bales of hay. Starting to get the picture?

Don't despair! Building this kind of conditioning is easier than I thought at first and than you may be thinking right now. It just takes a little focused planning, commitment, and the creation of new habits that not only help you in your horse activities, but have a positive effect on the rest of your life as well.

▓ Isn't riding a horse exercise enough?

The answer to this obvious question is both"Yes" and "No." Although riding a horse *is* very good exercise (see sidebar, p. 58), it is not enough to actually *gain* the fitness level you need for safer and more effective riding. In other words, riding can help keep you fit and round out a general exercise plan, but to become a *better rider*, you need something more. And that's not all. If the only exercise you do is ride, you put yourself at risk for repetitive motion or referred strain injuries in your back, muscles, and joints caused by strength imbalances in your body.

Whether you're a beginner, a "weekend warrior" returning to horses after a long absence, or a seasoned professional who is starting to notice body wear-and-tear, a simple, solid, and consistent conditioning program will keep you riding longer and better, and will help you enjoy it more.

How Riding Keeps You Fit

> ❯ An hour of trotting can blast 400 to 600 calories (in your body, not the horse's!)

> ❯ Mounting a horse uses every single leg and butt muscle you possess.

> ❯ Sitting on a horse simulates an extended squat, constantly working quads, hamstrings, abductors, and aductors simultaneously.

"Everyone who rides should incorporate a cross-training program and proper nutrition in their regimen to stay fit and healthy and prevent injury," writes Mary Midkiff in her book *Fitness, Performance, and the Female Equestrian* (Howell Book House, 1996). "Riding alone does not provide the fitness required for performance, especially if you only ride occasionally. Like any sport, riding requires other athletic activities be added to the mix."

▥ So what does this mean to the returning or "green as grass" rider?

In a nutshell you need a consistent and balanced training program that addresses the special needs of riding a horse: strength, flexibility, balance, stamina, alignment, and body awareness. You can create this by putting together a calculated cross-training program that fits your life, interests, and time constraints. With a little bit of upfront research and planning, and by revisiting your program and individual goals every six weeks, you can get the fitness ball rolling—and keep it rolling. The results, both on and off the horse, will amaze you.

Sound complicated and impossibly time consuming? It doesn't have to be, agree the experts I consulted for this book. (I kept looking for one who would say we didn't really have to do all this, but no such luck.) The consensus seems to be that mixing an aerobic activity at varying intensities with simple, targeted strength training (I offer examples of specific exercises on the pages ahead), along with "core work," such as Pilates or yoga (see p. 311 for ideas, exercises, and resources) is just the right blend for developing the oddly contradictory qualities of relaxation and strength that make you fit for the saddle (and lots of other stuff, too!).

A well-thought-out weekly mix of these elements can achieve what you need with a minimum of time invested. The bonus, it seems, is the overall impact on the rest of your life. I don't know about you, but middle age has not been kind to me, metabolically speaking. That 15 to 20 pounds I've lugged around—and meant to do something about—for most of my adult life has now blossomed into 30, and I'm finding extra "me" in places that never harbored fat before. I have to admit I was excited to find a way to blend a much needed "lifestyle solution" with my passion for horses and better horsemanship.

Options for getting started

▥ Pay for a pro

If your budget can take it, hire a certified personal trainer to put a plan together for you. This individual doesn't have to be a horse person to help you jump into your fitness program—just take him or her a list of your intended activities, fitness goals, and time and scheduling particulars. For an additional fee, you can arrange for the trainer to "coach you through" until you get the hang of the prescribed exercises. This can ensure you perform them correctly for maximum benefit and minimum chance of injury. There are also lots of physical trainers who actually specialize in working with equestrians, so if you're serious and have the funds, search your area for one with expertise particular to your interests.

Another option is the myriad of books and DVDs on fitness in midlife and fitness for equestrians now available. I've listed a few good ones in the *Resources* (see p. 311), and I have a feeling I only scratched the surface. Many of the creators of these published programs are also available for private consultation or will even come to your barn or training facility to put on a workshop for a minimum number of participants.

⦀ Go DIY

Don't worry—if you really want to get fit for riding (and life) with almost no outlay of cash, you can easily put together your own program at home with a decent pair of athletic shoes and a pair of 5-pound dumbbells. If you like treadmills, stationary bikes, weight machines, by all means use them...or just stick with the "equipment" you were born with and keep it simple.

There are tons of daily fitness programs on most cable and satellite systems; record a series and follow along for six weeks, then record a new series, and go for another six weeks. (You can of course watch the program "live" if your time allows, but the advantage of recording is you can be sure to fit in your daily exercise whenever your schedule allows.) Be sure to rotate exercises and alter intensities—most bodies respond best to changing things up about every six weeks in order to keep progressing toward your fitness goals.

In addition to looking better, feeling better, and creating enough energy for your new "horsey" lifestyle, developing a good basic training regimen that you do every day without excuse (a personal trainer once told me to think of it like brushing my teeth) will:

⟩ Decrease your risk of muscle and joint injury, strain, and fatigue.

⟩ Improve your confidence and focus while riding, making you more effective in the saddle.

> Increase your flexibility and help you move with the horse.

> Build greater body awareness, balance, and muscle control.

> "Reset" your muscle memory and sense of correct alignment.

> Build quicker reactions and more precise cues.

Talk is cheap...let's get moving!

Although there are a-million-and-one options for equestrian exercise routines out there, when I decided to get back into riding, I wanted to create one that would be the most effective, the easiest to perform, and the simplest to remember without requiring professional help. I wanted it to take no more than 30 minutes a day and no equipment beyond, maybe, that dusty old set of dumbbells hiding somewhere in my garage.

In the course of researching "top exercises for the equestrian," I found the following recommendations duplicated in one form or another in many different places. Experts advise that we start with one or two (approximately) 30-minute sessions a week, and work up to including five a week, every week. Of course, it goes without saying that you should consult your doctor and have a thorough checkup before embarking on any new exercise program. And, where physical limitations apply, work with a licensed physical or occupational therapist to develop the best modifications and overall program for your safe, optimum conditioning.

Build your weekly exercise foundation

Day 1: Build staying power
Regular aerobics keep you in the saddle stronger and longer. It doesn't

matter what sustained activity you do, as long as you do it with enough intensity to get your heart pumping while still being able to carry on a conversation or sing a song (to yourself, please!) without being winded. The simplest of these is brisk walking or jogging, but you can plug in whatever activity you like. If you're a "gym rat," mix and match those machines-to-nowhere to your heart's content. Personally, I like to take a walk and talk to my dog. He's a great listener, and the walk does him some good, too.

Day 2: Get strong to the core
Pilates greatly improves your balance and stability. Classes, books, DVDs, and cable/satellite exercise shows abound—just pick a good basic one that doesn't last longer than 30 minutes or require what appears to be a medieval torture apparatus.

Day 3: Find your balance, flexibility, and "relaxed strength" through regular hatha yoga practice
Hatha yoga improves flexibility, alignment, body awareness, and relaxation. To build a base of yogic fitness, just find a DVD, show, or series of asanas you like and do them for about 30 minutes.

Day 4: Hoist that saddle, toss that bale, step lightly onto the horse
Weight training equips you to do all this and more. The key here is light weights, high reps to build muscle endurance, and targeting the muscle groups specific to riding—or to balancing those you'll use when riding to avoid injuries to the weaker set. While there are no hard-and-fast rules here, try to keep your weight-training routine simple so you'll stay with it. (Check out the sidebar on p. 64 for the routine I found that streamlines everything you need into your allotted 30 minutes.)

Day 5: Enlarge your energy reservoir
Intense aerobics thrown in once a week or so increases your aerobic capacity enough to work harder, longer—and still keep a "burst of

energy in your tank" so you can respond even when you're tired. This is easy to describe, harder to do, but hang in there—it's worth it. Just do 10 minutes of your Day 1 aerobic activity (see p. 61) followed by 15 minutes of amped-up effort that makes it too hard to carry on a civil conversation (my dog hates this part) but not to the point of exhaustion. End with a leisurely pace for a 5-minute cool down.

Specific targets to meet specific horsemanship goals

While choosing the exercises that target specific muscle groups is not exactly rocket science, there are a few rules about how (and how often) to work each muscle group for best results. On p. 313, I've listed some good basic weight training references for women. With their help, along with a few online sources and the work I did with a personal trainer during one particularly insecure and narcissistic spell during my thirties, I gathered a few ideas for building strong hands, arms, upper back and shoulders, chest, lower back, glutes, abs, and legs. Again, consult a certified trainer or a good reference book for step-by-step how-to guidance, reps, rest periods, and how to put these exercises together for optimum results.

Your Muscle and the Horse's Mind

In addition to improving your riding and effectiveness in the saddle, there's another big benefit to becoming a physically strong rider. Believe it or not, the quality of your muscle strength helps control a horse mentally, as well as physically. In her online article, "Equestrian Weight Lifting and Strength Training," Linda Leistman, President of the North American Horseman's Association (NAHA), writes, "A horse can easily decipher if a rider is weak and ineffective. Not only will a horse sometimes simply not respond to a weak rider, but he can also react badly because the weak and ineffective rider is incapable of giving the horse the confidence for which he looks to the rider to provide at uncertain moments."

Who knew? Is that the "Rocky" theme song I hear playing in my head?

TARGET	EXERCISE
Hands	Hand grips and wrist curls with light dumbbells to help with rein control.
Arms	Bicep curls, hammer curls, tricep kickbacks, tricep extensions, and cross-face extensions to help with halting, half-halting, one-rein stops, and turning.
Upper back and shoulders	Upright and bent-over rows, rhomboid squeezes, and external rotations to help your balance, posture, and overall control of the horse.
Chest	Dumbbell flyes to improve posture and rein control.
Lower back and glutes	Lying butt lifts to provide strength and stability in stopping, slowing, and using your lower body to control the horse.
Abs	Crunches, curl ups, and leg raises that will pay off big time in the sitting trot, controlled canter, and staying with your horse when he spooks or shies sideways (see sidebar on p. 65 for crunch instructions).
Legs	Outer and inner thigh raises, corkscrews, leg extensions, leg curls, calf raises, and the good old "Thighmaster" (don't despair if you got rid of yours in a long-ago garage sale—you can still find them very easily online) will give you strong legs. You'll notice a big difference in your cues, posting, and generally moving well with your horse, no matter where he goes and at what speed.

EXERCISE

What to do when workout time "escapes"

When, despite your best intentions and ironclad commitment, your workout time somehow gets away from you, here are a few quick exercises to squeeze into the odd moment and keep your fitness program on track:

▸ **Good old pushups** work all of your chest, arm, and back muscles at once. If your "pushup strength" is less than optimal, start with standing pushups against the wall, progress to "girl pushups" from your knees, then, when you're strong enough, go for the full body pushups from your toes with your palms beside your shoulders. When you find yourself experimenting with hand position—turning your fingers in or out, or pushing off your knuckles instead of your palms—you may be in line for a Golden Lasso. Start by doing as many as you can with good form, then add one more every day. Basic instructions for a full pushup are:

- Lie chest down on the floor with your palms flat and slightly more than shoulder-width apart and your feet together, toes down.

- Straighten your arms and push your body up off the floor (look forward, not down). Don't arch your back.

- Pause, then bend your arms and lower your body back toward the floor.

- Pause when your chest touches the floor, then repeat.

▸ **Crunches** are easier on your back than old-fashioned sit-ups. The key is to lift straight toward the ceiling using your abdominal muscles—don't use your neck or pull with your hands. Give yourself a quick, full ab workout in no time by:

- Starting with a set of regular crunches, lie on the floor with your knees bent and your hands behind your head or across your chest. Contract your abs, bringing your shoulders a couple inches off the floor, pause, then lower back down. Repeat 15 times.

- Following with a set of reverse crunches to target your lower abs. Extend your legs straight up from your hips and place your hands on the floor beside your body or behind your head. Use your abs to push your heels toward the ceiling 15 times.

- Returning to the regular crunch position with your knees bent and your hands behind your head, and working your obliques (the muscles that crisscross the sides of our abdominal area and give us a waistline...or used to!) by using your abs to alternately pull your body up and across so you can touch one elbow and then the other to the opposite knee. Perform 15 reps each side (so a total of 30).

▸ **Squats** are invaluable because, as I mentioned earlier, the simple act of getting on a horse requires every leg and butt muscle we own. Strengthening your legs and glutes will help get you up in that saddle without a lot of tugging and hanging and swearing, so be sure to incorporate plenty of squats into your program. To do a basic squat:

• Start standing with your toes pointing forward, feet about shoulder width apart.

• With arms extended forward for balance, sit down as if you are sitting in a chair, taking care not to let your bottom go below your knees.

• Stand back up and repeat.

That's it. Do sets of 10 with your toes straight ahead, then 10 with your toes pointing in to work outer thigh muscles, and 10 with your toes turned out to work your inner thighs.

▸ **Lunges** round out your leg-and-butt workout, and in combination with squats, help you "rise to the riding occasion" (get on your horse) in a more graceful and efficient manner. They'll also strengthen your seat in the saddle, keeping you on board and making your cues clearer to your horse. To do a simple lunge:

• Stand with your feet together, then take a giant step forward, bending your forward knee to a right (90-degree) angle (do *not* flex so far that your knee extends beyond your ankle). At the same time, your back knee will bend, too.

• Return to your starting postion and repeat with the opposite leg. Alternate lunges until you have done 10 on each side. (Note: There are a lot of variations on this exercise, using weights and even walking forward, but this is enough to get you started. Go ahead and up the ante when you're ready.)

Getting even *more* specific

In her book *Learning to Ride as an Adult* (Cadmos Books, 2003), Erika Prockl presents a training method for getting your muscles ready to ride that offers some interesting insights, particularly in the areas of body alignment, muscle relaxation, and resetting your muscle memory. When I ran a few of Prockl's exercises past several women who have ridden all their life, both in English and Western disciplines, the consensus was that the following is very good information for all of us to remember.

▓ Get a broad seat

No, not the kind you get by eating more cheeseburgers. What this means is learning to deliberately relax the adductor muscles (inside your upper thighs) and your butt muscles to make a closer, softer, but more solid connection with your horse's back. These are the muscles that can squeeze a horse uncomfortably when we get tense.

> ❭ Sit backward on a straight-backed chair and consciously tense and then relax your adductor and butt muscles while keeping your upper body aligned and your lower back straight. Feel your body sinking into closer contact with the chair.

> ❭ Next, try the same exercise on a stability ball, straddling it as you would a horse's back, and again, paying attention to your upper body alignment and lower back. Practice tensing and releasing, then see how long you can sit, keeping these muscles relaxed. Monitor your muscles and when you feel the tension coming back in, make them relax.

> ❭ Now try keeping those muscles relaxed as you bounce gently on the ball. It's harder than it sounds—one of my barrel racing friends got "bucked off" a stability ball during this exercise. Go figure.

"You will be able to maintain a broad seat on your horse in different situations only after this position has become familiar," Prockl says, adding that when "you get good at localizing and deliberately relaxing these and other areas of tightness in your lower body, you will be able to move better with the horse and help him relax and trust you as his leader."

Another bonus to this exercise extends all the way down your legs. Remembering that familiar command by riding instructors to "keep your heels down," simply relaxing your adductors and butt to create a "broad seat" automatically puts your feet in the position instructors are looking for—without force and resulting tightness in your legs.

▥ Reposition your thoracic girdle

If you, like me, didn't even know you had one of these, it may interest you to know that in our habitual daily activities we tend to do things that shorten our chest muscles, causing us to hunch over our keyboard, book, and, to our mother's horror, sometimes even our dinner plate. What's worse, when we get nervous on a horse, the first thing we do, in addition to clamping down with our bottom and legs to give the horse an uncomfortable squeeze, is to hunch forward, seeking, I suppose, the fetal position for protection. The culprit of this natural physical tendency, it appears, is the "thoracic girdle," or the group of muscles that sits at the top of your chest.

> ❭ To locate and reposition this key to better alignment, Prockl advises us to simply pull our shoulders up to our ears, then let them sink slowly back and down as far as they will go. Hold them there for a moment and let this feeling sink in (if it feels weird, this is an exercise we probably need to do a lot!)

Realign your thoracic girdle as often as you think about it—and whenever you catch yourself slumping or hunching your shoulders forward. Being conscious of this important group of muscles and training it to stay properly aligned will go a long way toward keeping you in better position to control your horse in all kinds of situations.

▥ Swinging circles

This exercise for your shoulders, elbows, and wrists, Prockl tells us, is designed to keep your hands light, and keep your arms relaxed and moving with, not against the horse in whichever riding discipline you choose.

> ❭ Relax your shoulders and make big forward circles with your arms. Make the circles progressively smaller until your arm isn't moving at all, but in your mind you are imagining tiny rhythmic circles inside your shoulder joint. (I know it sounds weird, but try it. You'll be surprised at how easy it is.)

> ❭ Now, hold a set of imaginary reins and mentally extend your rhythmic imaginary circling into your elbows, circling them in time with your shoulders.

> ❭ Do the same thing into your wrists. You should now "see" tiny circles in your shoulders, elbows, and wrists, all swinging in time with the gait of your imaginary horse. Hold the image in your mind as long as you can. Then repeat the exercise.

> ❭ Once you are proficient on the ground, try this exercise when you ride. You'll be amazed at how it keeps your arms relaxed and rhythmic, giving you a light, flexible, and elastic contact with the horse's mouth.

▥ Three lower back/pelvic exercises worth learning

Two common resources for equestrian-specific conditioning exercises are the website from the creator and founder of Women & Horses™ fitness and performance program, Mary Midkiff (www.womenandhorses.com), and her book *Fitness, Performance, and the Female Equestrian* (Howell Book House, 1996). Mary introduced me to a series of equestrian ball exercises that isolate and target the muscle groups in the lower back and pelvic area that we've already identified as needing to strengthen, control, and—perhaps most importantly—relax. The following three exercises, done consistently, will make an amazing difference in your ability to follow the natural motion of your horse.

Pelvic circles

Due to a scarring experience in a YMCA Belly Dancing class during the 1980s, this exercise is, for me, best practiced alone. However, if you ever developed any skills with a hula hoop (which I admittedly never did), you'll find the exercise a piece of cake, as it is much the same motion.

>) Sit on an exercise ball (several experts recommend using the 75-centimeter core stability ball you can buy almost anywhere for around 25 bucks. Get the 85-centimeter version if you're tall or especially long-legged.)

>) Put your hands on your hips and, concentrating on your hip bones, but keeping your legs and upper body as still as possible (easier said than done—have someone hold on to your knees at first if you need to), "circle" your hips slowly in one direction.

>) When you master one direction without the help of a spotter, try the other way. Concentrate on keeping your circles smooth.

>) Spiral down to smaller-sized circles, then up to as large a circle as you can make. Do 20 to 30 circles of varying sizes in each direction.

Pelvic tilts

In the pelvic tilt you roll the exercise ball back and forth, using just the muscles of your lower back and pelvis.

) Sit on the ball with your hands on your hips.

) Concentrating once again on those hipbones, tilt your belly button up toward your chest to make the ball roll forward.

) Now arch your back to push the ball backward.

) Repeat, keeping your rolls smooth and even. Complete 20 forward/backward repetitions.

Side to side

A physical therapist actually recommended this one to me when I was rehabbing a lower back injury. (Quick lesson: When you're halfway on a horse and he starts bucking, don't bail off backward thinking that landing on your hip in soft dirt is the preferable outcome...)

) Sit on your exercise ball with your hands on your hips.

) Using just your pelvis, roll the ball to one side by bringing the opposite hip straight up toward your shoulder, then slowly roll it back.

) When you get about back to center, bring the other hip up toward the other shoulder.

) Repeat 20 left-right repetitions, noticing any unevenness or tightness. On the side that's tighter, do a few more each session until the feel starts to even up and you can complete the exercise in even, side-to-side arcs.

Hidden paths to equestrian cross-training

Quite by accident I discovered two things on my own with regard to fitness and horses. (No doubt you will too, so keep your eyes and your

Find your alignment

Creator and founder of Women & Horses™ fitness and performance program Mary Midkiff tells us how to find our alignment so that maintaining our place of balance both in and out of the saddle will soon become automatic.

- ▶ Place one hand at the center of your lower back.
- ▶ Bend forward until you feel the bones of your spine start to protrude.
- ▶ Now, bend backward until you feel your spine disappear. Somewhere in between these two extremes is your straight spine.
- ▶ Keep one hand in the center of your lower back and place the other in the center of your chest. Slowly allow your chest to come forward into your hand without lifting your rib cage. Notice how your lower back feels now. This is your place of perfect alignment. Take a breath and blow it out like you would a birthday candle. Close your eyes and memorize this balanced feeling.

mind open!) After several years of devotion to Bikram yoga (Bikram Choudhury himself calls his trademark series of postures—or *asanas*— a "torture chamber") I realized the truth to the dialogue that instructors repeat during every class: The time you spend keeping your body in tune is like putting deposits in your checking account. The activities and stressors of your daily life are writing checks on that account. As long as you put more in than you take out, you stay strong and healthy and are able to enjoy your life and whatever you choose to do with it. When you start to overdraw this account, you invite disease and injury.

It never occurred to me while I was standing in that 110-degree room for 90 minutes at a time, doing those same 26 postures every day, that the "bulldog determination and Bengal tiger strength" I was building— along with the "nothing can steal your peace" place of stillness in my mind—was also perfect preparation for work with horses. Not to mention it brought me the body awareness that makes it easier to consciously relax certain muscle groups while using others to the max (an ability referred to in a very colorful manner by reining clinician Greg Dial as "pinto bean butt" (now there's an image that will stick with you!). Now I see the unmistakable connection. It may very likely be the same for you— once you know the conditioning requirements particular to effective horsemanship, you can most likely look around your life experience and current activities and find something you already make time for that is perfect equestrian cross-training material.

Modifying yoga with the rider in mind

In their book *Yoga for Equestrians* (Trafalgar Square Books, 2000), authors Linda Benedik and Veronica Wirth deliberately integrate yoga with horsemanship to help riders of all disciplines to build balance, flexibility, body awareness, and use of breathing to enhance their ability to move in rhythm with the horse. Using meditations, visualization, and detailing the yoga postures that are key to improving a rider's seat and communication with the horse, the routines presented in this book can be done at home, at the barn, and some even on the horse. A specific breathing exercise, called pranayama breathing, also detailed in this book, is very helpful in getting rid of tension and calling for that "place of stillness" that calms both you and your horse whenever necessary.

Another cross-training surprise for me—albeit one that takes a "horsey" activity and finds the inherent fitness benefit within it—are the aerobic and strength conditioning benefits of doing Australian horse trainer and clinician Clinton Anderson's groundwork exercises. Due to time constraints, when I decided to "start over on the ground" with my midlife horse Trace, I traded my morning exercise time to work through Anderson's groundwork exercises one by one, exactly as prescribed in his books and on his DVDs (see p. 311 for a list of these). Spending 30 minutes a day hustling my horse's feet (and my own) through deep sand, swinging that gosh-darned "Handy stick," and "bumping" on the lead rope gave me a big surprise: I found myself often leaving the arena sweatier than my horse and, consequently, in the best shape of my recent life. I was easily doing things I had not done since my physical peak in my twenties. While I was concentrating on getting my horse to do his groundwork exercises correctly, my own conditioning just snuck right up on me.

So where else can cross-training work its magic as you try to massage your days to accommodate your horsey activities and your fitness needs? Come to find out, there's no end to the ways you can "double down" on the little tasks that make up your equestrian hobby.

▓ Make barn chores count twice

In the spirit of the old Benjamin Franklin quote, "Chop your own firewood; it will warm you twice," here are a few hints on barn-friendly cross-training from the article "Minutes to a Fitter You" by Helen Peppe, which appeared in *Practical Horseman* (March 2010):

> ❯ Filling water buckets is an opportunity for "stallside squats": Hold the bucket at mid-chest and keeping your back straight, feet shoulder width apart, weight in your heels, and chin level, bend your knees and sit down until your thighs are parallel to the floor, taking care not to let your bottom go below your knees (see instructions for squats in sidebar, p. 66). Hold this for a count of 12 if you can, then slowly stand up. Repeat 10 times. You can also do this exercise with two half-full buckets. (Notice my optimistic outlook.)

> ❯ Work your biceps, shoulders, and waistline with the "one man bucket brigade": Grasp a full(ish) bucket in your left hand, palm up, and bend your elbow to raise the bucket waist high (a bicep curl), then slowly lower the bucket, twisting your palm clockwise as you move your hand behind your back. When you reach the midpoint

(behind your butt) grasp the handle with your right hand, palm facing back, then twist it clockwise as you bring the bucket forward and up, bending your elbow to bring it waist high on the right side. Reverse and repeat, working up to 10 repetitions.

﹥ Work your abs and glutes as you muck stalls by consciously tightening both at the same time every time you pull the pitchfork or rake toward you. Rake at an angle and turn to empty the fork to work your obliques (sides of waist), but take care to protect your lower back by keeping those abs pulled in ("Press your belly button to your backbone!" one of my yoga instructors used to say) and your knees soft.

﹥ Add spurts of aerobic activity anywhere you can by jogging with the wheelbarrow (full or empty), and while leading your horse to and from the pasture or arena.

Above all, be creative and look for ways you can up your fitness quotient in everything you do. "There are many benefits to working out in short blasts," says fitness pro and certified sports nutritionist Amy Bento, who places a big value on the mental benefits of this kind of "sneaky workout" as well. "When you have to schedule time to go to the gym, getting fit can seem overwhelming," she adds. Bento believes that by dedicating 10 minutes here and 10 minutes there during the course of your day, you can gain the benefits of a gym workout without adding to your already hectic schedule. (Bento's conditioning DVDs and more 10-minute fitness solutions can be found at www.nrgfitness.net.)

Take it easy and you'll get there faster

As I mentioned at the beginning of this chapter, you should have a thorough physical checkup before beginning or "amping up" your exercise and conditioning program. It's also kind of fun to pay a little extra

A Full Belly Isn't a Flabby Belly

When improving your fitness level and losing weight, fitness pro and certified sports nutritionist Amy Bento says you shouldn't deprive yourself (even of chocolate!) In fact, when you have a busy day with plans to ride after work, you need to be sure to keep eating—every three hours is best to keep your metabolism stoked and your energy reserves full.

"Make good choices when you do eat," Bento advises. "Use portion control." And of course, "Be prepared." Take the time to pack a cooler with healthy snacks when you plan to spend the afternoon at the barn or at a show. This helps keep you fueled up and away from the siren call of those vending machines and fast-food drive-throughs.

(depending on your idea of "fun" and depending on your insurance) for a full panel of bloodwork to show you exactly where you rate in terms of blood pressure and cholesterol, for example. After a few months, you can have bloodwork done again, and you'll likely be amazed and pleased at the improvement in your numbers.

Your pre-fitness-program physical is also be a good time to discuss with your doctor any vitamins, supplements, or bodywork you may need to consider as you venture into the world of riding and working with horses on a regular basis. "Horsey" activities can be hard on muscles, ligaments, bones, and joints—not to mention the effect of the occasional spill. (There are some who say if you're not falling off you're not riding, but I really don't agree with that!) Nevertheless, injuries happen and as we get older, we need to do what we can to speed up an unavoidably lengthening recovery time.

To return now to the sage advice from our friend and midlife role model, Dara Torres, while Torres is the first to say that at this age and beyond we can be strong and fit and do all we want to do, she is quick to remind us we have to be smart about how we go about our physical conditioning. This will make the difference Torres tells us, between pain and performance.

Be sure to break in slowly to your new fitness routine—add one thing at a time, and build up gradually to the workout you have in mind. If this means you only do one or two modified pushups the first day, so be it. Start wherever you are and flirt with the fine line between "enough" and "too much" to keep yourself moving forward at the right rate for your body. Whereas a coach may once have barked, "Give me 10!" now your body is the boss, and you have to respect it—even when you're going for 10 and your body says, "I'll give you seven-and-a-half...."

Give yourself extra warm-up and cool-down time, and allow greater recovery time between workouts. Make sure you ingest plenty of fluids and replace lost electrolytes. When we're young we can get away with pushing this envelope—and when we're excited and in a hurry to see changes in our body it can be easy to overdo. Just *take it easy,* build up your program gradually, and you'll get there much faster than if you have to stop and recover from overuse injuries.

The moral of the fitness story

"We owe it to our horses to be as fit and flexible as we expect them to be," says Gina Smith, Canadian Olympian and Assistant Chef d'Equipe of the Canadian Dressage Team. And, whether you plan to ride dressage, Western pleasure, or just for fun on the trails and in your own pasture, Smith is absolutely right. To be safe and ride well takes a calculated, dedicated, and committed effort to getting fit. By educating yourself on exactly what these specific needs are, then looking around your life and experiences to find the activities and programs that can get you there from wherever you are right now, you will do right by yourself and your horse.

5

Find your happy trail

Maybe you still have your childhood jumping saddle stashed away under a pile of your kids' outgrown clothing. Maybe you've always pictured yourself out in Big Sky Country, galloping across an open field on the back of a horse. Maybe you want horses in your life, but can't ride for any number of reasons. Maybe you have no idea. What will your happy midlife trail look like? In this chapter we'll take a look at some of horse-related activities and disciplines out there, so you can take the next step on your exciting journey of self-discovery.

THERE ARE MOMENTS OF PURE JOY that stand out for me on my midlife horse journey, aside and apart from all the digging around I've done in my own soul. They rank as "firsts" in my life, and looking back on them, I am so glad I took opportunities to broaden my horse experience.

I took my first real trail ride on my midlife horse, Trace, on a ranch just out-side Paradise, Texas (an irony that didn't escape me even then), and it was truly one of the most magical rides of my life. Galloping across a hayfield at sunset with a half-dozen newfound friends, we all laughed out loud together, the joy-ful exuberance of the moment spread-ing between us like wildfire. Afterward, when I slid down off Trace, I hugged him and whispered, "Thank you" into his ear.

Another great moment came in a pen of cattle at a local ranch sorting "practice." What we did that day was, in fact, a kind of fun I have never had before and can't wait to have again. I've always loved the idea of working cattle, but I thought it completely out of the question with neither cows nor the "deep pockets" required to be a cutter. Ranch sorting turned out to be the perfect low-budget alternative that gave me everything I was looking for—and more.

Trace and I entered a large, covered arena. He was, as usual, on high-headed alert, but for some reason, the closer we got to the figure-eight-shaped sorting pens and the cattle, the more he seemed to calm down. I felt the opposite.

As I observed the first few rounds, my attention was diverted from watching the cows, to watching *Trace* watch the cows. Ears pricked forward, he followed every movement inside the pen with a level of interest I had never before seen in him. So, for 25 bucks I (and my riding partner in this madness, Susan) got a sticker with a number on it. The cows had numbers on them, too. When the announcer called our number, one of us had to go into the herd and "get" (that sounds simple, doesn't it?) a cow and move him through the 12-foot opening, or "gate," that connected two 50-foot round pens. The other guarded the gate—and since cattle like to stay with their friends, the guard's job was to "peel off" any cows that tried to come through with ours. Then we had to switch roles and continue to sort the cattle in numeric progression until the buzzer (mercifully) ended the round. The number of cows sorted in the proper order was our score.

Fortunately, Trace knew exactly what to do. When I pointed him toward the rear flank (as instructed by well-intentioned ringside hollerers) of the cow we were after, he got in there, got on it, and pushed it against the fence, all the way around to the gate. "That's good! Use that fence—it's your best cowhand!" someone shouted. When it was our turn to guard, it was another story. There's just no good way to describe facing down a herd of panicked cattle and trying to block a fairly large hole they are desperate to get through—let's just say, this part wasn't our finest moment, although it did get easier when we figured out which direction to face (I told you it wasn't pretty).

By the end of this first outing, I knew I had found my thrill and a source of the intoxicating magic called "having fun with my horse." And what was even better than the actual event was how much fun *my horse* was having (and for once, his fun was not at *my* expense!) I had experienced what author Linda Kohanov would call "partnering with a horse [that feels like] music in motion." I don't know exactly what song we were playing that day, but I do know I want to "play it again."

The other great moment of midlife "ah" came on the last morning of a three-day "horse camping" trip. I woke before everyone else and looked through the flap of the tent to see my two horses on the picket line just a few feet away. The sun was coming up behind them and the early morning air carried that feeling of promise—a soft sweetness that made me feel very, very grateful to be right where I was in time and place. When my horses saw me emerge from the tent, they both nickered. Now, I know their greeting was more about the hay I was about to give them, but just for a moment I let myself think that they, too, were glad to be there, glad to see me, glad we were on this adventure together.

Soft nuzzling noses. The smell of the barn. Large, soft eyes watching you, waiting to see what you have in mind. Contented grazing. Friends, campfires, picnics on a hill, and loping across a spring meadow. Fall leaves shuffling under hooves on a clear crisp day. Hosing off a sweaty horse. Stacking sweet smelling hay. New leather. Old spurs. Where will you find *your* music?

Saddle is to discipline as egg is to chicken, or....?

Now that you've reinvented yourself, gotten fit, and discovered your path to midlife authenticity, I think it's high time you take a look around at what's available and find the kind of fun you want to have with horses. While that "Happy Trail" for each of us is probably going to be a little different, in the next pages it is my hope that you will find plenty of things to make your heart sing and your spirit soar. That is, after all, what we came here for, right?

But before you can get in the saddle, you need to decide what that saddle looks like! Whether all you want to do is a few jogs around the arena or pasture, practice basic reining-styled maneuvers, hit the trails on the weekends, following the clinic circuit to keep increasing your training skills and abilities, or try your hand at any number of equine sporting endeavors, there is an amazing amount of opportunity out there at all levels. And (here's the kicker), all of them use different kinds of tack and equipment, different kinds of horses that are bred to specialize in various pursuits, and require a different "outfit" on your part.

The challenge, it appears, is to find what interests you, set your course for gaining the skills and knowledge you need (aligned, of course, with your financial, time, and access resources), and go for it. (Then, get the right outfit.) The Internet opens the doors to opportunities to us as never before. Just use your favorite search engine to find the association for every horse breed, every discipline, and every horse-related event that's interested you over the years.

If you are a returning rider, you very well may have a past area of specialization or interest that you are planning to rediscover. This means you know whether you want to ride English or Western, whether you want to jump or keep all four feet on the ground, and perhaps even the breed of horse you prefer. If you are a long-time dreamer who is finally making horses your reality, perhaps you have the sweet, delicate profile of an Arabian firmly in your mind, or you've long heard talk of the silky smooth ride offered by a gaited horse and you're desperate to give one a try. In addition, our horse-related interests are impacted by our geographic location: You're more likely to "get into" eventing in certain areas of the East Coast, and you have a better chance of being bitten by the roping bug in the West.

The thing is, determining what you want to *do* with horses is a complicated equation. It depends entirely on what *you* bring to the table: your skills (or lack of), your preconceptions, your fantasies, what calms you down, what gets your blood pumping. One thing begets another: Your choice of saddle impacts your choice of discipline impacts your choice of horse. And, your choice of horse impacts your choice of discipline impacts your choice of saddle.

Since there are many excellent books out there that give you the lowdown on horse breeds around the world, and thousands of instructional books that provide the fundamentals for basic English or Western riding, I'll focus on the different activities you can enjoy from the back (or side) of a horse on the pages ahead.

So, what are my choices?

Bet you'll be glad we honed our decision-making skills in chapter 3 when you get through with this one! Honestly, though, if every activity I describe sounds like heaven and every discipline sounds too good to be true, don't panic...just pick a place to start, and jump right in. There's no reason one equestrian activity can't lead to another; there's no reason to feel you might be trapped in a sport you don't like. Professional riders accrue new skills, branch out, and experiment on a regular basis, and so can you.

If you do feel that you are drowning in riches, I advise you begin in your comfort zone: Try groundwork before you ride; walk before you run; focus on pleasure before competition. But other than that, just *find your thrill*.

▥ Are you *just* a trail rider?

"Okay, that's it, enough is enough!!!!" read the blog post by Minnesota trainer and clinician Liz Graves (www.lizgraves.com). The exaggerated use of multiple end punctuation caused me to stop and wonder what in the world had gotten her so worked up. Speaking directly (if a little sternly) to those of us who regularly trail ride, Liz's post went on to say she sure wished we'd all describe our preferred horse activity differently.

Trail riding, it turns out, is really not the piece of cake some people think it is. True, you don't necessarily go fast and make hairpin turns around some object. (Unless, of course, we're talking about me riding my midlife horse, Rio, and something out there looks like it might be a little bit "flappy.") But trail riding, just the same, requires a certain amount of horse and rider ability—in some ways, much more than people generally give it credit for.

"Somewhere along the way the horse industry has, it seems, made some of those who trail ride as their main pastime feel like second-class citizens," Liz observed. "That is absolutely not true in any way, shape, or form!" Right-e-o, sister!

A good trail horse is...

A horse that is good on trails has been exposed to all kinds of unexpected things he would never see hanging on the rails of an arena. Wildlife pops out of the bushes. Branches blow off trees in front of him. Tall grasses and sunflowers tickle his belly and his "you-know-what." All of this can and does happen on even the shortest afternoon trail ride close to home. (Ask me how I know this!)

Trail horses have to be in good enough shape to carry our midlife butts long hours (especially when we get lost without a trail map on a 35,000-acre National Grassland), up and down creek banks, over logs and discarded tires (hopefully more the former than the latter), under branches, across creeks (sometimes backward—did I mention Rio doesn't like water, either? Well it turns out he'll back through it...*don't* ask me how I know this).

Trail horses sometimes have to go for long periods without water or food (usually when the rider is lost due to, again, the lack of a trail map), and then, if it's an overnight trip, they have to stand quietly, tied to a picket line, while we humans eat and drink and giggle with our friends.

A good trail rider is...

As trail riders we have a lot of responsibility. We have to make sure we pack right (trail map, anyone?) and that our horse's tack fits well and doesn't rub or chafe, even after hours of riding. We need to be prepared for emergencies involving both people and horses. We have to be in shape, keep our horses in shape, and pay attention to what's going on in front, to the sides, and behind us the whole time we're in the saddle.

Now, there are some "just trail riders" who give this particular equestrian pursuit a bad name. They ride in their shorts and tennis shoes and then complain when their legs get scratched up or they hang up in the stirrup and get dragged 10 feet when they fall off their horse. Most of the time, they don't wear a helmet. They gallop their horses on unfamiliar terrain and run up behind others. They're out of control, take stupid chances, and are a danger to themselves and others. If you ever find yourself riding in a group of these folks, *any* time is a good time for an alternate route...or a rest stop that turns into a nap in the sunshine.

Why be just a trail rider?

Trail time is a way to rest and refresh your mind from nine-to-five work, from arena work, and from the cares and troubles back home or in the office, but it doesn't have to be the brain-dead vacation some people make it out to be. It can be creative time, a space to sort through a problem, and an interactive way to see and appreciate the natural world around you.

Getting out on the trail is good for the horses, too. Liz says that a big part of her training program for all her show horses has always been trail work, and she credits this mix with a huge part of their success in the show ring. "It keeps the horses fresh and happy, so they aren't just drones, and it also kept us fresh as teachers for the horses." And, since just about all advanced ringwork (from *any* discipline—yes, you can piaffe outside the dressage arena) can be done on the trail, too, Liz firmly believes the trail offers best possible training ground for the horse. So, if you choose trail riding as your midlife equestrian pursuit, take it on with pride and dignity!!!!! (This time, the exclamation points are all mine!)

Note: There are also ways to turn trail riding into a competitive venture—see below for more on this.

The Birth of the ACTHA—A New Equestrian Sport

When two middle-aged friends, Karen VanGetson and Carrie Scrima, began riding together in the spring of 2004, they began to talk about how they wanted to ride beautiful trails, take it slowly enough to enjoy the scenery, yet find challenges along the way to satisfy their competitive spirit. They wished there was some sort of friendly competition that could incorporate all these elements, include friends and families, and create a community of trail enthusiasts of all ages to ride together in some of the prettiest parts of the country.

So what did Karen and Carrie do? They started a sport. (Did I mention this midlife horse thing makes you bold *and* creative?) It's called the American Competitive Trail Riders Association (ACTHA) and its event, the Competitive Trail Challenge (CTC), directs a portion of entry fees back to horse rescues— a cause both of them feel strongly about supporting (see more about rescues on p. 101). In addition the ACTHA raised $68,000 in the first day of a dedicated fundraiser called "Ride for the Rescues."

Today, the ACTHA sponsors rides all over the country, and it sanctions "affiliate" CTC rides for other organizations that want to raise funds for their favorite cause. Fifty percent of all profits go to equine rescue facilities. What is especially exciting to Karen is the broad reach their brainchild now enjoys nationwide: "ACTHA is getting so widely known that anybody who can trail ride is able to enjoy their horse and take part in fun competitions," she says. "Our CTCs can encompass any kind of rider, from the fierce competitor who wants a national record to the occasional rider who wants to be with family and friends and take in the scenery."

For more information about the ACTHA, to become a member, or to find a ride near you, visit their website: www. actha.us.

▥ More fun in the great outdoors

Horse camping
One of the most relaxing, exhilarating, exhausting (in a good way), and bonding experiences I've ever had with horses is taking them camping. The feeling of waking up, looking out the tent flap, and seeing them right there, just a few feet away, waiting expectantly for you to get up and get moving, is a marvelous one. Tending to horse chores with, if somewhat makeshift and primitive methods, the supreme satisfaction of figuring out how to get the job done, then saddling up for a good long day of unhurried exploration, a picnic in a shady spot, and coming back grubby, hungry, and happy to sit with your friends around a campfire, laugh, tell stories, and share a night under the stars, can make you feel there's no better place on earth.

The secret to this kind of experience, more or less, lies in the preparation. If you think horse camping is for you, here are a few ideas, tips, and resources that will lead you to the information you need to get started enjoying the great wide open on horseback.

) **Read up** The Certified Horsemanship Association (CHA) has published a comprehensive guide to trail riding, camping and packing out with horses and mules, the *CHA Trail Guide Manual*, which is a must-have for every horse camper's shelf. This comprehensive guide compiled by leading trail guides from across the United States and Canada covers (with plenty of illustrations, photos, and "how-to" info) everything you need to know to be safe, have fun, and be good stewards of the trail and wilderness areas still left to explore in North America.

Horse Camping (Washington State University, 2009), the timeless classic first written in 1981 by George Hatley, is also required reading for anyone interested in camping with horses. It covers such topics as planning your trip, what you need and how to set up camp, details on gear, food, and provisions, as well as Hatley's wisdom gained from years of leading pack and wilderness camping trips.

) **Surf for info** Some great information and resources for horse camping are also available online. At www.campingandhorses.com (go figure!) you'll find links and information about destinations all over North America, as well as a number of organizations, guided trips, and opportunities in just about any location you can think of to explore on horseback.

And, for been-there-done-that horse camping know-how, check out www.infohorse.com/horsecamping.asp, a great site compliments of Melisa Snipe, president of Mountain Horse Incorporated's online store, Horsin Around Outdoors, where you can find many camping products, including picket line kits, hobbles, corral kits, and portable stalls.

Finally (and believe me, this just scratches the surface) www.horse-traildirectory.com ("trail riders helping trail riders") provides detailed information and links to horse trails and campgrounds in the United States, Canada, and even a few in Central and South America, and www.trailsource.com gives you an online guide to more than 1,200 horseback riding trails and campgrounds in 10 countries, with printable trail maps and specific tips for each area.

Foxhunting

Remember Gail from chapter 3, whose midlife horse calling was answered by an off-the-track Thoroughbred named Jamaica? As you may have guessed, her adventure didn't stop with some nice jogs around the pasture.

When Gail found Jamaica, she was in Texas, far away from the Virginia hunt community she grew up in. There, foxhunting—riding on horseback along with a pack of trained scent hounds as they track and chase a fox—was (and is) ingrained in the culture. Gail wondered what she could do to recapture the physical and mental excitement of a day in the open with your horse and a bunch of baying hounds out to give chase.

"There really is nothing like a run," she says, eyes glowing at the recollection. "When those hounds start baying and the horns start blowing and the horses are moving out—it really makes the hair stand up on the back of your neck!"

Gail discovered that in Texas there are hunt clubs that help area ranchers thin out the exploding coyote population in return for the privilege of riding on their land. However, the truth is, people who love "the hunt" really are not there for "the kill." Gail explains: "Foxhunting is really more about watching the hounds work, enjoying the land and the wildlife, and of course, the big breakfast afterward, which is an important social aspect of a traditional hunt."

Let a mystery unveil the mysteries of foxhunting

Avid foxhunter Gail says that a great way to learn about the atmosphere of a true hunt—along with the rich traditions and emotions that go along with it—is to read the novels in Rita Mae Brown's Foxhunting Mystery Series (Ballantine Books). In Gail's opinion, these mysteries set in Virginia with strong foxhunting themes and backdrops reflect Brown's deep understanding of the hunt and are very accurate portrayals of this area of horsemanship and the people who love it. Even as seasoned as Gail is, she says she always picks up knowledge when reading them!

While the Texas-based hunt Gail joined was somewhat different from those in Virginia, it provided Gail with a way to get out in the open, enjoy time with Jamaica, and be with others interested in the same activity. (Even though it wasn't quite what she had set out looking for, as many of us discover when we return to our first "horsey thrill," the midlife lens has a way of refocusing your priorities.) So, wherever you are in the country, if galloping cross-country after a pack of baying hounds makes your heart pound (in a good way), do an online search for local hunt clubs—you never know what you might find.

▦ Fast and fun: gymkhana, "O-Mok-See," and playdays

The name, "gymkhana" most likely originated in India, and these "timed games on horseback" began as a way for English military to let off steam with their horses on Sunday afternoons. The National Saddle Club Association (NSCA) adopted "O-Mok-See," the sport of "pattern horse racing" that originated with the Blackfoot Indian Tribe (who describe it as "riding big dance") to encourage families to compete together.

These action-packed competitive "horse show" events, often geared toward kids and ponies, are designed for fun and improving horsemanship with such things as obstacle courses, races, relays, and other speed events. They are a great way to enjoy horses, find a source of community, and get the competitive fire burning without spending a lot of money.

"Playdays" are great family fun for competitors (young and otherwise) just starting out or those not yet ready for the higher caliber competition found at gymkhana and O-Mok-See competitions. They are often sponsored by breed associations.

The actual classes at gymkhana, O-Mok-See competitions, and playdays vary from region to region, but here are just a few of the common events featured.

Barrel racing
Barrel racing is a timed event in which participants follow a "cloverleaf"

pattern around three barrels in a triangular formation. Contestants must choose either the right or left barrel, circle it, and go on to the next barrel, completing the course after circling the third barrel and running home. Barrels are permitted to be touched, but if one is knocked down during the course of the run, a five-second penalty per downed barrel is added. The fastest time wins. (For the official scoop on barrel racing, visit www.nbha.com.)

Pole bending

Pole bending is a timed event similar to a slalom ski race—horse and rider run to the far end of a series of six poles spaced 21 feet apart, turn, weave in-and-out as they work their way through one set, turn again, and weave their way back to the far end, then race in a straight line toward the finish line at full speed. A five-second penalty is added for each pole knocked down. (For more, go to www.polebending.org—I know, but I *told* you there is an organization for *everything*!)

Keyhole race

The keyhole race is a timed event executed over a pattern. The pattern is usually "drawn" with white powder, commonly flour or powdered chalk, in a "keyhole" shape on the surface of the arena. The horse crosses the timing line, enters the keyhole, turns in either direction "inside" the keyhole without stepping over the chalk outline, then races back to the finish. Participants are disqualified any time they step on or over the chalk line. This is a very popular gymkhana event.

Stake race

The stake race is another timed event, and it is really a variation of pole bending, but with only two poles. The two poles are set 80 feet apart and a timing line (defined by two markers) is set between the two poles. You race between the markers to the first pole and go around it in either direction, then across the timing line again to the second pole, which you circle in the opposite direction. The race ends when the horse crosses the timing line the third time. Participants are disqualified if they knock over a marker, and a five-second penalty is added for each pole knocked down.

▥ Are you one for the show?

Sure, gymkhanas and playdays are fun, but maybe you've always secretly longed for the intensity of the horse show ring. Here's the good news when you look at this kind of horse experience through the midlife lens: According to Jennifer Forsberg Meyer in her January 2010 article, "Get Going Showing," in *Horse&Rider* magazine, there's no time like the present to get into—or *back* into—the competitive spirit of things.

"Opportunities for newbie and returnees abound," she writes. Explaining that even though the economy has tightened our budgets over the last few years, it has also led equine breed and sport associations to reach out more to first-time exhibitors and mid-life returnees, offering them comfortable and fun ways to compete in all kinds of disciplines, all across the nation. You can now find "walk-trot" classes for adults (instead of just kids), more lead-line divisions to get multiple generations involved, novice-only shows, introductory shows, clinic/show combinations, and other semi-competitive offerings outside the usual realm of traditional show ring competition.

Crediting the influx of new and returning show enthusiasts to the "ever-expanding reach of cyberspace," Forsberg Meyer writes, "It's easier all the time to connect with others who share your specific interests and can offer help and advice—on rules and regs, turnout trends, in-ring protocols, and so on." (All of these topics make great online search terms, by the way, when combined with the breed or event you're interested in.) She also points to blogs written by new or returning show enthusiasts who invite you to "ride along" as they prepare and compete (check out 50plushorses.blogspot.com).

So what do *you* need to do if you think a little competition would be good for your midlife soul? First, find your sport/discipline of choice.

Next, find a trainer to help you prepare yourself, and quite possibly your horse, for the rigors of the show ring. (I talk a bit more about taking lessons in chapter 11—see p. 255.)

It can be a lot more fun learning something new if you have a like-minded gal pal willing to tag along with you. So find a buddy and attend the type of event you are interested in as a spectator before you try to become a competitor. Volunteering at local shows can be another great way to learn the ropes by watching.

Finally, once you've found a breed or discipline that is "right" for you, halfway through life, join the associations and organizations related to it. These groups tend to have divisions dedicated to education and outreach, and they can be a good source of finding a mentor, as well as the go-to hub of information regarding events and shows in your county or state. Don't be shy. Be a joiner.

I've provided *very* brief summaries of some of the different areas of equestrian specialization that invite serious competition at different levels. For lack of a better method of organization, I've listed them in alphabetical order. Note: Most require entry fees (some higher than others) and not all include prize money in the winnings (although some of those that do offer an impressive amount!) So read up on each and find out what kind of time and financial commitment is required before "falling for one"...although who knows which horse sport might be the source of *your* thrill.

Carriage driving

Hitching a horse or pony to a buggy or sleigh and driving him along country roads or across fields can be a lovely way to pass the time. This equestrian activity can be an ideal choice for those who cannot or do not want to ride their horse, or for those adults who may have a preference for vertically challenged equines, such as Shetland Ponies and Miniature Horses. There are many areas in which to compete a horse in harness, including pleasure driving and combined driving, and at a variety of levels. (For more information, visit www.americandrivingsociety.org.)

Conformation (halter)

"Halter" describes competitive horse show classes where the horse is shown "in hand." This means the "handler" (rather than "rider") leads him from the ground, rather than directs him from the saddle. The purpose of this kind of competition is to select individual horses in the order of their resemblance to their breed ideal with the most positive combination of balance, structural correctness, muscling, and movement. In other words, it is a way of judging "breeding stock." Classes are typically divided by the horse's age and sex, and may necessitate demonstrating the trot (or a specialized gait) in hand, and sometimes at considerable speed. Conformation classes can be a nice way for individuals who don't want to ride but would like to compete to get involved.

Cowboy mounted shooting

The Cowboy Mounted Shooting Association® calls theirs "the fastest growing equestrian sport in the nation." This activity involves mounted contestants running in a timed event, where they must follow specific patterns and shoot a designated number of balloons using two .45-caliber, single-action revolvers loaded with specially prepared blank ammunition. (To learn more, or to find a club in your area, go to www.cmsa.com.)

A REAL-LIFE, MIDLIFE HORSE STORY *SUSAN*

There are few things more enriching and colorful to the midlife horse experience (especially when you grew up in the city as I did) than getting to know a "real cowgirl." Susan grew up on a Montana ranch, and while trying to keep up with her two older brothers, learned how to ride (often at great speeds) anything with hair and hooves. How Susan survived her childhood, I'll never know, but in the words of our mutual riding buddy, Walter, "that girl can *ride*."

It is Susan who introduced me to trail riding, horse camping, and ranch sorting. When it comes to horses, there is almost nothing she wouldn't try if it struck her fancy. And lately, something new struck her fancy as nothing has before. (This just goes to show that even someone who has pretty much done it all can still find a new passion in some little corner of the horse world.)

Now, Susan loves speed events. In addition to childhood O-Mok-See days, she rode racehorses, and later parlayed that into training barrel horses. Then, after a career as a flight attendant she married her husband, Bruce, and settled onto a 30-acre place in Texas, where she began buying and selling horses and planned to compete in area barrel racing events. Except something always got in the way. First one thing, then another, and the years went by without her really having the time to pursue the sport she loved.

Then one day she saw an event that got her blood pounding again. Cowboy mounted shooting, if you've never seen it, is (as I might classify Susan herself) just a little bit crazy. Running at a full-out gallop, often dressed in vintage Western clothing and sporting a pair of six-shooter revolvers, riders run a pattern around (ironically, in this case) barrels that anchor a number of helium-filled balloons. Shooting black powder (with just enough charge to pop the balloon but not hurt a spectator—or so they tell me) the rider is judged on how fast she pops the balloons in a specified sequence.

"It's just you and your horse out there, going fast, riding and shooting at the same time—it's a lot more complicated than you'd think," Susan says. "With barrel racing, there's a lot to pay attention to—three cans, your legs, your hands, your body position, the pattern. But with this, it's a whole lot more challenging. You've got all that, *plus* all these clothes and accessories—chinks, hat, belt, guns. You've got the speed, the pattern, the noise, the adrenalin, both yours and the horse's. Your horse has to run faster than you think will give you time to shoot, so your timing has to be perfect. It's a different kind of feeling than I've ever had before, and I'm addicted to it!"

This addiction is obvious—Susan now hauls two shooting horses (she's trained three of them herself) somewhere almost every weekend, and most recently, has had more than a few top finishes in her division. Susan will be the first to tell you, however, that it's not about the ribbons and trophies. "I've won a lot and lost a lot through my years of competition," she says, "that's just the way it is. I'm really not worried about that anymore—I'm just so excited to be out there doing it!"

Cutting

In this often high-stakes event (but not always), a single horse and rider separate a cow of their choosing away from a herd and then must keep it away from the herd for a short period of time. This event relies on the innate ability and athleticism of the horse, the instincts and abilities of the rider, and to some extent, the luck of the draw in terms of the cow. (For more information, check out www.nchacutting.com or www.achacutting.org.)

Dressage

Founded on a French term that means "training," this discipline of (usually) competitive horse training holds events at all levels, from novice to Olympic. Its purpose is to develop through progressive methods, a horse's natural athletic ability and willingness to perform while remaining calm, supple, and attentive to his rider. Competitors are judged on their ability to perform a memorized "test," or series of required movements at specific points in the ring. (Learn more at www.usdf.org.)

Endurance and competitive trail riding

If your heart is on the trail, but you're hankering for the kind of affirmation competition offers, endurance riding and competitive trail riding may be where you're headed. Endurance riding asks a horse-and-rider team to complete a 50-, 75-, or 100-mile course in the fastest time possible, usually in a single day. Terrain is often varying, and at the advanced levels, very difficult. Veterinary checks are required along the course where the horse's fitness and ability to continue is evaluated.

Competitive trail riding covers a long distance, as well, but usually over a number of days. Competitors are expected to cover a specific distance each day, and veterinarians and horsemanship judges provide reviews of horse and rider conditioning and evidence of partnership on the trail. (For tips on getting started in endurance riding, check out www.aerc.org. For more about competitive trail riding, visit www.natrc.org.)

Eventing

This high-intensity sport originated as a way to test cavalry and ensure mastery of multiple types of riding. Eventing has three phases: dressage (see p. 96), cross-country (a timed course of anywhere from 12 to 40 "natural" fences over a long outdoor circuit), and stadium/show jumping (see p. 98). Penalties are accrued for each horse-and-rider team as they complete each phase (often over several days). You can compete in the sport of eventing from the beginner levels up through the Olympics. (Learn more at www.useventing.com.)

Hunt seat equitation (on the flat and over fences)

Hunt seat equitation evaluates the performance of the English rider—specifically her position and effectiveness. The performance of the horse is only a factor in that it betrays the ability of the rider to communicate with him. Individually, contestants must work a predetermined pattern on the flat consisting of maneuvers such as changing gaits (walk, trot, canter), traveling in a figure-eight pattern, and backing-up, as well as ride in a group along the rail of the show ring performing gait changes at the judge's discretion. Over fences riders are judged on their ability to establish an even "hunting pace" over a predetermined jumping course, as well as their position and effectiveness in properly influencing the horse.

Hunters (under saddle and over fences)
Hunter under saddle is the preliminary class for English riding disciplines—judges evaluate the horse's way-of-going on the flat, at a walk, trot, and canter. Horses circle the perimeter of the arena, performing each gait at the judge's discretion. The ideal hunter-type horse is smooth-gaited, well-mannered, and attractive. Over fences he should move freely and easily, while performing safely and jumping "clear."

Jumpers
Also known in other countries and sports as "show jumping" or "stadium jumping," this discipline offers competitive opportunities from lower levels through the Olympics. Jumpers are judged on their ability to clear a course of jumps cleanly and in an allotted amount of time. Speed and athletic ability win over style and grace. This can be an exciting spectator sport as the jumps get higher and the times get faster. (For more information, check out www.usef.org.)

Ranch sorting
This event originated out of the basic ranch need to separate cattle from the herd for doctoring or branding. Calling itself "the funnest family sport on a horse," ranch sorting is a timed event in which two 50-foot pens are connected with a 12-foot opening, and 11 calves must be moved, one by one, from one pen to the other by a team of two riders. (Learn more, find instruction and events, and watch videos at www.rsnc.us.)

Reining
The easiest way to understand reining is to compare it to figure skating.

All reining patterns include stops, spins, rollbacks, and lead changes (just as figure skating programs require certain jumps and spins). Each horse performs the pattern individually and is evaluated on movement, mastery of the pattern, and attitude (again, like a figure skater). Although born in the United States, reining has gained an international following and is now recognized by the Fédération Equestre Internationale (FEI) and is part of the World Equestrian Games, which are held every four years. (Read more about this sport at www.nrha.com.)

Saddle seat

The tradition of riding saddle seat developed when those who bred and rode horses with "flashy action" needed a way to show these horses to their best advantage. This style of riding is usually limited to certain horse breeds, such as American Saddlebreds, Tennessee Walking Horses, Morgans, and Arabians. Riders sit farther back on the horse than in other disciplines in order to encourage high-stepping front leg action.

Showmanship

While the "halter" classes I described earlier judge the horse, "showmanship" focuses on the handler's ability to turn her horse out properly and present him in hand. Judges evaluate the grooming and condition of the horse, and the expertise of the handler in presenting the horse to the best of her ability. Contestants must also work a predetermined pattern consisting of maneuvers such as walking, trotting, pivoting, backing-up, and "setting up" the horse according to his breed type (placing his feet in the position that best shows his conformation). This can again be a way for a "non-rider" to compete her horse.

Team penning

Faster moving and wilder than ranch sorting (see p. 98), this timed event calls for teams of three horse-and-rider combinations to humanely separate particular cows from a large group and herd them into a designated penning area. (Find out more at www.ustpa.com.)

Team roping and calf roping

These fast-paced sports based once again on ranching tradition involve horse-and-rider combinations (in team roping there are two riders on two horses, and in calf roping, there is only one) chasing a single steer or calf, lassoing it and "throwing" it as quickly as possible. (Find out more about team roping at www.ustrc.com.)

Trail

This show event brings the joy of trail riding into the show ring! Trail horses must be accomplished in numerous obstacles, such as passing through gates, crossing bridges, and handling other situations—usually in the confines of an arena—that might occur on an outdoor trail ride. Trail judges focus on the horse's willingness, and the skill, ease, and grace with which he negotiates the course.

Western horsemanship

Like hunt seat equitation does for English riders, Western horsemanship judges the Western rider's ability to follow a prescribed pattern, consisting of maneuvers such as walking, jogging, or loping in a straight or curved line, and pivoting, stopping, or changing leads, as well her position and effectiveness when riding in a group "on the rail."

Western pleasure

Western pleasure horses are judged by whether they appear to be— as the name implies—a pleasure to ride. Contestants compete simultaneously, traveling around the perimeter of an arena at a gait chosen by the judge. A Western pleasure horse should display quality of movement, consistency of gait, and a calm, responsive disposition.

Working cowhorse

Also known as "reined cowhorse" or "stock horse" competition, in this event a single rider works a single cow in an arena, performing specified maneuvers such as circling the cow, turning it in one direction or the other, and performing a prescribed reining pattern (see more about reining on p. 98). (Find out more about working cowhorses at www.nrcha.com.)

Is helping horses your midlife soul's "calling?"

There have been many days since I added horses back in my life that I've wondered, "Why? What's it all for?" These musings most often come on the heels of a long day or a long stretch of work that has kept me from my horses and the related "connection" that, when you step too far away from it, can seem like more complication than salvation. For some of us, it may very well be that owning our own horse in order to meet the challenges of competition only leaves us asking more questions when all we're looking for is answers. It may be that finding some *other way* to have horses in our life, one already laden with significance, is the best route "home."

Many of us have heard vague stories of horses starving and neglected, or abused and left to die. We feel sad. We feel helpless. Those stories break our horse-loving hearts. But what can we do? How do we get involved? What are our options? Is it safe to adopt a rescue horse? How do we take that first step?

▥ The story of Cider: twice unlucky, three-times blessed

Before she was even a yearling, Cider, a small Palomino, was rescued from starvation by Habitat for Horses, one of the largest equine protection organizations in the country. After being brought back to health, she was adopted by a well-intentioned new owner who, after a while, fell on hard financial times and Cider had to be rescued again from neglect. By this point, she had no reason to trust humans, nor did she have any reason to want to connect with them. At the age of six, she had never worn a saddle or bridle, wouldn't lead, wouldn't be tied, and above all, wouldn't get in a trailer.

"The first time I saw Cider was after her foster caregiver told me what a great horse she was," says Jolene Castillo of Habitat for Horses. "I took one look at her and said, 'Oh my gosh, what is that?' She was so thin—and her head looked way to big for her body."

Habitat had matched Cider with Jackie Hardin of Greenville, Texas, who has fostered more than 27 rescue horses in recent years. (Before being deemed ready for adoption, rescue horses are first brought back to health in foster homes.) Of all these horses, Cider was his favorite, and for the first time, Cider knew what it was to be cared for and to bond with a human.

Although Cider's recovery didn't happen overnight, her first night with Jackie did provide a turning point. "The day I picked up Cider," Jackie recalls, "it took me five-and-a-half hours to get her into a trailer." He ended up borrowing a stock trailer and leaving his two-horse trailer in Oklahoma. He and Cider got to his place around 11:30 pm—and then she wouldn't unload. "So I just backed the trailer up to the barn, opened the back of it and left her there for the night, figuring she would eventually come out on her own," Jackie says. "She stayed in that trailer all night, but when she heard the hay and feed being distributed in the barn the next morning, she came out."

Jackie quickly realized that food and treats were the way to get Cider's attention; he used them to cultivate what became a beautiful friendship, and Cider began to follow Jackie around like a puppy. "She'd get to where she'd always come to me, because most of the time I had either feed or treats for her," Jackie says. "She's a sweet horse," he adds, getting sentimental. "I really miss her. She's going to make someone a really good horse."

I learned about Cider's story when I was working for Australian horse trainer Clinton Anderson. He had decided to include a series featuring a rescue horse on his top-rated weekly RFD-TV show, and Cider was chosen to star in it. "First, I want to show people that you can actually get very good horses from rescues," Clinton says about his decision to include an example of a horse rescue on his television show. "If you're willing to put in the time to work with them and train them, you can not only improve their life, but you can also get a really nice horse. Many rescue horses—not all of them, of course—are good horses just waiting for someone to put some time into them."

Second, Clinton wants people to see how well suited his training method is to developing a relationship, building trust, and earning the respect of a horse that has been abused or neglected. By reclaiming "lost horses," enjoying them, and giving them a good life, people who love horses have a great opportunity to make a difference in a world that is seeing far too many horses abandoned, abused, and neglected. "We all have a responsibility and opportunity here to use what we know about horses and give something back to the world," Clinton says, "I am happy to have the chance to work with Habitat for Horses to show people just how to do that."

At the conclusion of the RFD-TV series, a truly transformed Cider was given to a carefully chosen adoptive home—a well earned blessing after a long road traveled.

▓ So, are you interested in fostering or adopting a rescue horse?

If Cider's story got you where it counts and you think you'd like to adopt or foster a rescue horse, visit Habitat for Horses online (www.habitatforhorses.org) and download the free instructional booklet "From Seizure to Adoption," by Jerry Finch, the organization's president. There you will find everything you need to know about the process, the rules, and the procedures.

Jolene Castillo says that before fostering or adopting a rescue horse it is important to educate yourself on all aspects of that horse's care. Castillo recommends you take plenty of time to learn about equine nutrition (see chapter 8 for more on this subject), veterinary care, as well as consider all the expenses associated with owning a rescue horse.

"A lot of well-intentioned people adopt rescue horses because they think it would be fun to save a horse, but they don't really take the time to understand what they're getting into," Castillo says. "That's what happened in Cider's case, at first, and it happens more often that it should. By educating yourself and learning everything you can *before* you take that horse home, you have a better chance of creating a successful relationship with that horse."

▥ The many other ways you can help

In the process of writing about Cider, I had several conversations with representatives of Habitat for Horses, and I asked what those of us on a midlife horses "service quest" could do to help—besides, of course, fostering or adopting. Here's what we can give:

) **Cash** Monetary donations, of course, make the rescue world go around—and no amount is too small.

) **Horse items** Can you buy one extra sack of feed every trip to the feed store? What about that extra halter hanging on your wall gathering dust and rot? Got extra grooming tools? Wash them up and donate them.

) **Time** Almost as pressing as the need for funding is the need for human hands to help. Just commiting to a few hours a week of barn chores could really help your local rescue and do your heart good. It doesn't have to be a permanent, full-time, or even consistently part-time time donation. One afternoon will do, once a month, once a quarter, once a year—just go.

) **Service** Do you have a professional talent? Offer to help out for an afternoon, doing whatever it is you do best, in order to help the organization help our equine friends. Are you an electrician? They probably could use some help with a wiring problem or the addition of outlets. In advertising? Who couldn't use a little pro

Caring through the end of times

Nobody wants to think about her horse reaching the end of his time here on earth. But let's face it. It happens. And while *we* know *we'll* be there for our horses and take care of them until they draw their very last breath, what about the horses that aren't so fortunate? What happens to those that have outlived their usefulness and have no one to see them through the gate to the "rainbow bridge"?

Recently in her monthly newsletter, world-renowned author and creator of the Tellington Method® Linda Tellington-Jones told of a special program she discovered in Santa Fe, New Mexico, called Kindred Spirits Animal Sanctuary (www.kindredspiritsnm.org), a 501(c)(3) non-profit organization that offers eldercare and hospice for dogs, horses, and poultry. After spending several hours there with her friend, holistic veterinarian Dr. Ella Bittel, Linda wrote, "You might expect this to be a sad place, but actually, it was the opposite...I was very touched by the feeling of joy and honor that pervades the atmosphere."

In providing a final refuge for animals that have nowhere else to go, Kindred Spirits welcomes animals previously unwanted because of advanced age, health problems, or trauma they have experienced. Some come from owners unable to care for them, others come from shelters and rescue groups because they are unlikely to be adopted. The furthest thing from "just a place to go to die," Kindred Spirits offers these animals a caring and nurturing *living* environment some have never had before.

bono campaign? Architects, engineers, teachers, accountants—you name it, we all have something to offer.

To learn more about horse rescues, visit the Unwanted Horse Coalition (www.unwantedhorsecoalition.org) to see what the needs are nationwide. Another good source of information is the American Association of Equine Practitioners (www.aaep.org), where you can download all kinds of information about volunteer opportunities and guidelines for horse rescues. Finally, thehorse.com (www.thehorse.com) operates its own adoption center that has placed more than 400 horses to date, as well as providing a wealth of information, guidelines, and resources for adoption, fostering, volunteering, or making monetary donations to all kinds of rescues and veterinary relief initiatives.

Having horses *without* having a horse

Who among us doesn't like to talk about horses? My family knows that if we're out running errands and I happen to run into another horse person, it's going to be a while. Horse people, it seems, never run out of things to talk about, stories to tell, and new things to discuss, argue about, and prove wrong.

It used to be that to be involved in horses you needed a horse—and usually, that included being ready, willing, and able to ride. But the birth of the Internet has brought with it a strange new option—a whole world of "horsey" fun awaits today's new breed of horsewoman: the Armchair Equestrienne. What can you do online that is (almost) as good as being at the barn?

> ❭ **Make friends** Watch the hours slip away as you meet others on any one of the many message boards, live chats, forums, podcasts, webinars—you name it. My Google search for "online horse communities" yielded 43,400,000 results. If there's a kind of horse, a discipline of riding, a part of the country, or a particular interest you have in this horse world, there is an online community that now supports it.

> ❭ **Do high-level research** If you are interesting in breeding and bloodlines, just about every breed registry is now online, and you can trace the lineage of any registered horse you choose. Show results (and often, thanks to YouTube, the show performance

itself) can be tracked, as well as training histories. A friend's mother enjoys following famous horse families online so she can "watch" the babies grow up and eventually compete. Go figure.

) **Buy, sell, trade** You can buy, sell, and trade horses, trailers, and tack online. You can locate any product, manufacturer, catalog, or brick-and-mortar store you can think of. You can see demonstrations of new equipment, find out what's wrong with the equipment you already have, and determine what you should get instead. Then you can surf around, because you can probably find the new piece of equipment cheaper somewhere else. When you buy it, you'll eventually discover what's wrong with *it*, but the good news is you can go *back* online and sell it for as much, if not more than what you bought it for.

) **Learn** There's no way to even count the hours of horse entertainment and educational viewing you can watch or download—entire training DVDs; past television shows featuring your favorite horsemen; plus winning runs, big wrecks, and heat-of-the-moment interviews. Top manufacturers of horse-related products recognize that they need to provide quality educational content in order to attract business to their website, so in almost all cases you can glean an amazing amount of information from the simple process of searching for the right kind of fly spray for your geographical region (for example).

) **Connect** I've mentioned manufacturers' websites, but I haven't even touched on club and association websites. We haven't scratched the surface of blogs, Twitter, Facebook, Myspace, and LinkedIn. Nor have we considered all the online groups and organizations you can pay a fee to join. And what about newsletters? Most anyone worth their salt has a digital newsletter—and also email alerts you can sign up to receive, just to make sure you don't miss a thing.

) **Opportunity** From job searches, to looking for the right educational experience, to launching a new career in support of the seemingly endless array of occupations, activities, and avocations now available in the wide world of horses, opportunity abounds on the Web. Do you have a goal? There's support for it somewhere online—and most likely, that lead can connect you with a *real* person in the *real* world, as well.

Once you join the non-mounted brigade, you'll find rabbit trails you never dreamed of (believe me, I was on a lot of them while researching this book!). Armchair Equestriennes have new keys to the kingdom—a virtual option to experience almost everything the horse world has to offer, right there in the comfort of their own home. (I should mention here that I was once bucked off my rolling chair—although it wasn't the chair's fault. I had it coming. I just pushed it too far.) As it turns out, these days you can be "all hat and no horse"— as long as you *do* have a computer, Internet access, and at least occasionally, electricity

finding the magic

*Now that you've
made the life-altering
decision to follow
your dream, and
you're beginning
to have an idea of
what your horse
experience might
look like, what's
next? Do you run
right out and buy
the first pretty pony
you lay eyes on? Can
you learn how to ride
without taking the
plunge into horse
ownership? Most
people don't realize
the many options
that exist for today's
horse enthusiast.
Here are a few tips
on determining
what to do next,
depending on
which midlife horse
experience is the
right one for you,
your riding needs,
your lifestyle, and
your budget.*

AS BAD A JOB AS I DID CHOOSING MY
first midlife horse, I did a very good job
with the second. Rio belonged to a friend
of mine and I knew his whole history. He
had been lovingly raised, well-trained, and
cared for; he was healthy, well-bred, and
had a sweet, willing disposition.

But the funny thing was, I didn't
want to give up on Trace, who had—as
I'd half-expected—turned out to be not-
quite-perfect in the midlife horse department. Rio was like that nice boy who
keeps asking you out, and Trace was
like the bad boy who can't quite commit but who you can't stop thinking
about. While I definitely didn't have time
or resources for two horses, I knew I
needed a safe and willing "go-to" horse
I could ride anytime, just about anywhere without a big hassle. So in a way,

I decided to buy Rio in hopes he could help me become a good enough rider to eventually handle Trace.

The result was truly a good-news- bad-news situation: As perfect as this pair was for my continuing horse education, I never stopped to consider the time, resources, and support required for caring for, riding, working, and paying for two horses. I literally made myself crazy, knowing all the things I should be doing with my "boys," but always having legitimately compelling "big picture" items (work, family, relationships) blocking my path to the barn. I agonized constantly, and ultimately, because of my erroneous all-or-nothing thinking when it came to my horses, often ended up doing nothing—with either one of them.

Like so many women I spoke with while writing this book, finding ways to work something as large—literally and figuratively—as a horse into your life takes creativity, flexibility, and determination. Where do I keep my horse? When can I ride? How much is enough? What can we let go of? How do we put our whole self into this important new journey without forsaking the other important parts of our life?

The answers, it turns out, are not that cut-and-dried. And while many options exist, it is up to us to keep turning the knobs, wiggling the antenna, and kicking the set until we get the picture we're looking for.

Baby steps

What most of us don't realize when we make the landmark decision to add horses to our life, is that there are *many* ways to enjoy this unique relationship without actually *owning* a horse. Lessons, leasing, half-leasing, sharing, and afternoon/day rental are all viable options that give you time and experience in the saddle without the commitment of ownership. What's more, equine retreats, weekend clinics, horse vacations, equine-assisted therapies, and the volunteer opportunities that often go hand-in-hand with each, make it possible to enjoy being with horses at virtually all levels, styles, and disciplines without actually riding them!

Certainly, that "wind in your hair" lure is strong for most of us who love horses, and riding, more often than not, eventually becomes our focus. Still, proceeding with caution through the myriad of decisions that surround efforts to find "midlife horse magic" will serve you well in the long run. Using the life-evaluating skills we talked about in chapter 1, consider all the options available to you and what will be your best course in the "10-10-10" light (see p. 38). Remember, you are at the halfway point in your life, so time is of the essence. You want to make the choices with the highest "ROI" (that's Return On Investment, for the uninitiated) so you can start enjoying a life with horses but still maintaining the highest possible degree of safety.

So what *is* the best course to get back in the saddle (or in it for the very first time) with minimal damage to your body and wallet?

▥ Get schooled

Lessons first, most of the experts I polled agree. Not only will taking a few lessons acquaint you with your own riding abilities, it will give you a pretty good idea where to go from that point forward. For some, lessons will be "plenty of horse" for a while. When you think about it, going to a stable, riding a horse with instruction in whatever discipline you choose (see chapter 5), as many times a week as you can afford, is not a bad way to begin. Your commitment is minimal, enjoyment high, and you really get to test the waters mentally and physically to see if this is something you like to do.

To begin with, your best bet is a series of lessons in basic equitation (that is, position in the saddle and correct application of cues to communicate with the horse) at a local barn. Many experts agree that starting out in an English saddle can help you gain balance and awareness of how the horse's body moves, but it really doesn't matter. You just need to find a program that gives you a safe, solid foundation—or reinforces what remains of your childhood riding prowess. (We'll talk more about finding facilities and instruction that fit your needs, abilities, and goals in chapter 11, p. 239.)

In addition to individual or group, weekly or biweekly lessons, many lesson outfits offer longer excursions and additional opportunities as your riding level becomes more advanced. These may include weekend trail rides, playdays, and clinics to further hone specific skills. Some performance-related barns (if you've decided you really do want to pursue that reining career) move you up the ladder to higher levels of competition—all without your ever having to bite the bullet and buy a horse.

▦ You can lease a *horse*?

When you've had a few lessons and you're feeling confident and ready to take the next step, slow down, consider your options, and kick those decision-making tools we learned in chapter 1 into high gear. If it's your first horse—or your first one in a long time—or your time and money is limited, you may want to consider leasing for a while. Leasing presents a good opportunity to "test drive" horse ownership and get more time in the saddle as you decide what kind of horse you want, what you want to do with him, and whether or not it's the right time to make the full-time commitment ownership entails. In addition to "straight leasing," you can also half-lease or "share a ride," especially in performance barns.

I had never heard of leasing a horse (call me naïve) until after I had already bought Trace. It turns out it is a very common thing in the horse industry—and in times of down economies, it is a great win-win solutions for those who don't really want to sell their good horse and those who aren't quite ready to buy but want a good horse to ride. While these arrangements can be tricky and your agreement with the owner must be spelled out clearly (more on that in a minute), leasing can provide a perfect solution for the budding midlife horsewoman. In my case, in which I knew how to ride, but wasn't sure how well, and I had no idea what kind of horse I wanted or what I wanted to do when I had one, leasing would have been the perfect solution. Live and learn.

After looking at a few sample lease contracts, it seems that specific basic points should be covered (duration of arrangement, fee, division of expenses and responsibilities, termination of lease, and what happens if the horse becomes ill or dies during the period of the lease), and everything else is pretty much fair game and up to the individuals involved to hammer out. A good rule of thumb, however, is that if a particular point is important to you, make sure you write it into your lease agreement. (See the resources on p. 311 for more information about finding leasing contracts and information on the Internet. The book *Horse Economics* by Catherine O'Brien, CPA, is also a great reference for contract summaries and specifics.)

So, how do I find a lease horse?

Finding the right horse to lease is not quite as easy as it sounds. The good news is that you can consider a horse of "advanced age," which you might not be willing to do when buying. In fact, in the case of leasing, "aged" is a plus. Many old horses make perfect teachers for short periods of time while you're learning or solidifying your basics.

Sources agree that the Internet is a good place to start your lease candidate research, as are local feed or tack shops, boarding stables, performance barns, and even horse shows. Talk to trainers, owners, and competitors in the discipline that interests you and ask them to be in touch if a lease opportunity comes along. Check with area riding schools to see if they lease out their lesson horses during slow or off-season periods. And, if there's a particular horse you have your eye on, talk to his owner. Sometimes on an individual basis an arrangement can be made to benefit both you and the owner—not only do you get a horse to ride regularly, but the owner's expenses are reduced and her horse gets more exercise. Qualities to look for in a lease horse include:

) **Experience** He should have it, both under saddle and in the particular discipline you have interest in exploring.

) **Temperament** Look for a horse that is quiet, has a willing disposition, and displays characteristics of easy manageability. No horse is perfect, of course, but look for one that doesn't have any obvious nasty habits—and that is easy to catch!

) **Size** It's nice for a "first horse" to be one that is a manageable size for you. While experience and temperament are still paramount, if you are able to see over the horse's withers, you will have a feeling of control.

) **Condition** While this isn't by any means a beauty contest, make sure the horse is in reasonably good health, and his physical appearance reflects that he or she has been well taken care of. Before you sign a lease agreement, do a vet check, just as if you were buying the horse (see p. 181), and seriously consider acquiring theft and mortality insurance (again, see *Horse Economics* by Catherine O'Brien for more about this).

Types of Horse Leases

Full lease The lessee pays for boarding costs (and sometimes an additional lease fee), farrier, and vet care in return for being able to use the horse whenever and however often she wants to. There is usually no restriction on riding days or times, and often the lessee is free to take the horse off-site for rides or shows. The lease fee for a full lease is usually about 25 to 30 percent of the horse's value.

Share lease Less expensive than a full lease, this arrangement usually allows each person (owner and lessee) about three days a week with the horse. Boarding and other expenses are usually split evenly. Riding times and special circumstances such as shows are best spelled out in writing, as well as the routine care responsibilities. Share leases usually split boarding fees (and sometimes vet and farrier expenses) fifty-fifty.

Are you ready to own a horse? Are you sure?

It goes without saying that owning a horse is a big commitment. Of time, of money, and especially, of energy and focus. You may think you know all about what's in store, but once that trailer drives away and you stand face-to-face with your new horse, the reality of it hits you— it's not unlike the moment you're released from the hospital with your newborn baby. Up until that moment, someone else (usually more knowledgeable) has been with you every step of the way, helping you care for the "bundle of joy" whose safekeeping and happiness is now your responsibility.

There are a lot of variables here, too, and we'll wade through the main issues, one by one, in this chapter. But the fundamental questions are:

) What basic skills do you need?

) How much time will a horse require?

) How do you recognize the "right" horse for *you*?

) Where will you keep your horse, and how will you care for him?

) How will you pay for all this?

Like many people, I got so caught up in the excitement of fixing my midlife malaise, I leapt before I looked. Blindsided by my desire to do everything at once, I skipped a bunch of steps that would have made my new horse life a whole lot easier and much more fun. Fortunately (and somewhat miraculously), I was not seriously hurt, help came along at just the right time, and now I am happily-ever-after sorting things out.

There is a much *better* way than my way, however, so with a little help from trainer and clinician Clinton Anderson's *Horsemanship 101* DVD series, and the wisdom gleaned from a wide spectrum of online research, here are a few pointers to send you down the right road to horse ownership.

▥ What basic skills do you need?

When you own a horse, as opposed to taking lessons or leasing, it's "all on you" to do the things that are oftentimes done by others. Granted, most lessons worth their salt incorporate basic horse care into their curriculum, teaching you to safely halter and lead, groom, tack up, clean hooves, cool out, rinse off, and turn out a horse. Some may even teach you the ins and outs of feed and nutrition. But always there is someone right there to tell you what to do, in what order, and more than likely to hand you the proper piece of equipment. With the midlife horse owner in mind, I get more into the nuts and bolts of horse care in the chapters that follow, but for now make sure you know how to do the following in a safe and correct manner:

> Catch and lead

> Groom (this means cleaning him all over—including his feet!)

> Feed and water

> Tack and untack

> Mount and dismount

In addition you should also probably know:

> Basic groundwork skills (leading, lunging, backing-up, yielding both hind and forequarters).

> Riding (and stopping) skills at the walk, trot, and canter.

) Basic first aid so you can deal with common horse injuries and ailments. (This includes having an equine veterinarian's number stored in your cell phone and posted in your kitchen and/or tack area.)

If you don't have a handle on these basics yet, don't fret. We'll cover them in the chapters ahead, and I'll give you tons of good resources for further education.

▥ How much time will a horse require?

This may sound like a ridiculous question, but it's one worth asking. While most of us will want to spend EVERY WAKING MINUTE with our new companion, life has a way of expecting us to keep showing up other places. I know. It's just not right.

So, realistically, using the tools I gave you in chapter 3 (see p. 45) you need to have found yourself a little "spare time" before making the decision to lease or buy a horse. A lease, obviously, is somewhat less of a commitment, depending on your particular arrangements, while a "horse of your own" is more time-consuming—although again, it depends on certain details in your horse management scenario (we'll get to these in a minute).

Even if you board at a full-care facility (I explain what this means on p. 136), you're going to want to stop by and (at least) check on your horse every day. This means, at the very minimum, you give him a light grooming, check him over for nicks and scratches (especially if he's turned out with other horses), and maybe do a few barn or tack chores, for good measure.

On top of these visits, you should commit to some combination of groundwork and ridden work, at least three times a week. If your horse is turned out for at least part of every day (which he should be!), he probably gets a little bit of exercise, but a conscientious owner makes sure he gets about 30 minutes of sustained activity (walk, trot, canter) nearly every day, with about 15 minutes before and after for warming up and cooling down.

All the above most likely adds up to anywhere from 10 to 15 hours a week, give or take.

An important tip from horse trainer Clinton Anderson is that the amount of time you spend with your horse is not nearly as important as consistency. "If I had the choice between spending 15 minutes every day with my horse and three hours once a week," he is fond of saying, "I'd take those 15 minutes a day, anytime."

Avoid "Mondayitis"

Horse trainer Clinton Anderson always recommends that no matter how many days a week you work with your horse, you should try very hard to make it on consecutive days. This is because of a condition he calls "Mondayitis," which he discovered when he worked with his own horses on a Monday after he'd been away teaching a clinic all weekend. It always took a little while before his horses "remembered" where they'd left off in their training the week before.

Clinton found that if he worked with his horses again on Tuesday, he could pick up right where he left off at the end of Monday's ride, but if he waited until Wednesday, it was as if it were Monday all over again—he had to go back and review Monday's lesson.

So, save yourself time! When planning your horsey schedule, include time to work with your horse several days in a row. You'll get better results—that means more training advancement *and* more fun.

I noticed the value in this advice when working with my own horses. When I was able to get out in the arena and do groundwork for 15 minutes (several days in a row—see the sidebar on "Mondayitis"), I was amazed at how many exercises we practiced in a very short time once my horses knew the program. We'd start with reviewing all the exercises learned up to that point, then I'd start a new one. Obviously you can't ride in just 15 minutes, but if you can string together a few

15-minute days with a couple hour-and-a-half riding days, the next thing you know, you're seeing some wonderful progress!

Another valuable tip from Clinton and the Downunder Horsemanship team is that on "riding days" you can make the most of your time in the saddle by practicing some basic groundwork and "manners lessons" the minute you get to your horse's stall or paddock. For example, Clinton recommends "flexing" your horse's neck, left and right, when you first put his halter on, so I've made a habit of it. (Now sometimes when I go into Trace's stall just to say, "Hello," he starts flexing, without any cue from me. Overachiever.)

In fact, I have a whole groundwork routine I do with my horses, straight out of Clinton's program: After flexing, I ask them to yield their hindquarters and forequarters in both directions outside their stall, side-pass down the center aisle, then back up all the way to the saddling area. Yes, people *do* snicker and stare and wonder what the heck I'm doing to my poor horse, but it's become our routine, and by the time I get Trace or Rio saddled, we've covered important groundwork fundamentals, my horse's attention is 100-percent on me, and we can get right to work on whatever seems to be the order of the day. (Another great thing about middle age is that I—finally!—really don't give a rat's patootie what other people think. I say it's about time.)

The point to all this is, you can accomplish a lot in short periods of time simply by staying focused, and having a plan and a variable routine both you and your horse enjoy (most days). So it is possible to keep one foot in your old life, yet still have enough time to give your own horse the time and attention he needs and deserves.

How do you recognize the "right" horse for *you*?

One of Clinton Anderson's favorite sayings is, "Your first horse should be a 23-year-old, crippled-up, one-eyed, ugly gelding." He's making the very important point that you should steer clear of the shiny, black, off-the-track Thoroughbred that you will undoubtedly be attracted to—and more often than not, get hurt or frightened by. "It may sound cold," he admits, "but your first horse should not be one you love." This makes it easier, he says, to learn what you need to know, pass that great old gelding to another new rider, and *then* go get the horse you really want to ride.

This is sound logic, but unfortunately, most people don't heed such advice. Instead of buying first the horse we *need*, we tend to buy the one we *want*—the one we won't be ready for until a year or two from now. This scenario causes a lot of tears, broken hearts, and plenty of broken bones. The truth of the matter is that women tend to fall in love with horses—and that's just the way it is. Sometimes it's because of a pretty face, sometimes it is a romantic notion of how riding a horse with spirit will renew our own, and sometimes it is something more.

As Linda Kohanov observes in her book, *Riding between the Worlds*, sometimes traumatized people and traumatized horses are drawn to one another. "This person feels at home with this animal and insists on buying him over the safer, quieter one she needs," she writes. Comparing this process to how alcoholics and survivors of abuse tend to "find" one another in relationships, Kohanov observes that this phenomenon doesn't always end badly—sometimes each facilitates the healing of the other.

And let's not forget—this is our midlife horse. We hear that arthritic clock ticking, and we don't know how many good riding years we have left in us. A sense of desperation takes over and this is, after all, our biggest and most cherished dream. Who dreams of a 23-year-old, one-eyed, ugly gelding? Not any horse-crazy, middle-aged woman *I* know. (And, because of the softness of our heart at this time of life, something in us realizes that chances are, if we buy that one-eyed gelding, we'll end up getting attached to him, and he'll more than likely outlive us.)

So what can we do? Sure, I may *know* that what I need is that 23-year-old, one-eyed, ugly gelding, but I also needed Brussels sprouts instead of French fries with my dinner last night, and that didn't hap-

pen either. When it comes to matters of the heart, the truth is that
we don't usually want what's best for us, no matter how much sense
it makes. However, because statistics show the wisdom in Clinton's
advice—and because of the complete train wreck that can be the result
when we buy a horse for the wrong reasons—I'm here with a practical,
four-step way around this issue:

1   Do some soul-searching. If you have emotional stuff to work out,
    go find one of those cool, equine-assisted therapy workshops or
    retreats I mentioned in chapter 2, and heal yourself with a horse
    that does it for a living.

2   Once you're past that and you've had some lessons, start your
    horse hunt with a very specific set of criteria in mind (see the
    "Who's Your Horsie?" sidebar, p. 123). Do your homework, be
    patient, and above all, TAKE YOUR TIME and find the right horse
    (he can have both eyes, as long as he's a quiet and calm and will-
    ing teacher). Ask around, talk to trainers and instructors, join an
    online community, read all you can, attend shows and, if possible,
    an equine exposition or breed fair where you can walk around and
    observe many different types of horses and compare their charac-
    teristics. (This is a good place to note for the newbies that different
    breeds do have different personalities—just try a brisk, early-morn-
    ing fall trail ride on a Thoroughbred...and then, if you survive, do
    the same thing on a Quarter Horse. You'll see what I'm sayin'.)

3   Make a list of the qualities of your ideal equine companion, just as
    you would your ideal mate. Then maybe, just maybe, the horse you
    buy won't be like that "bad boyfriend" who is handsome, exciting
    and fun, but ends up breaking your heart because he just won't
    commit. After all the living we've done, surely we're "over" the
    good-looking heartbreakers. Aren't we smarter than that by now?
    C'mon girls, let's show it!

Clinton Anderson's Tips for Smarter Horse Shopping

(From his DVD series, *Horsemanship 101*)

1 Don't go by yourself. Take someone with you who knows horses and whose opinion you trust. Listen to them.

2 Don't buy the first horse you find, unless you look at other candidates, let some time pass, and ride him again—*several times*.

3 Stay away from sale barns and always get a vet check. You don't need X-rays unless the veterinarian sees something he doesn't like. The vet should, however, drug test the horse.

4 Don't let prettiness blind you. Seriously.

5 Buy a horse that has been ridden by someone of your approximate size and ability, and who has been doing with the horse what *you* want to do with him.

6 Ride the horse as much as possible before you buy him, in as many different environments as you can, and especially the one in which you will ride him most.

7 If the seller is agreeable, take the horse home for a two-week trial (you may need to pay a lease fee and draw up a contract for this); this could turn out to be the smartest money you ever spent.

8 If you can't afford the right horse, don't buy one at all. Instead, lease one for a year, take more lessons, and save your money for the one you really want. Remember: Leasing isn't wasting money— it's buying experience and the opportunity to find out what kind of horse is right for you.

9 There are only three ways to get a well-trained horse: buy a well-trained horse, pay someone else to train him, or train him yourself. But if you choose the latter, make sure you have the time, experience, and knowledge to get the job done.

10 Money doesn't always buy a better horse, but be willing to spend enough money to get a horse that has a good temperament, a good mind, and is safe and quiet.

EXERCISE

"Who's Your Horsie?"

Imagine a photograph of you smiling, holding the lead rope of your brand new horse. Just envisioning this horse—you have a magic wand and money is no object—helps solidify exactly what you're looking for...but there is a trick to it. The photo has to be you, exactly as you are today. In other words, the dream horse you are holding must be one you can get on right now with complete confidence. With this in mind, "build" your dream horse with this quick "wish list" quiz:

▸ Do you want a mare or gelding? Why?

▸ How old is she/he?

▸ What breed?

▸ Describe her/his color and physical characteristics. (I hesitate to put this on here because it could cause you to fixate on looks—but, since this *is* a "wish list"...)

▸ Describe her/his temperament and disposition.

▸ What kind of training has she/he had?

▸ What is her/his life story?

▸ Who owned her/him before you did, and what did she/he do?

Got it? Good. Now, close your eyes and imagine turning out your dream horse and watching him in the pasture. Visualize how he moves, behaves with the other horses, the look in his eyes. Picture yourself walking out into the pasture, catching this horse with no trouble, saddling, bridling, perhaps doing a little groundwork, then getting on. Imagine riding this horse, doing whatever it is you want to do. Feel the horse moving underneath you, the wind and the sun, hear the sound of his footfalls at the walk, trot, and canter. Imagine yourself moving with the horse, free and easy as he canters big looping circles on a loose rein or perfect voltes on the bit.

When searching for the right midlife horse, return to this scenario as often as you can, and you may be surprised at the horse that actually does show up!

4   Think about what a horse can teach *you*. Regardless of your riding ability, if there's something you want to learn how to do with a horse, there's a lot to be said for letting a dead-broke "schoolmaster" teach you what he knows. Then, when you're ready to advance to whatever inspires you, you'll be ready to shop for the horse you really, really want. Want to learn reining? Buy or lease a retired reiner. Cutting? Let a horse with experience teach you the dance. Eventing? A sound oldtimer who isn't fast enough for upper levels but with a lot of cross-country miles under his feet can help keep you safe as you give the sport a whirl. All disciplines have their "old pros"—what better way to learn than at the hands of a master? You find these horses by asking around, listening to stories told by great trainers and competitors, getting involved in online communities, and by putting the word out at shows.

▥ Where will you keep your horse? How will you care for him?

I was driving myself crazy, spending every day waiting for the magic window to open up so I could spend time with my horses, but when it did, having to choose which horse to go see, because they were in different places. As silly as that sounds now, it just happened that way, and finances, logistics, and reality kept colliding in such a way that it made some sort of convoluted sense.

This was about the time I bought Rio, and knowing how much more my dad would enjoy him than my "problem-child" Trace, I moved Trace to my friend Susan's where there was an arena with lights, a trailer, and her willingness to haul me and my horse to trails, camping sites, and ranches to ride. The potential fun in all that was hard to ignore. The trouble with my horsekeeping decision, I quickly found out, was that Susan's barn was about 30 minutes from my house. And, depending on the time of day, with traffic, this could easily become a 45-minute commute each way. It didn't take advanced math to realize that by the time I got ready, drove to Susan's to ride, caught Trace, brushed and saddled him, did a little groundwork, then rode for an hour or so, cooled him out, fed him, and made the drive back home, that just "going for a ride" was a half-day event.

If I had nothing else to do, or only wanted to ride a couple times a week, this all might have been okay, but the forehead-smacking reality of it was that enough "half days of bliss" a week to keep Trace and me both happy cost me late nights trying to make up lost work time, grumpy mornings due to the aforementioned late nights, time away from my family, neglect of other responsibilities, and, over time, the foggy-headed realization that there just wasn't enough time in the day for all my "stuff."

Instead of the exhilaration that can be a byproduct of midlife horse ownership, I felt trapped, continually thwarted, and it was about then that I almost gave up. Every attempt at a solution seemed to take me farther from the peace and joy this experience was supposed to bring. For the life of me I couldn't remember why I thought I needed a horse (never mind two)—but still, something inside willed me to hang on.

As I ran the gauntlet of horsekeeping solutions, I realized how many options there are out there—even within the "board" or "home" spectrums. How do you decide which horsekeeping option is right for you and your horse? And how can you do this without spending an unnecessary fortune?

Let's begin by assuming you've made a very wise "10-10-10"-based choice (see p. 38), and decided to buy your first horse. You've gotten yourself in reasonable physical shape, taken some lessons, developed some good basic riding skills, and now know your way around a barn. You've whittled your commitments and carved out enough time to own a horse, researched and found the perfect mount for you *right now*, and so here you are, face to face with a velvety muzzle and an exciting future.

The most pressing question on the block is one of accommodations. Where will you keep your horse? Who will be responsible for routine care? What kinds of facilities, features, or amenities are on your "must have" list? If you're already "dug in"—in the country, the city, or the suburbs—the rest of your life has most likely made this decision for you. Others of us have to thrash around a bit to find the best solution.

There are basically two choices: boarding your horse (paying a fee to keep him at a professionally or privately operated facility) or keeping him at home. There are good and bad points to each solution. I talk a little about them here, then examine both a good boarding scenario, and a good home scenario, more closely in the next chapter (see p. 135).

Is a "horse country club" right for you?

While juggling two horses in different places, along with all the rest of my life, and staring yet another "crisis of self" right in the face, I remember driving around in my car, thinking—in my typical black-and-white fashion—"I need to either get in or get out." In other words, find a place in the country where I could have my horse "in my backyard," or sell everything and call it a day. "It would be nice," I then thought, "if there were some high-quality boarding stable close to my house where I could keep both horses, and have good places to ride and fun people to ride with, all onsite."

I figured this solution was complete fantasy on my part and that if such a place did exist, it would likely be impossibly expensive, have a 10-year waiting list, and be filled with uppity riders who wouldn't give me—or my "scrub" horses—the time of day. Imagine my surprise when the door to this exact scenario (without the imagined drawbacks) appeared! After an online search and visits to several boarding facilities, I discovered a private "club" boarding facility just 14 minutes from my house, with nice, well-kept barns, 20 acres of daily turnout, full care (including feed and hay) for a reasonable fee, a large covered and two open arenas, several round pens, tack lockers, wash racks, hot walkers, and all kinds of riding amenities. The people there were of all ages, abilities, and disciplines, and they couldn't have been nicer or more inclusive.

"Keeping your horse at a place like this is like the difference between having children and having grandchildren," one of the other boarders told me the first day I saddled up in the covered saddling area.

"How's that?" I asked.

"When you keep your horse at home, it's like having children," she explained. "A lot of the time you spend with them is taken up by feeding, watering, cleaning troughs, mending fences, plowing, mowing, mucking out stalls, and dragging pens. Your time to ride and enjoy them is just part of all that, and there are always other things that need to be done first—or instead—of riding. Here, on the other hand, it's like having grandchildren. All that caretaking is done for you, and 100 percent of the time you get to spend with your horse is purely for enjoyment. We come out on our own terms, saddle up, ride, rinse them off, love on them, give them treats, and then go back to the rest of our life. It's the best of both worlds!"

Another advantage: Whatever time, day or night, I went to this "horse country club" (as another boarder put it) to ride, there were others there to ride with, talk to, or just acknowledge with a wave. It was a sense of community that I realized was important to me, but one that came without strings attached. When one person, or a specific group, is waiting on you to join them for a planned ride, it adds stress to a busy workday. But when there's simply always someone around to ride with (or to call 9-1-1, we all joke), you don't feel pressured.

Boarding, I'll admit, almost feels like cheating because all the hard stuff is done for you (mucking stalls, hauling hay and feed, spreading shavings, cleaning troughs, fixing fences, plowing arenas, clearing brush, spreading manure), but if you live in the suburbs or the city, or if, like me, you have a lot of other responsibilities pulling on you, it may be the only way having a horse seems to make any sense.

There are many different boarding scenarios, and they range from simple to extravagant. You can make a deal with a neighbor who happens to have an empty stall in her four-horse barn, or you can rent your horse a modest corner in a 60-stall stable, complete with indoor riding arena and groomed riding trails. You can find "rough board" scenarios, where housing is provided but you are responsible for part (or all) of your horse's care, and there's the "full board" option (such as I've described), when everything is taken care of for you.

Boarding prices vary depending on the scenario that is best for you and your horse, and also your geographic location. It can seem expensive, but if you really analyze the costs and what is included in your boarding situation, most often you'll find that it is a reasonable price to pay for convenience. For many midlifers, boarding their own horse is likely the perfect scenario.

A horse "just outside your back door"

Yes, boarding can be downright ideal. Except for one thing. I found that when deadlines raged, weather was disagreeable, and my many commitments started once again to overlap, the fact that my horse was *so* happy and well-cared-for at his boarding facility backfired. When I didn't have to participate in the daily hands-on care, it became easier and easier just to run by for a quick check on him, and maybe do a little groundwork, but I put off riding until I "had time." Well, guess what? Days, weeks, and yes, I'm ashamed to say, *months*, passed. Trace was spending his days "just being a horse," grazing and frolicking with his friends, while his evening hours were spent in a barn with clean shavings and an all-you-can-eat hay buffet, and being ridden (and thus becoming a better riding partner for *me*) was the furthest thing from his mind.

Worse, I was once again becoming miserable enough to consider giving up. Even my "perfect" solution wasn't working. While boarding took the day-to-day pressure of horse care off me, having a darned-near perfect boarding facility was making it *way* too easy to slack off, lose site of my training goals and riding plans, and slip back into my old habit of letting my life live me, rather than the other way around.

A long talk with a friend whose horses were "just outside her back door" confirmed something I suspected: Even though day-to-day, hands-on horse care is time-consuming hard work, its necessity guarantees a few hours with your horses, every day, rain or shine, no matter what else is going on in your life. I was missing out on the good stuff, my friend informed me.

After this conversation, I realized that if you have to haul your butt outside first thing every morning and feed your horse, you end up starting every day by saying good morning to him. If you're smart, you'll take a cup of coffee with you, turn that bucket upside down, and watch the sun come up. If the last thing you do every night is a "barn check," you also then end every day on a sweet note. True, in between those two blissful moments there's a lot of just plain old, back-breaking, physically hard work to do, and your real life obligations are still there, yapping at your heels like a pack of impatient terriers. So what if you don't get to ride as much—and maybe your time with your horse *does* become more janitorial than exhilarating—but at least you get to put your hands on your horse *every single day*.

However, taking advantage of the "just outside your back door scenario" requires that your back door open onto a decent amount of land, and not a suburban cul de sac. It means the view out your window is a mountain vista and not a city skyline. Perhaps you have the makings of a perfect horse property already, but if you're like me, following this dream to the end requires a physical relocation unlike any you may have experienced before. I was completely intimidated by the learning curve that would accompany a "move to the country" at my age. I'd lived my whole life in the city. I didn't even know what I didn't know.

Which path is the right one for *you* and *your* midlife horse? Take an informed look at both the boarding and the backyard scenarios. Then, read the next chapter on "good horsekeeping." There I provide clues and topical inspirations for further exploration on your own to help you keeping both yourself and your horse safe, healthy, and happy—without sacrificing your sanity.

▦ How will you pay for all this?

While the question "How much does a horse cost?" is a kissing cousin to "How big is a ball of string?" and the question, "Can you afford a horse?" is equidistant to "Can you afford to have children?" there are definitely a few things you should know when creating a budget for your dream:

1   Buy as much horse as you can afford.

2   Know the difference between *needs* and *wants*.

3   Make the most of every horse dollar.

Buy as much horse as you can afford
We're not talking pedigree and bloodlines, here, although sometimes that does make a difference. And, depending on your goals, it may well be a consideration. But for the average midlife horse owner, what you're looking for is a quiet, respectful horse with a good mind, solid training, and a willing disposition. And a horse like this isn't cheap. As we discussed earlier, know what you must have, what points you are willing to compromise on, and what are deal-breakers—and then stick to your guns.

While there are plenty of good horses out there that aren't expensive and plenty of expensive horses out there that aren't that good, just keep in mind that price isn't everything. And if a horse seems too good to be true, he probably is. My old tennis coach used to say, "There are no bargains in life," and I thought this statement to be quite cynical and negative until I understood it better by living though a few "bargains" of my own. So scrimp on other things, but buy the best horse you can possibly afford and make up the difference elsewhere.

Know the difference between needs and wants
Here's the real kicker: Whatever you end up paying for your horse, the

purchase price is only one part of the cost of keeping him...and it's the cheapest part.

Huh? Yep. Consider this: After the initial vet check (which can range from a few hundred to a few thousand dollars depending on what you have done), you have monthly board (unless you already have a place to keep him), feed, and regular farrier and veterinary care. One wise friend with a lot of horsekeeping experience advises you to immediately escrow $1,000, and then sock away an additional $100 each month for unforeseen vet bills. This is not for routine care, but for the emergencies that *will* happen, and that often require payment at the time of service.

You'll need tack, transportation (if you plan on riding, or regularly taking your horse off-property for any reason), and most likely continuing education for you, the horse, or ideally, both (trainer, instructor, coach, clinics—see chapter 11, p. 239). Then there's the cost of all these shows, trainers, clinics, and associated travel, not to mention all the incidental expenses along the way. In a nutshell, an average monthly horse budget *must* include:

〉 Feed and hay (amount and type of feed varies, but budget for about 30 pounds of hay, per horse, per day)

〉 Bedding (if your horse is in a stall part of the day)

〉 Farrier service—trim and/or shoes (every six weeks, unless specific conditions dictate otherwise)

〉 Deworming (four times a year, unless otherwise prescribed by your vet)

〉 Routine veterinary care and vaccinations

〉 Illness or minor emergency (budget for two of these a year and hope you don't need it!)

) Miscellaneous horse care products (shampoo, fly mask/fly spray, wound dressing, hoof dressing, and the like)

) Lessons (plan for two a month at $40 per hour)

) Books, magazines, dues, and subscriptions (continuing education is priceless!)

While costs vary greatly with horse breed, the activities you participate in, and the part of the country you live in, according to all-abouthorses.com, the following applies: A 1,000-pound horse kept for recreational riding and general enjoyment only and stabled at home might cost a conservative annual average of about $4,000. If you board (at an average rate of $300 per month) you can add another $3,600 to that. If the cost of your board includes feed/hay and bedding, you can adjust the grand total down a bit. This budget does not include land maintenance (or purchase) and related equipment or insurance. It does not include tack, travel, vehicle expenses, or cute riding outfits. It does not include entry fees or other expenses related to showing. (For some terrific horse budget worksheets, check out *Horse Economics* by Catherine O'Brien, CPA—see p. 313 for information.)

Make every horse dollar count
Discouraged? Don't be. We rarely do the math on the real costs of things we do, whether out of habit, convenience, or love. It is estimated that every person who has a hobby spends at least $5,000 per year on it. Using the tired old coffee-shop example, if we spend $3.50 a day on coffee and a muffin on the way to work, it adds up to $12,600 over 20 years. Every mile we drive our car costs about 50 cents over the life of the car—that's $15 for a 30-mile commute, and if we do it twice a day, five days a week, we're out $600 a month. Do we think about that? Nah.

The Internet helps us out here, with plenty of sites devoted to helping save money on horse-related expenses. Some trainers will barter for professional services (write the terms down in advance so everybody feels like they got what they needed at the end of the day), and some boarding facilities offer reduced rates in exchange for help with the barn chores a few days a week. Options are out there—don't be afraid to ask for them.

Factor Your (Horse) Joy Dividend

Author Martha Beck, who we met in chapter 1, offered a wonderful bit of advice on spending our money in her monthly advice column in the August 2010 issue of *O Magazine*. Although I'm quite sure Martha intended this advice for all-purpose life application, I realized upon reading "The Joy Dividend" that it also fit perfectly with horse budgeting.

Martha created what she calls a "two-by-two matrix" that "assesses the psychic value" of our expenditures. Using Martha's matrix, we are able to cull "all but the deepest needs and highest loves" from our budget. With this stark but wonderfully cut-and-dried measuring stick, we see all our potentially complex financial trade-offs organized in a way that begins to make sense.

1   Begin by drawing a large square on a piece of paper. Add a vertical and horizontal axis so there are four equal boxes within the square.

2   Label the top left square "Category I," the top right "Category II," the bottom left "Category III," and the bottom right "Category IV."

3   In Category I list the horse-related items you both NEED (notice the caps) and LOVE (ditto). Beck gives us a green light to pay top dollar for these things and budget for them before buying anything extra. ➡

4   Category II are those horsey things you NEED, but don't necessarily LOVE. Beck recommends "pinching pennies until they scream for mercy" on these. Shop, bargain, barter, use coupons, buy generic, she says. Do whatever it takes to cover these needs with the lowest possible outlay.

5   In Category III write down those things you don't really NEED, but that you do LOVE. These are the equestrian extras—you may have to wait a while on these, but keep them as a goal.

6   Category IV consists of items you neither NEED nor LOVE, but somehow inevitably acquire. "Don't spend a red cent on anything in Category IV," Beck writes. This, it seems, is the stuff that becomes the clutter that chokes us, overloads our grooming box and tack room, and detracts from our enjoyment of other purchases. Beck describes Category IV purchases as "piles of mediocre, creeping stuff that actually decrease quality of life," which immediately makes me think of all those extra saddle pads, the second set of reins that aren't quite right, even the saddle that really doesn't fit me *or* my horses, but that I keep because it's "a good saddle that was a bargain." Digging past all this Category IV "stuff," kept around just-in-case-I-one-day-fall-in-love-with-it, is just plain silly, and it makes it hard to get to "my favorite things" I use all the time. I don't know about you, but this revelation makes me want to go clean out my tack room. And my house. And my garage.

7

Good horsekeeping

While entire volumes can be—and are— written on how to properly care for a horse, here are a few key areas to consider along with important questions to ask the experts as you remodel your life to include a horse.

NO MATTER WHERE THIS MIDLIFE horse journey takes us, one thing I have noticed is this: "Success" looks quite a bit different to us at this time in our life than it may have in our younger years. Sometimes it means reigniting an old passion in a new way. Sometimes it's finding something completely new and different that somehow strikes familiar and beautiful chords within us. Some-times it starts with the familiar and then moves into a whole new area of self-exploration we never imagined could be waiting for us in a relationship with a horse.

In some ways, for some of us, the greatest "success" imaginable will now be creating the best living situation pos-sible for our horse, and then doing our part each day to keep him fit, healthy, and contented. There is really nothing quite like the sounds and smells of a barn after feeding time, when warmth, comfort, satisfaction, and a sense of general happiness pervades.

Boarding school

In the last chapter, I told you a little about my own experiences boarding my horse, and I summarized the basics for those new to the horse ownership scene. But even if you've settled on boarding as your horse situation's best solution, there's still plenty more to know about it. Visiting lots of boarding barns, talking to other boarders, asking the right questions of staff, and inspecting a few key areas are important steps in deciding the best one of the many (very different) facilities that are likely available in your area.

In order to compile a checklist of things you should consider when choosing a boarding barn, I spoke with Tom Blackmon, the onsite manager and caretaker at the Fort Worth Horseshoe Club in Fort Worth, Texas, for the past 27 years. Blackmon has seen a lot over a lifetime of dealing with hundreds of horses and owners. He believes a smart horse owner asks plenty of questions and does her own homework *before* selecting a boarding facility. The following areas deserve your particular attention:

) **Safety** First and foremost, you want safety, he says. Good indicators of a safe environment include good quality horse fencing (no barbed wire); "no climb" wire fencing is preferable, but smooth pipe is an acceptable alternative, as is smooth wire in pasture areas. (Wood and vinyl fencing is safe and attractive, although it can be cost prohibitive.) Safety rules should be clearly posted and upheld. If stallions are permitted, specific rules should apply to them, and they should be handled only by experienced individuals. You should know if a manager or caretaker is onsite at all times, and if a staff member checks over each horse, every day for injury or illness. While this last point is ultimately your responsibility as the owner, you can't be there all the time, and it's a definite bonus to have other eyes on your horse so if something happens you can be notified sooner rather than later.

⟩ **Structure material** Are the barns and other facility structures of metal or wood? While metal is hotter in the summer, it doesn't burn. After a fire at the Horseshoe Club years ago, Blackmon explains, all the barns there were rebuilt with metal. However, metal structures need to be in good shape—no sharp edges or torn panels. Wood structures, too, should be sturdy, and without rotting or sagging sections, or exposed nails.

⟩ **Body condition** If you are considering a full-board facility (all aspects of care are provided), Blackmon recommends walking around the place and noting the body condition of the horses. (I explain how to do a body condition evaluation on p. 178.) Are any of the horses underweight? Do any sport rubs, sores, scratches, bumps, missing hair, or a rubbed tail? This in itself is not necessarily a strike against a place—things do happen—but if more horses are skinny than grass-fat, if coats are dull instead of shiny, and if scabs and bald spots are prevalent, the red flag should be up.

⟩ **Bedding** Look at the stalls. Is there plenty of bedding? Is it dry? Whether the stalls are bedded with shavings, straw, sand, or some other material isn't as important, Blackmon says, as whether it's dry. Ask how often bedding is changed, how often stalls are cleaned, and whether the owner is expected to contribute to this task.

⟩ **Manure management** Believe me this is a hot topic and some people's area of expertise! Is the manure spread or piled? Is it composted or hauled away? If it is composted, where is it stored? If it is spread on pastures where horse's graze, is time allowed before horses are turned out in those areas to allow for decomposition?

) **Ventilation** Another important consideration is the air circulation in the barn. Each stall should have at least one window that opens, barns should have a layout that allows for cross-breezes, and fans (out of the way of all equine residents) should be employed as necessary.

) **Water** Is there plenty of fresh water in the stalls, paddocks, and pastures at all times? How often are buckets, troughs, or automatic waterers emptied and cleaned? What some people don't realize is that water that looks fine to us may have soured if your horse dropped a little grain in it; some horses won't drink water that tastes soured—and not enough water is a key concern in several serious horse health issues, including colic.

) **Feeding** What is the barn's feeding schedule? Horses should be fed at the same time every day. If it is a full-care facility, what brand and types of grain do they use? Take a look at the feed room. Is grain stored in a cool dry place with adequate protection from rodents? What kind of hay do they feed, and is it available to horses any time they are in their stall? Is the hay stored under cover and free of mold and dust?

) **Insect control** Is there some kind of fly control system employed at the facility? Are their strips in the barn or other measures taken? Are fly masks and fly sheets put on, and fly spray applied, before horses are turned out?

) **Blanketing** In cold weather climates, horses might wear one blanket inside, a different one outside, and no blanket at all on warmer days. All this blanket changing adds up to a lot of time, and is often an extra charge, even at full-care facilities. Ask about blanketing policy if applicable.

) **Tack and equipment storage** Is there a secure place to store your saddle, bridle, pads, boots, and brushes? Is there space for a tack trunk you can lock, or do they provide lockers? Is it protected from weather and rodents?

) **Turnout and exercise** Where and how are the horses turned out? Are they turned out in groups or as individuals? How long do they stay out? Are there hotwalkers? Does staff offer hand-walking or lungeing for an additional fee?

) **Riding areas** Look at the indoor and outdoor arena(s) and round pen(s). The ground should be level and free of rocks and debris. How often is the arena plowed and/or dragged? How is drainage handled? An indoor or well-lit outdoor arena is wonderful for stretching the hours in a day or taking advantage of cooler night temperatures during hot summer months, and shelter from rain and snow gives you a place to ride when the weather is not your friend.

) **Community** Does the facility allow guests? Instructors? Clinics? Is there onsite instruction/programming? How about social events or parties? Is there a balance of disciplines, or is the clientele strictly English or Western? Are boarders primarily recreational or competitive riders? Does the facility host horse shows? What events are represented?

) **References** Ask for the names and phone numbers/e-mail addresses of several who board at the facility you are interested in. Find out if they are happy and how long they have been there. Request their assessment of the care/handling of the horses, maintenance of stalls and facilities, barn politics, and management responsiveness. Any problems to report? How are complaints resolved? What can they tell you about the other people who board there? Is it a "closed community," or do they welcome outsiders?

"When it comes right down to it," Blackmon says, "a lot of what makes a facility 'right' for you and your horse is personal preference." And, while no one place is going to be perfect for every person, by asking enough questions and assessing the answers and information you gather, you increase your odds of finding a safe, convenient boarding facility that's a good match for your individual circumstances, meeting as many of your needs as possible.

Goodbye city life?

Given my preponderance of "escape to country life" fantasies, and given the fact that after my boarding debacle I determined that indeed the "all or nothing" route was the way I needed to go if I was really going to have horses at midlife, I decided to ask a couple of friends who were "living the dream" what they might say to someone considering such a move. While this is by no means a scientific sampling, I do believe they raise some common issues and questions and, once again, give us all a few places to dig for the answers *we* need to address our unique set of needs and circumstances.

‖‖ Emily

When Emily moved to the country, she was glad she didn't know what she didn't know. Most of us have no real idea of what it takes to live the "simple country lifestyle" until we actually bite the bullet, roll up our sleeves, and go for it. Emily reports that through quite a lot of trial and error, plenty of calls to her county agricultural extension hotline, endless

10 Tips for Being a Good Boarder

Developing a good working relationship with the management of your boarding facility—and with other boarders—can be key to making sure your horse is happy and well cared for. Feeling part of the community, and having it be one in which someone is always looking out for your horse when you're off dealing with the rest of your life, equals considerable peace of mind. Sure, it takes a village to raise a child, and when you're learning the ropes of midlife horsemanship, it sometimes takes a barn full of friends to get you from "green-horn" to confident horsewoman. Here are 10 tips with building these special relationships in mind:

1 Be aware of other people's use of your boarding facility, and be mindful that everyone's time may be as limited as yours.

2 Don't block the aisles or walkways with your tack and equipment scattered about.

3 Be efficient in your use of shared amenities, and respectful of other people's supplies.

4 If you have a problem with some element of facility management, go straight to the manager instead of just complaining to fellow boarders who can't do anything about it.

5 Pay your bill on time and keep up with incidental expenses.

6 Drive slowly in and out of the premises and around any horse areas. Never exceed 10 to 15 miles an hour on the grounds, even on paved roads.

7 Avoid any sudden or excessive noise or movements that might spook an unsuspecting horse and rider.

8 Communicate with management and staff. Let them know if you're going to be out of town, if you have a concern about your horse, or if there is any question about or change in his care, feeding, or routine.

9 Stay current on your horse health issues, and let the manager know if there's a concern or if you need help. Many barns offer shared vet calls for routine vaccinations and worming, and if you need additional services, this can usually be done at that time with advance notice.

10 Clean up after your horse. Yep, all horses *do* poop in the wash rack or in the saddling areas and in the aisles, even after they've been ridden all afternoon in the great big outdoors. Get over it. It's what they do. And while it's one thing to step in your own horse's poop, it's quite another to encounter a pile left there by someone else. Take that few extra seconds and be a good barn citizen by scooping your own manure. Little things often mean a lot, especially when it comes to poop.

visits to the feed store, and tractor and hardware stores, and mining her personal network for referrals and information, she slowly began to fill in the gaps in her country-living knowledge.

"I followed people around, I asked a lot of questions, and I studied every subject as if my life or the life of my animals depended on it." She laughs, and adds. "That was because, for all I knew, it could!

Over a period of months and years, Emily acquired basic carpentry skills, plumbing know-how, as well as the ability to operate various pieces of farm equipment safely ("I just took them one at a time and learned everything I could about how to operate them," she says). Focusing on safety, and paying particular attention to body mechanics when hauling, lifting, and pulling on things too heavy to handle, Emily is a role model for all of us who might not be as physically strong and agile as the average 25-year-old. With all the determination, wisdom, and self-preservation skills of our intervening years, she is living proof that this transition can work—and it can work very well.

She learned the art of manure management (and believe me, it is an art); how to keep the watering troughs clean; how to deal with weather (and how important that weather report becomes); how to patch broken fence in the dark; how to plow; how to mow; how to fix leaks and repair holes; and how to protect her horses and dogs—and herself—from predators. Spiders, snakes, and scorpions—and the occasional need to rid yourself of them—are very much a country-living reality.

And of course, somewhere in the midst of all this "personal growth," Emily found a way to create a place of beauty, peace, and harmony. Ah, midlife bliss.

▒ Barbara

When Barbara and her husband Ron, both in their mid-40s, traded in their high-powered city existence for a quieter rural life, their friends dismissed it as some kind of midlife crisis. Barbara and Ron laughed right along with the jokes but knew they were making the decision they *needed* to make. In the months and years that followed, Barbara learned some unexpected lessons of her own strength within the adventure they shared.

In her memoir of this experience, "Lessons from the Gap," Barbara describes moments of hair-raising realization: just how dark it is when you're alone at night on 175 acres; the exhilaration of holding your ground with the indigenous wildlife (from deer and coyotes, to a pair of grey wolves, to a rattlesnake in the barn); and nurturing skills and instincts heightened by sheer necessity (from saving an injured hummingbird, to milking an enraged, engorged—and verging on toxic—mama cow, to witnessing with awe the birth of goat triplets). Barbara describes what it means to find a new rhythm in a reinvented existence, moments of pure magic in the day-to-day rigors of country life, and the certainty, no matter what each day brings, that you have found the "right place."

Horses? Well, of course it was horses that, in fact, started the whole rural-life fantasy. As a child Barbara laid in the grass, side-by-side with her best friend, dreaming of the horses she would have, the place in the country, the handsome husband, and the beautiful life. And, it was while galloping across her own meadow one blissful afternoon that she realized she had found what she'd always imagined for herself. She describes the moment in "Lessons from the Gap":

> *I saddled Kit for an afternoon ride, and my other two horses, KC and Peno, trotted along behind. We picked our way past the overgrown trails I decided to leave for another day and came out near the stock tank. KC and Peno loped past us, scrambling up the levy like a couple of puppies, then tossed their heads, reared, and pawed the air like a Black Stallion remake, and charged down the levy into the belly-deep water. I sat for a while and watched them cavort in the water, laughing out loud at their teenage antics. Then I turned Kit back west for an easy lope into the setting sun across the old hay field. As*

we moved out, KC and Peno soon joined us, one on either side, matching our pace, beat for beat. "What could be better than this?" I thought, heart brimming with the joy of the moment. Then out of the corner of my eye I saw it. A hawk, sailing just overhead, glided gently along with us, bringing unexpected majesty to this moment I will replay like a video in my mind for the rest of my life.

▓ It's a "leap of faith"

When you take the bold leap of faith and make a move to country horsekeeping, remember that regardless of your luck, individual circumstances, or seat-of-the-pants solutions, you're choosing a whole new world full of both unforeseen complications and exhilarating moments you would never otherwise experience. Yes, it can work—and beautifully—regardless of your age or experience. And, although it is not an easy life, horsekeeping at home is an opportunity like no other to connect with your horse and find a new sense of balance rooted in the natural world.

Take your cue from Emily and Barbara. Seek out and find the information and help you need. And, to help you round up your own collection of resources, here are few hints inspired by authors Margaret and Michael Korda in their book, *Horse Housekeeping* (William Morrow, 2005)—which should be, in my opinion, required reading for anyone considering keeping a horse at home—as well as some points to consider when making this landmark decision. Believe me when I say there is far too much territory to cover here, but what follows should help get you started.

How much land do you want?
Real estate professionals tend to identify between 10 and 30 acres as "manageable" for personal use for someone who wants animals. Of course, when it comes to horses and having interesting places to ride,

more is always...more. A quick call to the county agriculture extension will tell you about the general soil conditions of the area (and once you buy you can have a sample analyzed to see what nutrients are there and which ones need to be but aren't); plants, trees, and grasses that are indigenous to the area, and what to encourage and what to watch out for. (See the resources on p. 311 for great ways to educate yourself regarding basic pasture management.)

What about the house?

Although I have trained my friends and family to tell me about a place's fences, barns, pens, paddocks, and arenas first, if you're going to live in the country you're going to have to have somewhere to rest your weary head. Horse people are notorious, as Michael Korda so eloquently writes in *Horse Housekeeping*, for tending meticulously to the needs of their barn and horses while letting their homes and personal appearance, shall we say, "slip a little" by city standards: "Hence, the number of houses of horsekeepers in which tack is hanging in the bathroom, dust lies thick on every surface," he says, "while the barn is a show place, off the aisle of which you could eat your dinner (and might prefer to, given the state of the dining room)."

It might also be noted that this is not exclusive to those who keep horses at home; in fact, I know one writer in the city (um, quite well) who boards and whose house is much worse than Korda's description... I like to think it is because when one has horses (and especially when one also *writes* about horses) *horse*keeping is far more interesting than *house*keeping.

What kind of house you need—or will settle for—is about as personal as it gets. But I guess it goes without saying to make sure it is safe, structurally sound, and as comfortable as it can possibly be within the constraints of your budget. It also should come as no surprise to you that the standards are different in the country, and things that may have been important to you in the city or suburbs are in fact minor or nonexistent issues in the country, while something overlooked or taken for granted (like the grossly important subject of sewage) suddenly becomes a big deal.

When you find a "country place" that deserves a more serious second look, be sure to involve someone you trust, preferably an individual with expertise in the area of architecture, engineering, or construction. This can make a big difference when choosing a "fixer-upper"—you need to make sure the improvements you'd like to make are actually doable.

Starting from scratch

Obviously, the more that has already been done (reasonably well) on the piece of rural landscape you're considering, the better it is in terms of immediate liveability and the fewer improvements you will have to make. However, sometimes it is easier and no more expensive in the long run to start from scratch. It is good to run the numbers each way and compare (the larger purchase price for what's already been done versus a smaller purchase price plus the cost of improvements you will have to make). When making such an evaluation, be sure to factor in how much knowledge and physical ability you'll have to improve *in yourself* (see Emily's story earlier) and how much time it will take to do that.

▥ Details, details

We covered some of this from a different angle when we talked about what to look for in a boarding facility (see p. 136). Review the section on boarding and consider what I add to it here—as you might imagine, when constructing the ideal horse property, it is all in the details.

Shelters and barns

The debate rages on whether horses are healthier and happier in enclosed barns with regular daily turnout or "free-choice" shelter in a three-sided "run-in" or "loafing shed" that provides a place out of the rain, wind, direct sun, or freezing precipitation.

If you go with the three-sided variety (or if that's what happens to be on the property you buy), it should be well-constructed and as large as possible (horses get claustrophobic easily, and you want this to be a place that is more inviting than scary). Ideally, it should face south, but really it's okay if it faces any direction but north. It is important to keep run-in sheds mucked out daily, with clean bedding added as necessary.

If a barn is more to your liking, do your homework and take no chances when it comes to structural soundness. While it's often easier to start from scratch than it is to renovate a saggy existing structure, both can be done well and safely if you take care to hire reliable help experienced in this area of construction. Some specific areas of concern include:

> **Soundness and safety** If using or renovating an old barn, have someone who knows something about construction and structural engineering check out the supporting structures and roof. Metal construction offers fireproofing; if the structure is not metal, it should have a fire system with overhead sprinklers located in each stall and several in hay and feed areas. In addition, make sure working (check dates and test annually) fire extinguishers are strategically located and easy to get to in a hurry. Stall flooring should be level and solid, and stall mats are a good idea.

> **Ventilation** There should be good natural airflow through the barn, and each stall should have a source of ventilation. In hotter climates, it is ideal to have horse-safe fans mounted in each stall and large fans strategically placed to keep air moving in the aisles. While it is important that horses in adjacent stalls are not able to hurt each other if there's a squabble, open space at the top of stall walls (or an upper level finished with bars or chicken wire) aids ventilation and improves the horses' social well-being by allowing them to see each other and touch noses.

) **Water** Automatic waters (with heaters in cold climates) are a definite plus, but if that's not in the budget, you just need a clean source of water that is easy for you to get to and that flows well. Outside water sources should also be easy to check and clean, and you need to educate yourself on how to keep algae at bay (horses won't drink water with certain kinds of algae in it).

) **Lighting and electricity** Make sure all wiring is sound and up to code, and any outlets that spark or are hot to the touch need to be replaced. Barn lighting is pretty much an individual preference, but equipping each stall and center aisles, as well as feed and supply areas, and entrances/exits, with adequate light is imperative in the event of a nighttime emergency.

Tool School

To help you keep up with your barn-care tools, Margaret and Michael Korda (authors of *Horse Housekeeping*) recommend making yourself a "wall of implements." This can be an elaborate pegboard construction with chalk outlines depicting where each tool goes, or as simple as pounding 10 big honkin' nails in rows along one or several horizontal two-by-fours. The point is to provide a place to hang up all your barn-cleaning tools and implements (pitchforks, shovels, brooms, nozzles, and so on) in one place so you can see them, reach them quickly, and put them back in the same place every time—or know exactly when one's gone missing at a glance. A horizontal wooden board or fence plank with large holes drilled in it (think of them as "tool cubbies") is great for storing your smaller hand tools, such as screw drivers, pliers, and hammers, for quick-and-easy retrieval.

Nail Down Your Barn Expectations Before You Call the Contractor

1   Where will you build the structure? Educate yourself on the prospective site and weather patterns, average temperatures, light, drainage, and so on.

2   How many horses will it house, what breed will they be, and what will you be doing with them? What kind of horse you're riding, and how you are riding him makes a difference as to what kinds of amenities you need and how much space everything will take.

3   Are there specific building styles or features you're looking for? A collection of cut out pictures and examples of elements you like can help you convey your vision and expectations.

4   What's your budget—*really*?

Vet Your Barn Builder

Make sure your barn builder knows horses. While lots of home builders can build a good-looking, quality structure, only someone who has built barns before and is familiar with horses and the horse industry knows what is important in terms of **safe**ty (yours and the horse's), convenience, and functionality. It also goes without saying that if there is something in particular you want based on your own needs and experiences, insist on it. This is you barn and you're going to be the one using it!

Fence finesse
From as long ago as the Old West to as recently as just last week, one of the biggest issues for horsekeepers (and other livestock-keepers, as well) is "looking after the fences." No matter what materials you use, how well it is built, or how impenetrable it is guaranteed to be, checking and maintaining fence lines (as well as keeping a well-stocked fence repair kit close at hand) has to become a regular part of your life.

Stay Charged

When you put new batteries in your electric fence charger, write the date on them with a permanent marker. That way you know when batteries are getting old and can check them regularly and replace on schedule to avoid hard-to-find sections of "dead fence."

Things to consider when it comes to fencing (whether you're starting from scratch or working with existing fence lines) include:

) **Layout of pens and paddocks** While the configuration of these areas is really about safety and personal preference, the main thing is to think it through in advance. You need access between fenced areas and the barn, if you're going to have one; and you need to determine how you like to keep your horses separated, and what your turnout plan will be. In addition, will there be grazing areas or riding areas or other special-use sections of your property that need to be fenced-in or fenced-out?

) **Width of gates** What kinds of vehicles need to get through your pasture and paddock gates from time to time? Tractor? Manure spreader? Truck? BIG truck? (Hint: The gate that leads to your manure pile needs to be big enough to accommodate a BIG truck. More on that subject later).

) **Material** What fencing materials are common and readily available in your part of the country? What is safe? What is affordable?

) **Pathways and roadways** As mentioned, checking fence is sure to be part of your regular—probably daily—routine. You can't check too often for loose rails, weak or wobbly posts, sagging wire, rusted metal, or dead batteries in your electric fence charger. Prepare for this responsibility with roads or tracks along the fence line that accommodate a horse or motorized vehicle—or a woman on foot—so you can follow and reach fencing easily.

Be a Prepared Fence Scout

Always keep a supply of extra fence posts and fencing material on hand. The need for fence repairs regularly occurs at the most inconvenient times—and usually when the lumber yard or supplier is closed. Even if you have a handyman who tends your fences, make sure you can handle basic repairs yourself in case he's not around. And, when you use your backup supplies, be sure to replenish for next time!

Pasture management
While it takes 4 to 5 acres of *unimproved* native grass pasture to support one mature horse for the entire grazing season, with rotation and good management, it takes just 1 to 2 acres. When it comes to growing—or encouraging the natural growth of—grasses, hay, or oats in your hay fields, pastures, and turnouts, you've hit upon an area of study that can be neverending. Consult your county agricultural extension agency for good resources and prepare to be both patient and diligent in your efforts. Describing pastures and fields as "needy," and advising constant and ongoing care, Michael Korda writes in *Horse Housekeeping*, "You can spend 20 years caring for [them], but forget [them] for six months and suddenly you will have a multitide of problems."

Good quality grass is best for your horses, but it does take some forethought and consistent effort to get it and keep it growing. In my research, the tips that came up consistently in expert sources included:

>) Keep pastures and paddocks (in use) mowed and dragged to spread out accumulating manure and encourage regrowth.

> Rotate grazing areas to allow a "rest period" and a chance for new grasses to take root and grow.

> Evaluate and mitigate your topography to take advantage of rain and natural water sources.

> Seed and plant strategically to use natural elements and barriers to your advantage.

"Burrito Skills" to Eliminate Pasture Leaves

If your horse(s) will be turned out in pasture areas that are wooded and you have a climate that results in dropped leaves, it's a good idea to formulate a plan to "get the leaves up." Some horses will eat *anything* on the ground and certain kinds of leaves—red maple and black walnut, for example—are especially toxic to horses, as is the mold that can gather as the leaves decompose.

Here's a trick from the Margaret and Michael Korda's book *Horse Housekeeping* for making fast work of pasture leaves. (Granted, its success depends on what kind and how many leaves you're dealing with.)

After a few sunny fall days (this works best if leaves are dry) use your tractor mower (sans blade) to "blow" the leaves into the center of the pasture, starting at the outside edge and working inward, making your circle smaller and smaller until the leaves are in a giant pile. Fork the leaves from the pile onto a large tarp, wrap the tarp like a giant burrito, and drag it out of the pasture for disposal (decaying leaves make great compost). Depending on how many leaves have fallen and the size of your tarp, this may take a few trips, but it definitely beats days of hand-raking!

In addition to fertilization and hydration, regular mowing is important to establishing good grass root systems. Mowing season starts in April in most areas and extends into the fall—as late as November in some parts of the country. Regular mowing is also a good way to keep a close eye on your land and topography (you can find holes and washed out places before they get too deep and pose a threat to your horse), as well as your fence line. It's also a good idea to run a weedeater around your perimeter fencing, gates, sheds, and buildings to eliminate fire hazards and places for snakes to hide, as well as give you a chance to eyeball your posts and structure foundations.

What's up with the water?

Are there wells, city water, tanks, livestock watering systems, irrigation? Are there pumps—and if so, what kind, how many, where are they located, and how old are they? Are warranty, repair, and parts information readily available? If there's a well, get the particulars—and if there's a water test available, ask to see it. If there's not and you're serious about making this country home your own, you'll want to get one and have it analyzed to be sure the water supply is dependable for you and your horse.

Keep convenience in mind when determining where water is or will be available. Try to eliminate the need to carry water buckets significant distances—this gets old in a hurry. Automatic waterers, water lines, and stock tanks in pastures, pens, and paddocks can all be part of your grand water plan. Just remember, you need to keep an eye on water level and quality to prevent sickness and dehydration in livestock, and it's also good to plan for a secondary source of water for horses that will be turned out for longer than a few hours at a time.

Sewage and sanitation

More than likely, your prospective horse property will have a septic tank or leach field, but you'll want to know exactly where it is located and how old it is, as well as how it is maintained. While this is not really what you want to think about when trying to put legs under your country dream, believe me, it becomes very important when you move in.

Is trash pickup and recycling available, or will you have to haul your own to a town dump or recycling center? Since dealing with garbage is a year-around proposition, you'll need to make provisions. This, too, may seem like a less-than-glam minor detail—until you're drowning in it.

Manure manifesto

And on related matters...

In England they burn it. Some barn owners and farm managers pile it indefinitely and allow it to compost (there's a lot more to this than just letting it sit—if you're interested, check out explicit instructions, along with other invaluable "green" tips in Lucinda Dyer's book *Eco-Horsekeeping*, Trafalgar Square Books, 2009). Others haul it off to approved disposal sites (usually landfills), while still others just take a backhoe and bury it (not good for the environment and a good way to contaminate your water supply, but it happens).

When you have horses, you're going to have manure. Did you know that the average 1,000-pound horse produces more than 30 pounds of manure a day, along with 20 pounds of urine? This adds up to more than 8 to 10 tons of manure per year, per horse. Add to that the bedding that generally gets scooped up with the waste, and you can see why this is a subject every horse owner needs to take seriously.

While manure in itself, when composted correctly, can be a great soil amendment prized by home gardeners and commercial growers alike, if not dealt with correctly it can contaminate area water, become a breeding ground for flies and insects, and make you a very unpopular neighbor, especially in more populated areas. The short course on manure management can be boiled down to a few simple rules. How you adapt these rules to your particular situation is the artistry part:

) **Remove regularly, preferably daily** This is necessary especially when your horse is in small confined area such as stall or small paddock. Try to minimize the amount of bedding material in your manure pile, as it delays decomposition.

) **Plan temporary storage** A concrete or other tight enclosure keeps the pile as compact and moist as possible, which helps speed decomposition. This storage area should be big enough to contain the total volume of anticipated manure to be generated within your "storage period"—that is, however long until the manure is removed or spread (for one horse, over one year, a 12-foot by 12-foot space, piled 3 to 5 feet high, should do the trick).

) **Location, location** The storage area should be located where both unloading wheelbarrows and loading large trucks is convenient, both for daily barn cleanup and monthly, quarterly, or annual removal from your property. The equation here is: Close enough to the barn to be convenient, but far enough away to minimize flies and odor.

) **Standing manure protection** Your storage area needs a roof or a tarp to prevent contact with runoff or rainwater. Care should be taken to make sure any water that does happen to leave the manure storage area is channeled away from clean waterways and groundwater locations.

) **Spread on pasture and cropland** Spreading 1 to 1½ inches of manure on your pasture just prior to fall rains improves the next year's vegetation (note: proper pasture rotation should be scheduled alongside fertilization). Incorporating about 2 inches of manure into surface cropland soil conditions the soil, improves nutrients, and prevents loss of nitrogen. And, 2 to 4 inches of manure can be used in landscape areas to suppress weed growth and conserve moisture.

▥ Foul weather fixes

Rain, drought, snow and ice, heat and wind—all extremes of weather bring new issues you must address when your horse is in your own care. When it comes to dealing with the weather extremes Mother Nature can deal, experienced horsekeepers instinctively know what to do and how to do it, but if you're new at this game, you need help getting a plan in place for whatever foul-weather-likelihoods exist in your geographical area.

When you move to the country, that weather report you used to mostly tune out on your way to work becomes the most vital information of your day. If you are moving to an area with a climate that is new to you, it would serve you well to talk to a few locals about weather patterns and concerns you should have when livestock is involved.

There are a number of weather-monitoring devices that work like satellite radios, which can help you keep an eye on incoming bad weather, monitor storms in the area, and keep tabs of the temperature so you can take necessary steps to deal with weather extremes (see Resources, p. 311). Compose a list of names and phone numbers of folks who can help you out in times of need—whether simply plowing snow and clearing fallen timber, or replacing wind-damaged structural elements and even evacuating your horses.

A REAL-LIFE, MIDLIFE HORSE STORY   *LIZ*

Acknowledging that many horses make it through just fine when turned out in extreme winter weather, Minnesota horse trainer and clinician Liz Graves says she'd rather have her horses "in out of the wind and cold, with fluffy bedding to lay on, warm water to drink, and where they can actually be comfortable." Realizing the key role we can play in our horse's life during long, frozen winters, Liz finds joy in the comforts she is able to provide.

"They seem so grateful to be in," she says. "It's so peaceful in the barn listening to them all chewing in contentment, playing with toys, soft, happy nickers to each other and not one giving any indication of wanting to go out to the frozen tundra. I love the feeling it gives me doing everything I can to make them very comfortable and content; it's just very fulfilling. This is the weather when they need us the most."

I have to admit it sounds quite romantic when you look at harsh winters in this loving kind of way. And it is Liz who shares one example of how to get clever in helping your horsey partner pass the time, even amongst the more serious and specialized challenges posed by the winter white stuff. "This is a good way to keep horses' winter boredom at bay, and for wood chewers, it's even better!" she says. The only requirement is you must live in a part of the country where you can freeze water solid at some point during the coldest months.

How to Make Horsey Ice Pops

Fill a 5-gallon rubber bucket three-quarters full of water. (Don't overfill it or the bucket will split when frozen water expands.)
Add:
1 cup chopped apple (The apple pieces will float.)
1 cup *shredded* carrots—note that sliced or chunked carrots can cause a horse to choke (The carrot shreds will sink.)
1 cup grain (The grain will sink.)
1/2 cup electrolytes
1/2 cup sugar (Liz uses raw sugar.)
Food coloring (Optional—Liz likes to use food coloring so the Horsey Pops stand out against the snow and she can see them when the horses are playing with them. For use inside the barn, food coloring is not needed.)

Mix well and place the bucket outside until frozen solid, then bring inside for about 30 minutes to let the sides of the bucket warm up just enough to slide the pops out.

Depending on the horse and the weather, one Horsey Pop should last one horse, one to two weeks.

▥ The heavy on farm and ranch equipment

Before you buy a lot of big equipment—or decide whether to keep or sell whatever comes with your new horse property—be sure to give some serious thought to your time, interest, and ability to actually *do* the jobs the equipment is meant for. If you're not careful, you can end up with a barn full of stuff you may not need.

From trucks and trailers (which I talk about in chapter 10, p. 227) to tractors and ATVs, from brush hogs and mowers, to plows and gators, you may find, once you've stepped into "Bubba's World," that you're more than a little bit out of your element. Not to worry. In time you'll learn which tasks you enjoy and want to do for yourself, and which ones are just as cost effective, and sometimes safer, to hire out. As one person that I interviewed (who would like to remain anonymous) found out, even the simplest farm equipment can be downright dangerous when you are unfamiliar with its rules of safe operation, and if you're unaccustomed to staying out of the way of its "obvious" hazards.

Basic equipment tips from those who've been there

1   Remember that *all* equipment, no matter how simple, needs periodic inspection and maintenance to keep things working properly and extend their usefulness.

2   Start an equipment notebook for each piece of heavy equipment, and keep all related receipts, warranties, repair records, maintenance schedules, and contact information for the manufacturer and your "repair guy."

3   Get in the habit of cleaning every tool after each use. Hose it off, give it a quick wipe with a rag and a squirt of lubricant, or *really* "take it apart and clean it" from time to time. Figure out what will

keep each piece of farm equipment in good working order and consider this maintenance part of the job. You won't be sorry.

4   Most pieces of farm equipment have an "off-season." Use this time for their thorough inspection, replacement of parts that may have incurred wear and tear, and make sure it is stored clean and ready to go again the following season.

5   Read and follow all safety instructions. Seriously. You'd be surprised how many people are "shown" how to use equipment by someone and never bother to read the manual and how-to instructions for themselves. (I know, those manuals are not the most exciting reading material, but if they can save your limbs, isn't it worth a little bit of focused study?)

VIPs

When you're living in the country and keeping your horse at home, you develop a whole *new* idea of what a "very important person" is. In a complete departure from the CEOs, executives, and white-collar professionals that used to run your world, the people on your new VIP list are those who can help you take care of things—especially when you get in a jam. And believe me, especially when you're new to the rural lifestyle, there of plenty of those.

It is a great idea to create a "personal farm or ranch directory" (I recommend hard copy as well as an electronic spreadsheet), starting with your realtor's referrals, of people in your area who offer specific services or are just good folks to call on when you need a hand. These are your country-living VIPs. The VIPs listed in your directory will vary, of course, with your individual needs, situation, and expertise, but they may include:

) Veterinarian

) Farrier

) Horse dentist

) Carpenter (preferably with barn/horse knowledge)

) Plumber (preferably familiar with livestock watering projects)

) Electrician (preferably with experience wiring barns, sheds, and workshops)

) Someone with welding expertise

) "Ranch hand" with a tractor and/or other heavy equipment to perform property maintenace you may not be able to take care of yourself

) Caretaker to stay on your property and feed/check on your horse when you need to go out of town (whether planned or unexpectedly)

) Equipment repairman

) Timber management service to cut and haul away trees, limbs, and branches

) Manager of the local feed store (make a point to become a regular so you have a go-to when you need additional resources or information, or an emergency delivery of grain)

) Hay provider (a valuable connection you'll want to make as soon as possible)

) Bedding provider (learn his regular delivery schedule, place a standing order if possible, and *always* be there to receive the load when he arrives)

Getting a (country) life

Okay, so you've taken the plunge, moved to the country, and brought your horse with you. You've settled into this whole new lifestyle and done a primo job making sure your fences are tight, your barn is sound, and your place is well-equipped. Now what?

Oh yeah—we started this journey in search of our "authentic self," right? The next question soon to cross your exhausted mind is likely, "Between all these *new* responsibilities, not to mention the others I brought with me (family, friends, work) how on earth am I going to have a *life*?"

When you're juggling a million different things, life in the country, as beautiful and different as it is, is in one major way no different from life in the city or suburbs. *Routines will save you.* You need a feeding routine (for horses, other animals, and people); a barn-cleaning routine (and, yes, you better have one for the house, too); a land-management routine; and last but not least, a horse routine.

Begin with daily routines for morning, afternoon, and evening to anchor each day (they will soon become automatic), and in between these anchors, any available blocks of time should be loosely assigned to specific goals. With a lit-

Install Barn Notice Boards for Important Reminders

Put up two dry-erase, chalk, or cork-style bulletin boards in your barn to keep handy the things you need to know at a glance. On one board, keep a current list of names and phone numbers for your VIPs. On the second, keep a list of the important dates on your calendar, including:

▸ Next shoeing or trim

▸ Next vet checkup

▸ Next deworming date

▸ Next equipment maintenance/service date

You can add a third board for messages and other reminders if you'd like, depending on how many people you have coming or going—or if you like to leave yourself visual notes as I do. Keep board information clean and clear of distraction so it is in your line of daily sight and you won't forget about it!

tle careful thought and planning, over the course of each week you'll care for all your new responsibilities and make some forward progress on your personal goals with your horse. Be gentle with yourself, take your time and remember that any step—even a small one—toward this midlife goal, counts.

It appears that the magic of country living for most people is found in those little pockets of joy they deliberately work into even the most mundane tasks: taking 15 minutes when you're done mowing to down a cold beverage and wriggle your toes in the freshly cut grass, or while checking fence, stopping under your favorite tree and watching your horse graze as you munch your own lunch.

Plus, when you take advantage of every opportunity to reap some side benefits, you may be surprised on what can sneak up on you: The best tan I ever had was the summer we painted all the pipe fence at my dad's ranch. The best physical shape I have ever been in was the summer I learned to work my horse from the ground in deep arena sand. Hauling hay is a deluxe upper body and core workout; ditto mucking stalls. My friend Terry laughs at me and my regimented trips to the gym—she says her "gym" is her barn, her "track" is the path between her house and the paddocks, and her personal trainer has four hooves and high expectations.

So with all this in mind, let's now take a look at the best routines of all...

Barn and horsekeeping routines

As I mentioned, you need to establish a set routine that you follow each day with your horses, rain or shine, snow, sleet, hail, or hot weather. Although this routine will change with the season, and will vary with the extremes of those seasons, figure it out, write it down, and stick to it. Once again, a notebook or spreadsheet divided by seasons, as well as daily, weekly, and monthly checklists posted in the barn or tack room, will keep you on track and help make sure everything flows together into some type of logical order. Your regular barn and horse schedule needs to address the following, which I've illustrated here in only the most basic of fundamentals (see Resources, p. 311, for more information on general horse care):

) **Feeding and watering** Feed the same time each day and change water twice a day (unless you have automatic waterers). Scrub buckets and wipe out auto waterers once a week.

) **Grooming and hoof care** *Coat:* first remove any mud you see. "Don't ever ignore mud, wet or dry," writes Michael Korda in *Horse Housekeeping*. "It can hide cuts, scrapes, and scratches that need to be tended to." Remove mud gently and carefully with a metal currycomb (if mud is dry) or a water hose (if mud is wet). Give a brisk, all-over rub (small circular motions) with a rubber curry comb to loosen dust and hair, followed by long strokes in the direction of hair growth with a coarse-bristled brush, then a soft bristled brush, and then, if you like, a slicker block or soft rub rag to bring up the shine.

Manes and tails: When I worked for horse trainer Clinton Anderson, his barn staff (who prepare all his horses for their clinics, demos, and television appearances) told me to never comb out manes and tails *except* after shampooing or applying product (otherwise, you break the hair off). About once a week, shampoo and condition body, mane, and tail with a good quality product.

Feet: Clean your horse's hooves daily, have them trimmed every four to six weeks, and shoe up front or all around depending on your farrier's recommendations and the condition of your horse's feet. Opinions differ on hoof dressings and hoof supplements— speak with your farrier and veterinarian before you use one.

Clipping: Whether or not your horse is clipped is an individual preference (depending on your horse's breed, your riding discipline, and whether or not you compete), as is exactly what is clipped and how. Since my horses are turned out all the time, I leave their whiskers (which protect the soft muzzle skin when grazing) and ear hair (which keep flies and insects out of the ears). I clip Rio's bridle path (it makes him look more like a cutting horse), and let Trace's grow (it adds to his wild brumby look).

) **Stall and aisle care** Pick stalls out (remove manure and wet spots in bedding and add a little dry bedding) daily. Strip stalls once a week. Rake or sweep barn aisles daily to keep things tidy, and keep a long handled dust mop on your "wall of implements" (see p. 148) to knock down any cobwebs that appear in stalls or tack and/or feed rooms. Tidy your feed room (especially the medicine/supplements shelf—keep labels facing out!) once a week to make sure everything stays in good order and you know to replace or replenish anything that's running low or expired.

) **Turnout** Just like people, horses need fresh air, sunshine, and room to run and kick up their heels—and the more they get of all of this the happier, and usually healthier, they are. At the very least, your horse should get a couple hours of turnout each day, and more if you can manage it. To make it easy on yourself, create a turnout schedule so you can plan other barn- and horse-related tasks (such as cleaning stalls, and vet and farrier appointments) around times you know your horse will be definitely in or definitely out. Remember that horses need a change of scenery from time to time and pastures need "rest periods," so rotate paddocks and grazing areas regularly.

) **Riding and training time** Clinton Anderson's assistant trainers say they try to spend 30 to 45 minutes a day on the ground, and then 45 minutes to an hour in the saddle with each horse they work with, six days a week. (That's an hour and a half combined groundwork and riding, each day, for a younger horse in train-

ing.) While my horses are neither young or in training, per se, I
do try to follow this guideline on the days I ride, and I try to string
my riding days together whenever possible to avoid the dreaded
"Mondayitis" (see p. 118).

When you can't ride, be sure your horse gets some kind of sustained exercise (on the lunge line, for example) for about 30 minutes, always preceded by a 5- to 10-minute warmup (groundwork
exercises work well for this), and followed by a 5- to10-minute cool-
down (a nice leisurely walk around the property is good for both
of you!). Several people I know swear by keeping a small calendar
clipped to the outside of their horse's stall or next to their saddle in
the tack room so they can plan what they're going to do with their
horse, days, weeks, and even months in advance (horses have a way
of rearranging carefully planned schedules, but if you keep moving
in the general direction, you'll get the job done eventually).

) **Tack/equipment care** I get into more detail about tack and
horse equipment in chapter 9 (p. 205), but a couple of basic rules
of upkeep are to wipe down tack (including bits, silver, and metal
pieces) after each use, then schedule a time once a week or once
a month (depending on how much you're riding) to give your
tack a thorough cleaning and inspection. This is how you avoid
wrecks caused by equipment failure, as well as preserve expensive items you won't really want to buy more than once, so don't
neglect this routine.

So now you're moved in, you're settled, and you've established
good routines to use your country living time wisely. Hang on—there's
a few more things you need to know about owning your own horse,
whether you're boarding or keeping him at home—and we'll cover
those in the next few chapters.

8

Healthy as a horse

Horse health is a subject as full of controversy as any you'll find in the equine world. From those who consider horses delicate creatures in need of constant care and coddling to the crusty old cowboy at the other end of the spectrum, knowledge and technology offer many options as we seek solid middle ground for the very best care we can provide.

BESIDES WHERE AND HOW TO KEEP my horse, the thing that confused me most, starting out as a horse owner in midlife, was the sheer volume of conflicting information that swirls around conscientious horse ownership. When it comes to horse health, not only is there a gazillion-dollar industry ready to tell you all the things you "need," but there are "experts" everywhere you look.

From the old "just put some salve on it and he'll be fine" cowboy modalities to MRIs and laser therapy, the choices here are staggering. What I realized is that within the wide range of information out there lie good answers a-plenty. Your job as a horse owner is to sort through them and figure out which ones are right for your situation.

When my horse Trace started acting up, getting spookier and jumpier and more reactive the more I worked with him, I knew something was very wrong. But what?

"Where knowledge ends, frustration begins," Clinton Anderson is famous for saying. My frustration with my lack of knowledge and paired with a journalist's curiosity drove me to discover that although there is rarely a single right answer to such a problem, if you keep digging, you can narrow the range of solutions down to a handful of good possibilities.

When I asked horse professionals about Trace's problem, most often, the dialogue began with, "What are you feeding him?" then moved on to " Is he on supplements?"..."How much turnout does he get each day"?..."Is he stressed?"..."Could he be in pain?"... "How are his feet?" ..."Does he have allergies?..."How about stomach ulcers?"... "Are you working him hard enough?"..."Giving him enough rest?"..."Keeping his mind busy?"..."Turning him out with the wrong horses?"

Sometimes, the questions people asked came with a side order of advice, something along the lines of: "Oh my God you're feeding him oats? You might as well be pouring pure sugar in his veins! No wonder he acts up!"

When I ran to my vet with this flash of insight, he just laughed and shook his head. "No," he said. "Oats actually have the lowest glycemic load of any grain. But if you're concerned about it, just feed him good quality grass hay. With as little work as he's doing, he doesn't really need grain."

But when I suggested "good quality grass hay" to my feed salesman, he had his own reason to laugh. "No such thing in this part of the country," he said. "There's just not enough nutrition coming out of the ground in grass hay these days. What he needs is a 12-percent pellet. I have several good ones right here."

"I think he needs a light senior feed," said the nutritionist. "And you might consider beet pulp and some ulcer preventative in case he has an acid problem."

"Don't give him that," my daughter, the vet tech, said, "you'll cause all kinds of problems if it's the wrong thing. Besides, I don't think he has acid or ulcers. I think he's just being a jerk."

"I feed my horse nothing but alfalfa, some in cubes, some in hay," said one friend. "He thinks he's getting grain, but he's really just getting hay with his hay. And not much—just a handful of those cubes is all he needs."

"Oh my God, don't feet him alfalfa—that's like horse crack!" one trainer told me.

"Alfalfa is all I ever feed my horses," said another trainer. "And if I'm working them hard I also feed oats mixed with Calf-Manna® and some flax seed."

What the hell is Calf-Manna?

By this time my head was doing complete 360s and I still had no idea what to feed my horse, or if feed even had anything to do with his escalating unmanageability. What I did know was I was getting a knot in my stomach every time I got on him, and I realized that it really was no longer a matter of if he bucked me off, but when. I had to get a better handle on the different elements of horse care and how they might play a part in this problem and its (hopefully) eventual solution.

The skinny on feed and supplements

After all the conflicting advice I got about what to feed, what not to feed, and how to feed or not to feed my horse, I was really perplexed by all the options and the lack of clear-cut answers. I wanted to do the right thing—I just couldn't figure out what that was.

Worst of all I didn't know who to believe. Most of the people offering advice were either selling feed, representing feed manufacturers, or (in the case of trainers) were sponsored by specific feed companies. I didn't think anyone was giving me *bad* advice, per se—I just wanted to find information that came from an independent source.

A friend introduced me to an equine nutritionist named Dr. Juliet Getty. Not only was Dr. Getty willing to talk to me, she had written a comprehensive book on the subject. *Feed Your Horse Like a Horse* (Dog Ear Publishing, 2009) has since become my horse feedin' bible. It pulls together some big ideas about feeding horses, and puts the advice I received (which all turned out to be pretty good, by the way) into perspective. The result made enough sense to help me make choices regarding my horse's diet with confidence.

▦ How a horse's digestive system works—in a nutshell

Like everything else I touch on in *this* book, this subject could be (and is) a book of its own. Fortunately for all of us, Dr. Getty's wonderful book explains the horse's digestive system in an easy-to-understand way (get it at www.gettyequinenutrition.com, and while you're there, sign up for her newsletter for additional feeding tips and information). In the meantime, here's the long-and-short of why we need to feed horses differently than most people do.

First, a horse's digestive tract is designed to have food and water running through it all the time. I tease my little Rio about his insatiable appetite, but in their natural state, horses really *are* supposed to eat 22 out of 24 hours a day. The remaining two hours is actually scattered into 10 to 20 minute increments when they doze, play, or run from tigers. (Or from me as I approach with a halter in my hand.)

Because a horse is supposed to have food and water in his stomach all the time, his body produces a constant supply of acid (unlike ours that only produces acid when we eat). When a horse stands around in a stall all day with all that acid in his stomach, waiting to be fed his "meals" (a human concept), it is not only very uncomfortable for him, it stresses him out because he is always worried about *when* the food is coming, *if* it is coming, and *whether* he'll still be alive to eat it. Dr. Getty says, "If a horse consistently goes for more than three hours without anything to graze on, the excess acid can produce ulcers, as well as diarrhea, behavioral problems, and even colic."

Another thing you need to know about a horse's digestive system is that they are "non-ruminant herbivores," which is a fancy way of saying they only eat plants, but unlike cows and other "ruminants" whose fermentation vat (where the food is broken down by bacteria) is at the *front end* of the digestive system, the horse's fermentation vat is at the *back end*. Therefore, horses need to consume a lot more grass and hay than, say, cows, to get the same number of calories—another reason they are meant to eat "forages" (hay and grass) constantly.

And here are a few other important points

>) Once food travels through the horse's esophagus to the stomach, the esophageal sphincter (a one-way valve) closes tightly and seals the stomach off. That's why a horse cannot vomit.

>) A horse's stomach, which is very small in relation to the rest of him, is not designed to hold very much, which is why feeding him too much leads to problems such as colic and laminitis.

>) From the stomach, the food goes to the small intestine, then on to the cecum, which, along with the colon, makes up the "hindgut." This is where hay, grass, and other fibrous parts of the horse's food are finally broken down, and in order for this stuff to move on through (and eventually be excreted), water has to be present. This is why it is so important that horses have a constant supply of water. Compaction colic is caused, Getty explains, when too much dry matter is present in the cecum and the fibrous stuff settles and compacts at the bottom.

Types of feed

There are really only two main types of feed for a horse: forages (pasture grass and hay, which is further divided into grasses and legumes) and concentrates (cereal grains, such as oats and commercial grain-based feeds). Of course, my midlife horses, Rio and Trace, would add a third category to this: treats.

"What the hay?" (Forages briefly defined)

Hay, pasture grass, and other at least 18-percent fiber material falls into this category. *Grass hays* include slightly sweeter cool-season grasses (timothy, orchard, and fescue) and warm-season grasses (brome and Bermuda). Grass hays are considered low-to-medium protein content (10 to 15 percent), and are especially low in an important amino acid called lysine. Alfalfa, the most common *legume hay*, has a higher protein count (17 to 20 percent) and the correct proportion of amino acids, including the lysine missing from grass hay. Because of this, Getty recommends feeding a mixture of the two, based on your horse's energy needs.

How do you really *know* the nutritional content of your horse's grass and legume hay? Believe it or not, there is something called a "hay analysis." The first hay supplier I knew (a sweet, older woman named Dorothy whom we affectionately called the "Hay Lady") was always eager to show me the nutritional analysis of her hay. I would smile, nod, and marvel over it without really understanding it—but now, I appreciate her efforts. She had gone to a lot of trouble to make sure her hay was of very high nutritional quality, and had paid to have it analyzed as proof. Today, with Dr. Getty's help, I can look at an analysis like those the Hay Lady used to share and see:

>) **Crude protein (CP)** While this doesn't tell you anything about the quality of the protein or the amino acids, it gives you an overall picture of protein content. Grass hay should be 10 to 15 percent, and legume hay should be 17 to 20 percent protein.

>) **Acid detergent fiber (ADF)** This measures how digestible the hay is and should be around 31 percent, although higher can still be acceptable.

) **Neutral detergent fiber (NDF)** The best estimate of total fiber content, this number should be less than 45 percent and not more than 55 percent.

) **Relative feed value (RFV)** Reflecting the overall quality in terms of digestibility and available nutrients, this number should be at least 100, but 150 is ideal.

) **Non-fibrous carbohydrates (NFC)** If your horse has insulin resistance or Cushings disease, you'll want an NFC value lower than 18 percent.

) **Non-structural carbohydrates (NSC)** If your horse needs to have a low sugar/low starch diet, look for less than 12 percent here.

) **Balance between calcium and phosphorus/calcium and magnesium** Ideally, there should be a 2:1 ratio of calcium to phosphorus, and calcium to magnesium.

"Concentrating" on nutrition

Traditional feed "concentrates" include cracked corn, whole oats, barley, soybean meal, sunflower seeds, flaxseed meal, and oil. Getty goes into each of these elements in detail in her book, with helpful charts that compare their nutritional compositions, and says in the end your best bet is still good ol' oats, preferably crimped, rolled, or steamed rather than whole. Small servings of oats are easily digested (see more about serving size on p. 176), but they are 44 percent starch, which in some horses (like mine, maybe?) can produce sugar highs and lows that can lead to behavior problems.

Although the majority of your horse's diet still needs to come from forage (remember—a steady supply of hay and/or pasture), commercial feed can take care of the rest of his nutritional needs. Commercial feed comes in the form of: sweet feed, which many horse profession-als no longer recommend ("Do you put sugar on everything *you* eat?" Dr. Getty asks), or in pelleted or extruded form. Once you learn to read commercial feed labels wisely (see below) selecting the right feed is no longer the difficult part—feeding the correct amount for your horse's size and activity to be sure he is actually *getting* enough of the nutri-tional elements printed on the label is what's tricky.

How to Read a Feed Label

According to Dr. Juliet Getty, author of *Feed Your Horse Like a Horse*, there are a few things we need to look for when we read the labels on commercial horse feed, including:

▸ **Order of ingredients** In horse feed, unlike in human food, these are not always listed in order of concentration. (Note: Getty says they are *supposed* to be listed in order of concentration, as it is required by law, but still, not all of them are. That's why it's important to stay with reputable feed companies who are most likely to comply with the laws governing their industry.)

▸ **Crude protein** As with hay and grass, this gives you a general idea of the the feed's protein content (and *not* the protein's quality), which should be 12 to 14 percent. Look for mention of two essential amino acids, lysine and methionine (soybean and alfalfa meals provide these, as well).

▸ **Crude fat** This is the balance between omega-3 and omega-6 fatty acids, ideally a 3:1 or 4:1 ratio.

▸ **Vitamin A** Beta-carotene is the magic word here. It's much safer than straight vita-min A, which can be toxic in too high amounts; beta-carotene is only converted to Vitamin A as your horse needs it.

▸ **Iron** Listed in your ingredients as ferrous sulfate, your horse is probably getting plenty of this from his pasture grass and hay. Deficiencies are rare, as is the need to supplement iron in horses.

▸ **Selenium** Typically your horse needs between 1 and 5 milligrams per day.

Pass the salt (often)

As you may know, horses need salt. Salt helps replenish the sodium and chloride the horse loses when he sweats (body salts known as *electrolytes*, and including potassium, calcium, and magnesium, as well). Too little salt can spell big trouble, and if your horse is working hard and sweating a lot, you may want to up his salt *and* give additional electrolytes. Ask your vet for guidelines.

Some horses like salt blocks, some prefer free choice table salt, others want you to stand over their bucket and add salt to each bite with a pretty little shaker. In all seriousness, horses need about two tablespoons of salt per day if they're not working—four if they are—divided into no more than two tablespoons per feeding, or provided as a "free choice" block or bucket of granulated table salt in the stall (if licking a block makes your horse's tongue sore). The popular red "mineral salt blocks" don't taste as good to the horse as the plain white ones, so avoid them, as well as any that are "sweetened" with molasses, which encourage the horse to bite off large pieces and increase his risk of choking.

A Word about Mold

There are several different kinds of toxic molds (mycotoxins) that can grow in feed and which can be deadly to your horse. Sometimes these are in the plant before harvest and just continue to grow in the bag, especially if it has been exposed to high temperatures or humid conditions. Pay attention when you open a bag of feed, and don't use it if it is:

- ▶ Crumbly, dusty, or caked into clumps (its separate pieces should flow easily through your fingers)
- ▶ Dark in color
- ▶ Foul or "funny" in smell (it should smell sweet and clean)

Use all open bags of feed within two months and sooner than that if the weather is hot and humid.

In cold weather, salt is still important because it encourages your horse to drink plenty of water. (Note: Don't ever add salt to your horse's water, even though in a way it does make sense.)

▥ How to feed your horse

You might be surprised at how many seasoned "cowpokes" get this part of horsekeeping wrong. How much, how often, how to measure it—all these areas of feeding horses are subject to wild fluctuation and often based on little actual knowledge or science.

As an example, consider this story a horse rescue worker told me: It seems that an owner whose starving horse was being seized by the Society for Preventing Cruelty to Animals (SPCA) argued with case-workers, tearfully insisting that he fed his horse every day, twice a day, and he had been worried sick about her because she just kept losing weight. "Something must really be wrong with her!" he wailed.

Curious, the caseworker asked what he fed the mare.

"A scoop of feed and a flake of hay, every morning and every night, just like they told me to," was his answer.

On a hunch, the caseworker said, "Show me."

The owner took the caseworker to where the feed was stored and inside the feed bin was a standard coffee cup—this was what he was using as a "scoop."

"Now show me the flake of hay you were giving her," the case-worker said.

The owner picked up the single fistful of hay he considered a "flake."

The reality is, while perhaps not so dramatic as to necessitate SPCA involvement, thousands of horses are under- and overfed because their owners just don't understand how to determine correct feed amounts.

How much food does my horse need?

When my vet first suggested I feed my horse Trace hay only, I asked him how much. "My horses eat hay free-choice," he replied, "and they each eat about 30 pounds of hay a day." He knew this approximate number because he put out a round hay bale each month or so, and he knew what the round bale weighed, then divided it by the number of horses eating it. The result wasn't exact, he assured me, but a decent guess.

As for concentrates, most experts agree that the coffee can you're probably using as a scoop is okay (and far better than a coffee *cup*) but it is important that you *weigh* your concentrate and mark the proper amount to equal the weight your horse requires on the can. Remember: Scoops measure *volume*, not *weight*. Even if it *is* a 3-pound coffee can, that doesn't mean filling it up gives you 3 pounds of horse feed. So scoop with whatever you like, but the first time you feed a specific concentrate, weigh it first to get the amount right.

Most commercial feed packaging provides guidelines as to how much to feed your horse, based on his weight (see p. 178 for help in accurately "guessing" your horse's weight), usually in pounds of feed per 100 pounds of equine body weight. Using a postage scale (if you have one) or a bathroom scale (oh, c'mon, you *know* you have one!), first weigh your scoop empty. Then fill it with feed and weight it again. Subtract the weight of the scoop from the weight of the scoop filled with feed and you have how much feed that scoop *really* holds. Any time you change feed type or brand, go through this process again, because different concentrates weigh different amounts (extruded feeds are much lighter, for example) and different companies process their product in different ways.

How do you know if you are feeding your horse the right amount? "Just look at your horse," my vet said when I asked how much concentrate (in my case, oats) I needed to feed Trace. "If he gets too fat, feed him less. If he gets too skinny, feed him more." (He also gently reminded me that since my horse was not doing any work to speak of, he probably didn't need any grain at all.)

I really expected a more scientific answer from a vet, but like most simple answers, it made a surprising amount of sense. "A healthy horse maintains a healthy weight," Getty writes in *Feed Your Horse Like a Horse*. "Just like people, horses can eat a nutritious diet and still be too heavy." And, just like people, things like metabolic rates, genetic tendencies, amount of exercise, overfeeding (or too many treats), and stress can all cause unwanted weight gain in horses. (Clinton Anderson says that his horse, Diez, can *look* at a bale of hay and gain weight!)

The first step in determining how much food your horse needs, Getty agrees with my veterinarian, is to "look at him." For the uninitiated, this actually means to evaluate his measurements. There are several ways to do this. You can:

> Measure your horse's length (from point of shoulder to crease of the buttocks), then around his girth (4 inches behind his front legs), then use the formula: Weight = (girth x girth x length) divided by 330.

> Or, you can buy an inexpensive and easy-to-use weight tape (slightly less accurate, but close enough) and measure your horse's girth (just behind the elbow and behind the withers), then use the chart that comes with the tape to determine your horse's approximate weight.

Body condition scoring

One widely used method of "looking at your horse" is the Henneke Body Condition Scoring System. Developed by Texas A&M University's Don Henneke in 1984, this is the method most professionals and horse rescues use to assess the body condition of a horse. Body condition scoring (BCS) considers the fat stored (or not) on six specific areas of the horse's body: neck, shoulder, withers, ribs, back, and tailhead.

On a scale of "1" to "9," with "1" being "extremely emaciated" and "9" being "bulging fat," body condition scoring works for all breeds. Horse owners should use both visual and palpated (touch) assessments to make sure their horse stays between "4" ("very fit") and "6" ("moderately fleshy"). For a " Perfect 5," here's how that shakes out:

Neck: blends smoothly into body
Withers: rounded
Back: level (no crease)
Tailhead: slightly spongy

Ribs: felt but not seen

Shoulders: blend smoothly into body

You can find out more about body condition scoring in Dr. Getty's book, and also in the book *All Horse Systems Go* by Dr. Nancy Loving (Trafalgar Square Books, 2006).

Tips for Feeding an "Easy Keeper"

▸ **Don't cut back on hay** Cutting calories is fine, but even the chubby horse still needs forage, for all the reasons mentioned earlier (see p. 170).

▸ **Avoid cereal grains** This includes oats, corn, barley, wheat, and pelleted feeds that contain these ingredients, and sugary treats.

▸ **Consider an all-forage diet** Be sure to provide a "carrier meal" (such as alfalfa pellets, beet pulp, or a low-starch commercial feed) for supplements (if necessary) and to keep your horse from feeling deprived when other horses he is stabled or pastured with are fed.

▸ **Provide free-choice grass hay/pasture grass** Your horse will self-regulate in about a week, once he knows the forage is always there. You may want to limit pasture grazing to mornings, when grasses have the lowest starch content.

How to (correctly) assess your horse's activity level

The only remaining question about what and how and how much to feed your horse comes in the area called "activity." Activity means different things to different people, so let's work under the guidelines provided by the National Research Council (NRC) and Dr. Getty:

Light activity One to three hours per week; 40 percent walk, 50 percent trot, 10 percent canter; recreational riding, weekend trail riding, occasional shows.

Moderate activity Three to five hours per week; 30 percent walk, 55 percent trot, 10 percent canter, 5 percent low jumping, or

Tips for Feeding a "Hard Keeper"

When a horse is underweight, particularly if he is very underweight from starvation or neglect, there are very specific "Do's" and "Don'ts" for bringing him back to optimal weight. Medical problems—including anemia, inflammation, ulcers, worms, and Cushing's disease—should be ruled out, and his teeth should be checked since poor teeth are the number-one cause of underweight horses. Engage the help of your veterinarian and a knowledgeable horse nutritionist when dealing with an extremely underweight animal.

▸ **Add calories, not amount** Do this slowly in very small meals, and choose a feed that will add calories without adding bulk. Limit concentrate meal size to no more than 4 pounds per feeding.

▸ **Add fat** Choose a commercial feed with at least 8 percent fat. Flaxseed meal is another good option, or canola oil—start with only one tablespoon per meal, and increase if necessary.

▸ **Provide an all-you-can eat hay/grass buffet** Don't overfeed concentrates, but do allow free-choice grazing/forage at all times.

▸ **Provide frequent nutritious snacks** Feed plenty of extra carrots, apples, or alfalfa cubes.

other skill work such as cutting; training and light ranch work also fall into this category.

Heavy activity Four to five hours per week; 20 percent walk, 50 percent trot, 15 percent canter, 15 percent gallop, jumping, or other skill work; serious ranch work, polo, show events, low- to medium-level eventing.

Very heavy activity Ranges from an hour a week of "speed work" to six to twelve hours of "slow work"; racing, endurance riding, and three-day eventing.

Each level of horse activity has different nutritional requirements. In addition to amount, type, and frequency of feedings, there are various additions and supplementations to consider for your "equine athlete."

As I found with Trace, horsekeeping is a "thinking woman's game." Be prepared to consider all facets of your horse's breed, body type, and discipline when analyzing his diet and constructing a feeding plan for ideal behavior and performance.

Vet check

When dealing with a "mystery problem," such as the one I faced with Trace, a natural (and necessary) source of information and advice is the first VIP on my contact list. My veterinarian. But "Doc" doesn't only play a role when something is going wrong; he or she is integral to maintaining your horse's health, in the first place.

While guidelines vary with breed, purpose, and geographical region, basic veterinary care for your horse consists of annual examinations and vaccinations, as well as diagnosis and treatment for any illness, injury, or physical condition you may not have the knowledge, skill, or experience to handle. Buck Neil, DVM, of Fort Worth, Texas, was kind enough to share his personal insights and opinons gathered during his 26-year equine practice in order to help you put together a sensible, affordable horse health plan.

▓ How to choose a vet

While admittedly a lot comes down to personality, choosing a veterinarian for your horse is much the same as choosing an obstetrician or pediatrician. How can I compare having a horse to having a baby? Because in terms of the emotional connection you feel for this "great big baby"—and the issues surrounding his care—the dynamics are very much the same.

Of course, referrals are always a great source of leads, and in calling a vet's current and past clients, you get a pretty good picture of him (or her) and what it is like to work with him. Ask if you can be present during an upcoming appointment so you can watch the vet in action and see how well his diagnosis and treatment philosophy aligns with yours. Ask the vet questions, such as:

> What is the extent of his education?

> What is his experience with the type of horse you own?

> Is he a member of the American Association of Equine Practitioners (AAEP) or another professional association? (The AAEP recommends veterinarians who hold professional membership because it shows they are involved in their field and interested in keeping up with the latest advances.)

> Is he available for emergencies at night and on weekends and holidays, or are you referred elsewhere? Will he make "barn calls," or do you need to truck your horse to his emergency clinic?

> Is he aggressive or conservative in his approach to diagnosis and treatment? Does this align with your own feelings?

> What does he charge for routine procedures, such as annual examinations and vaccinations?

> Will he provide instruction/support if you want to learn to give vaccinations and/or provide first-aid care yourself?

> Does he accept payment by monthly installment in the case of "big bills," such as those involved with surgery?

Once you have one or two candidates, make an appointment with your first choice for a standard checkup and see how the veterinarian interacts with you and your horse.

> ❯ Is he thorough?

> ❯ Are you comfortable with the way he handles your horse?

> ❯ Does he answer your questions clearly and willingly? Are his explanations easy for you to understand?

> ❯ While your vet doesn't have to be "BFF" material, is he someone you feel comfortable with—that is, do you think you would get along with and trust him in a difficult situation?

If for any reason you are not comfortable, try the next vet on your list of prospectives. Consider the cost of your horse's multiple "check-ups" a wise investment in his long-term health care.

▥ Vaccination primer

According to the AAEP, "It is the responsibility of attending veterinarians, through an appropriate veterinarian-client-patient relationship, to utilize relevant information coupled with product availability to determine optimal health care programs for their patients." At the top of the health care list are vaccinations, and you need to know a little about this subject to discuss core requirements with your vet.

Rabies is chief among the most important vaccinations available, Neil says. "Rabies is one of the few diseases a horse can give to his owner—or the vet who tries to treat him," he adds. Always fatal to horses and devastating if not fatal to humans (and anything else infected), rabies is a threat not to be taken lightly. Unlike with cats and dogs, rabies vaccine for horses is not required by law (and must be dispensed by a vet), so many horse owners neglect to do it.

Second on Neil's list is tetanus toxoid and encephalomyelitis ("sleeping sickness"). "Tetanus can be in the soil where you live, even if there haven't been any horses there for years," he adds. There are three strains of encephalomyelitis: EE in eastern regions of the United States, WE in western parts, and VEE (Venezuelan) in various areas of the country (although we haven't seen this strain since the 1970s.) All are spread by mosquitoes.

Finally, West Nile Virus is also spread by mosquitoes, and there are frequently new vaccines developed, Neil says. Apart from these core vaccinations, he refers us to the AAEP website for specific guidelines and official recommendations per geographical region.

▧ Administering shots

While there are many shots you can administer yourself, there are a few that have to be given by a licensed vet. "A lot of owners think they want to give shots," Neil says, "but then they realize that sticking a needle in their horse hurts him, and depending on the sensitivity of the horse, his reaction may not be something they've dealt with before. Some horses don't really mind too much and others react violently."

Being able administer a basic shot such as a painkiller can be good to know in the case of an emergency. If you think you'd like to take on this responsibility, ask your vet to show you how and where to give each kind of injection, then have him watch you do it a couple of times before you try it solo.

"Some vets will be happy to show you how to give your horse shots," Neil says. "I'd rather help my clients learn to give shots than have them not to immunize their horses."

▧ Deworming ("worming")

This subject gets a lot of press and is a constant source of controversy. For years, the advice was to paste worm (you are actually trying to *rid* your horse of worm infestation, but horse owners usually refer to the process as "worming" rather than "deworming") four times a year with rotating ingredients that address seasonal parasites. Then along came the advent of a daily wormer, followed by concern that parasites were becoming resistant.

Many now advise doing a fecal egg count (*you* don't have to do it—just send a manure sample home with your vet) on your horse each year to a) determine whether he has any parasites on board, and b) treat just those parasites with only the product designed to eliminate them. Of course, gone once isn't gone forever. Neil relates a story of a study at Kansas State University in which 30-year-old soil taken from a parking lot was found to still have viable worm eggs in it. Persistent little buggers, aren't they?

When faced with whether to worm your horse yourself or have your vet do it, again this is a matter of comfort zone and horse temperament. Personally, if the vet's doing shots and it's time to worm, I'm happy for him to do it. Other times, I do it myself.

First aid preparedness

There really is neither rhyme nor reason to horse injuries. While some horses can live for years in a barbed-wire pen with rusty farm implements scattered where they graze with nary a scratch, others, as my dad says, can hurt themselves on Kleenex. So, it pays to be prepared.

How prepared? It depends on your comfort level, your experience, and your interest in learning more about first aid, says Doc Neil. Above all, he adds, it is important in a horse emergency to keep your cool, call the vet the *first time* you wonder if you should, and describe *only* what you're seeing (not what you think happened or what you guess is wrong) to the emergency operator.

"A lot of horse owners think they're helping speed things along by telling their vet what they *think* is wrong," he says, "and sometimes they're exactly right. But if they're wrong, and this information sends the vet down the wrong road in terms of diagnosis, then it actually slows down the vet's response time."

Worming Your Way to Success

If you're having trouble worming your horse (and it is a horsekeeping task you want to do yourself), horse trainer Clinton Anderson provides this "sweet" process that will end your worming woes for good!

STEP 1: Desensitize the horse's face and mouth with your hands.

Use "approach and retreat" until you can rub his face all over, in different ways (once he gets used to it, he'll probably like this first step quite a bit), and until you can rub his mouth and chin and stick your fingers in the sides of his mouth (be careful!). This may take a while—so be patient and don't rush it.

STEP 2: Desensitize the air space around the horse's head with the wormer.

First find your "starting point"—that's the place where you can move the wormer around in the air and your horse will stand still and relax. Work your way in from there until you can wave the wormer, just a few inches off his body, all around the horse's head, neck, and body without a reaction.

STEP 3: Desensitize the horse's head and mouth with the wormer.

Once again find your starting point and then use approach and retreat. This time, however, actually touch the horse with the wormer dispenser. Keep working on this until you can rub the wormer dispenser all over the horse's head and mouth.

STEP 4: Teach the horse the cue to open his mouth.

Insert your thumb into the corner of your horse's mouth (find the space where there aren't any teeth). As soon as he opens his mouth, take your thumb out and rub him. (This cue is handy for getting him to accept the bit as well.)

STEP 5: Insert the wormer into the horse's mouth, and then retreat.

When you take the wormer out, go back to the previous step and rub the tube all over the horse's face. Then insert the wormer again, and again retreat and rub his face. Repeat this sequence until you can stick the tube in his mouth and leave it there long enough to dispense the wormer without a reaction.

STEP 6: Actually give the horse the wormer.

If a horse is difficult to worm, try "worming" him with a dispenser of honey for five days before the real thing, but be sure to follow up the actual worming with a few more days of honey in that dispenser so he remembers this as a sweet experience!

Plan ahead and start this process several days—and preferably at least a week—before you actually need to worm your horse. That way you can work on it a little bit each day. Don't tie your horse up when you worm him; instead do it in an area like an arena or roundpen where he can move his feet. (For more great Downunder Horsemanship training tips, see Resources, p. 311.)

To give you an example scenario: If you find your horse in an acute state of discomfort, don't call your vet and tell him your horse has colic. Tell him *only what you're seeing*, and be specific. Include such details as the horse's actions (rolling, trying to lie down, biting at his side), the horse's temperature, and his food and water intake (that you've witnessed) over the past 24 hours. Note: Keep a thermometer on hand and learn how to take your horse's temperature and compare it to his normal parameters (your vet can show you how).

When it comes to emergency horse care, establishing a good relationship with your vet is key. Over time he'll learn what you can take care of yourself, as well as your comfort level and capability. "Most vets are happy to help their clients learn what to do in an emergency, especially if you show interest," Neil says. "It's very important for an owner to know and recognize what they can handle themselves and what they can't."

I recommend acquiring a good basic equine first-aid book to have on hand when the unthinkable happens and you need to know what to do while you're waiting for the vet to arrive. You can see recommendations on p. 188.

Putting Together a First-Aid Kit

It's best to ask your veterinarian for his or her recommendations as to what to keep in your barn first-aid kit. This will vary greatly with your vet, horse, activities, as well as your own experience and abilities. Here are a few basics that allow you to care for most horse health issues until the vet arrives:

> Wound cleaner (Betadine®, chlorhexidine, or other non-stinging antiseptic)
> First aid ointment or cream (such as Corona® or Vetericyn®)
> Sterile gauze (roll and pads)
> Vet wrap
> Wound fly repellent (for example, Swat®)
> Thrush treatment (such as Kopertox®)
> Dosage syringe

When Dealing with Drugs

Follow your own vet's recommendations about the use of sedatives and anti-inflammatory medications for colic or lameness issues. (You can only get these drugs *legally* from a licensed vet, anyway.) These drugs can be very effective if used correctly—and very dangerous if not. Two examples commonly found in barns across the country:

▸ **Acepromazine** The sedative known as "Ace" is widely misused and often misunderstood—and it can be very dangerous to your horse, especially in cases of trauma and blood loss. When choosing to keep this drug on hand for use in an emergency, ask your vet for his recommendations and follow them, no matter what your neighbor says.

▸ **Flunixin meglumine and phenylbutazone** Banamine® and "Bute" are powerful non-steroidal anti-inflammatory drugs (NSAIDS) commonly used in horses for colic and severe joint pain. However, these drugs are not as harmless as many people believe, and can be subject to overuse.

▥ Teeth, sheaths, and other ticklish tasks

Now here's a strange combination of topics that has an odd common denominator. These are things that some people *try* to take care of themselves (and depending on the horse, many are able to do this successfully), but in Neil's opinion, unless you really know what you're doing, they are all an invitation to getting yourself badly hurt.

While it's true that geldings (and mares, too, although this is much less invasive) need their nether regions cleaned regularly (once a year or so for geldings), this ticklish chore can be dangerous, both to the owner (you are in a very vulnerable position for being kicked) and to the horse (by potentially opening the door to irritation and infection that is far worse than not doing it at all). Ask your vet for guidance on sheath and udder cleaning, and see how your horse responds to the procedure before trying it on your own.

As for teeth, horses need to have their teeth "floated" (the sharp points ground down) about once a year, and maybe more often as they get older. Most vets have a variety of methods and equipment they use depending on the horse and the problem, and there are equine dentists who specialize in caring for horse teeth. If sedation is involved, however, make sure you're dealing with a licensed vet or an equine dentist specially licensed to sedate (check www.AAEP.org for referrals).

▥ A safe vet is a happy vet

Most vets are pretty good at taking care of themselves and have highly-attuned self-preservation instincts. However—and especially if your horse is fearful, pushy, aggressive, or just reactive—bear in mind that you do carry some responsibility making provisions to help keep your vet as safe as possible during visits and treatments. Here are a few things you can do to hold up your end of the deal:

>) **Provide a good workspace** Have, at the very least, a clean, well-lit, debris-free area for the vet to work.

> **Have horse-savvy hands available** Additional help may be needed to hold your horse, so be prepared.

> **Pay attention** Know how to stay out of the way to keep yourself safe if things start to get ugly so the vet isn't distracted because he's worrying about you!

Hoof care

When, in the course of trying to solve Trace's mystery misbehavior, I called out the farrier to evaluate his feet (they were fine), I realized how little I knew about the subject. Should your horse have shoes or go barefoot? How do you know a good trim from a bad one? What is a healthy hoof supposed to look like? What does a developing problem look like? What do you do (besides call the vet or farrier) when you find something wrong with your horse's hoof? What's the difference between a problem that can wait and one that needs immediate attention? Honestly? I really didn't know!

I also realized that I wasn't doing a very good job of cleaning my horses' feet, and while I did "inspect" my horses hooves—supposedly looking for the obvious stuff like cracks, punctures, and swelling—I really had no idea what my horses hooves were *supposed* to look like or what to do when I found something that didn't look quite right or was just plain wrong.

Choosing a farrier

The farrier is the VIP of horse feet. Having a horse with healthy feet all starts with the right farrier. If choosing a vet is like choosing an obstetrician or pediatrician, then choosing a farrier is like choosing an orthodontist. Besides education, knowledge, and experience—and a "treatment" philosophy (shoes, barefoot, trim style) that aligns with yours and fits your purpose—the right farrier needs to have a personality that is easy and comfortable for both you and your horse to deal with.

Top 10 Ways to Make Your Vet's "A" List

Here are Doc Neil's tips for being the kind of horse-owning client a vet will drop everything for:

1   Be willing to admit what you don't know. Don't guess, don't try to impress, don't try to "save the vet time."

2   Give good information. Learn how to describe only what you're seeing, not what you think the problem is.

3   Stay calm and be rational—you can eat up valuable time with hysterics. Do that later, when things are under control.

4   Don't put yourself in danger. Remember that when a 1,000-pound animal is in pain, he can hurt you without meaning to. Sometimes when a horse is hurt the best thing you can do for him is call the vet and wait in a safe place.

5   Be as knowledgeable as you can, ask questions, and be willing to listen and learn. If you're willing to learn, chances are your vet is more than happy to teach you.

6   Listen to what your vet has to say, *then* ask questions and communicate your wants, needs, and priorities.

7   If you think you have a problem, don't wait. Go ahead and call your vet. You'll never err by calling, but you might by waiting too long.

8   When your veterinarian asks a question, answer only *that* question and wait for the next one. This gives the vet time to process what you're telling him without the clutter of too many observations at once.

9   Have your horse in the barn and ready when the vet is scheduled for routine care appointments. Even usually easy-to-catch horses become cagey renegades once the vet's truck pulls in the gate.

10 Try to provide a well-lit, reasonably comfortable place to work. (A cold drink if it's hot and a hot drink if it's cold is a nice touch. As are cookies.)

Seven Signs of a Great Farrier

These may seem like no-brainers, but you'd be surprised at the regular abuse I've witnessed as my horsey friends put up with surly, grunting, condescending farriers. It doesn't have to be that way, girlfriends! Expect the best, and you're more likely to get it.

Your great farrier:

▸ Is competent, knowledgeable, and up-to-date

▸ Arrives when he says he will

▸ Returns calls promptly

▸ Responds promptly in emergencies

▸ Resets lost shoes within 24 hours

▸ Listens to your concerns and needs

▸ Answers your questions in a way you can understand

▸ Treats you and your horse with kindness and respect

Matt Taimuty, CJF (www.fairhillforge.com), a certified Maryland farrier, offers us the following common sense advice for locating a great farrier. "Ask around," he says. "Your best source for information on farriers, whether you are new to the area or just ready for a change, is your veterinarian, followed closely by people in your sport who are consistently competitive with sound horses—whether you plan to compete or not. Most people just love to be asked for advice. Ask a lot of them. If one or two names crop up again and again, that's a good sign."

While most people I talked to agree that certification isn't the be-all-end-all (plenty of top-notch farriers aren't certified) it is a way to ascertain a basic level of competence and signifies that the farrier takes his craft seriously enough to stay up-to-date. A farrier with CJF (Certified Journeyman Farrier) after his name has been recognized (after taking a test and passing a performance evaluation) as complying with the

Questions to ask when interviewing a prospective farrier

What is your education, training, and/or apprenticeship background?

Are you certified, and with whom?

How long have you been shoeing?

How many horses do you shoe each year?

What disciplines or breeds do you regularly work with?

Do you know the shoeing requirements and rules for my breed/ sport/event?

What kinds of hoof problems have you dealt with?

Do you do therapeutic shoeing/hoof rehabilitation?

Is there a trimming theory that you subscribe to?

Are you available for after-hours emergencies?

What is the normal turnaround to reset a lost shoe?

What is your normal, usual charge for standard trimming and shoeing?

Do you have a list of references? May I call them?

rigorous, internationally recognized standards of the American Farriers Association (www.amfarriers.com). The AFA is also a good place to get the names of certified farriers in your area.

Price for standard trims or specialty hoofcare will vary with location, breed, and riding discipline (different sports and seasons require different kinds of horse shoes—think running vs. hiking and summer vs. winter in terms of your own footwear). As a general rule, remember that less is not necessarily more when it comes to shoeing or trimming. If a farrier seems too cheap to be good, he probably is. The ultimate cost of straightening out a bad farrier job (and all the associated complications it can cause) is far greater than just paying for a good quality job in the first place.

How can you tell if your farrier is doing a good job? The answer can be found, as when determining correct feed amounts, by looking at your horse. Is he happy, comfortable, and sound? Of course, lameness and/or performance problems may have nothing to do with the job the farrier is doing, but it is a definite consideration when seeking out an unidentified cause of behavioral change or discomfort.

▥ How to have a happy farrier tale

A solid, dependable relationship with a farrier you trust is a priceless commodity in the horse world. Here are a few tips gathered from a handful of farriers that will clue you in on the niceties they appreciate in their favorite clients.

- ❭ Be on time, and stay on schedule with your appointments according to your farrier's recommendations.

- ❭ Have your horse inside with clean feet and legs when the farrier arrives.

- ❭ Have an easily accessible (think truck), clean, level, reasonably quiet, well lit place for your farrier to work that's at least a 12- by 15- foot space and free of hazards. Water and electricity earn bonus points.

- ❭ If your horse doesn't like to stand for the farrier, work with him ahead of time, teaching him to tolerate having his feet picked up, his legs stretched out, and his feet tapped (see sidebar, p. 197). Be on hand to hold the horse and make sure he behaves. Tell the farrier about the horse's fear, insecurity, or bad habits so he is prepared.

- ❭ Contain children and pets during the appointment. They can get hurt or cause the horse or farrier to get hurt.

⟩ Pay promptly and in accordance with the farrier's policy. Don't complain about the cost (it's rude), but if you're truly having a financial problem, talk to him about it *before* he does the work. If you're a good customer and it's a temporary situation, he may cut you some slack. Don't abuse this kindness, though.

⟩ Inform your farrier of any problems or concerns—as well as loose shoes *before* they come off—but be mindful of his time and schedule and right to have a life. If it's a true emergency and he's a professional, he'll be there when you need him. But if he gets to your barn and sees your "emergency" really could have waited, next time he may not be so prompt.

⟩ Although tips are not expected, they are a nice way to say thank you for above-and-beyond service, such as in the case of an emergency.

⟩ A cold drink if it's hot or a hot drink if it's cold is a nice gesture. So is remembering him during the holidays. Thank you notes and cards are always a welcome surprise.

▥ To shoe or not to shoe?

Early in my midlife horse daze, most of the people I knew kept their horses shod. Some competed, some didn't. All I knew was it was a pain when a shoe came off and my friends couldn't ride, and they seemed to be spending a lot of time and money on farriers. "Horses are better off barefoot," my dad told me. I believed him, since in my experience, he was usually right about these things.

Then I caught one of Clinton Anderson's segments on RFD-TV one night, when he featured "natural hoof care" practitioner Pete Ramey, and even though I didn't understand much about it, this "natural hoof care" thing was interesting to me, especially when Ramey said: "I never meant to be a 'barefoot oddball,' but the horses themselves were pushing my thoughts hard in that direction!" Although Ramey's latest book, *Making Natural Hoof Care Work for You* (Star Ridge Publishers, 2005) is written primarily for vets and farriers, it explains the whole barefoot thing in a simple and straightforward way that makes it all much easier to understand. By learning more about what my horses' feet are *supposed* to look like, how they are *supposed* to work, and what a difference healthy feet make to the health of the whole horse, I was further intrigued.

Benefits of the shoeless hoof seem hard to ignore: "Recent blood-flow studies by Robert Bowker, VMD, PhD, show that the horse's foot gets at least twice as much circulation when he's barefoot on yielding terrain, as compared to when he's wearing a metal shoe," Ramey reports in a recent *Horse&Rider* article.

The article went on to dispel the only argument that made sense to me on the shoes side: We ask horses to perform sustained and concussive activities when we're riding them, such as sliding stops, flying changes, piaffe, and jumps from difficult takeoff points—things that they don't do much of in the wild (much less with the weight of a rider on their back). "The weight of the rider does have impact," Ramey explains, "it creates the need for more energy dissipation and shock absorption." That, he adds, is why bare feet (or padded boots) are better than metal shoes. Hmmm.

Upon further exploration of both sides of the great shoeing debate, I found passionate and logical reasoning on both sides that were equally convincing. The bottom line, once again, it seems, is that with the help of your vet and a farrier you trust, you have to figure out what is best for *your* horse.

With gratitude to Robert Miller, DVM, and the book he wrote with Rick Lamb called *The Revolution in Horsemanship* (Lyons Press, 2005), I finally adopted the following position on this issue:

1   Shoe only when necessary.

2   Shoe or trim at regular intervals (and to this I add "practice good and consistent daily hoof care"—see p. 200).

3   Provide barefoot "vacations" as frequently and for as long as possible.

How to avoid foot fights

Starting a couple of weeks before your farrier appointment, work with your horse on this for a few minutes every day and you'll be amazed at the difference it will make. The secret, horse trainer Clinton Anderson tells us, is in breaking the process into small steps the horse can understand, and taking into consideration his natural instincts. Here are his six steps to better hoof behavior:

1   **Desensitize the horse's front legs to a lead rope.**
     Stand a couple of feet from the front of the horse at a 45-degree angle. Gently and softly, see-saw the end of a soft cotton lead rope back and forth, up and down one front leg. If he starts to move, try to stand still (keep his nose tipped toward you), while allowing him to drift in a circle around you. Do not stop moving the rope until he stands still and relaxes. Rub him between the eyes. Now start again. Repeat until you can rub the rope all over both front legs while he remains still and relaxed.

2   **Desensitize the horse's front legs to your hands.**
     Next, starting at the top of one of the horse's front legs around his elbow and gradually working your way down, rub your hands up and down. If he starts to move, return to a spot where he is comfortable. Continue until your horse understands that he doesn't have to panic or run away when you touch his front legs—your hands don't hurt him.

3   **Teach your horse a cue to pick up his front feet.**
     Find the chestnut—the small, horny growth just above the knee. Place your thumb and forefinger on it and squeeze lightly. This will make the horse feel a little uncomfortable and he will probably shift the weight off that leg, and maybe even pick up his foot for a split second. As soon as he does this, take the pressure off the chestnut and start to rub his leg again. Remember: You are not trying to

pick the leg up just yet; you just want him to lift his foot up off the ground when you ask him. If at any time he starts to react badly, just go back to the previous step(s).

4   **Hold his front foot.**
    Once your horse understands the cue to pick up his front foot, slide your hand down toward his fetlock and try to hold his foot off the ground for a second or two. Now here's the trick. As soon as he lets you hold his foot, drop it and rub him. Then repeat the chestnut squeeze and hold his foot again, but for a little bit longer. Start with one second for the first five or six repetitions, then add a second for four or five repetitions, and so on until you work up to about 10 to 15 seconds of standing there holding his foot off the ground while he remains relaxed. Repeat on both sides of the horse.

5   **Rub his leg while holding his front foot.**
    Cue your horse to lift one front foot, and as you hold it, take your other hand and gently rub up and down his leg to desensitize him *while his leg is off the ground.* If he wants to move around, try not to restrict him—just move with him. Do not try to keep his foot still, but as soon as he stops moving his leg on his own, drop the foot, rub him, and start all over again. If he manages to pull his leg away from you and you are not able to keep it off the ground, just begin again, going over all the steps. Don't get into a fight with him—treat the whole procedure as a casual game. Repeat this many times on the front legs only. Anticipate your horse's actions to keep progressing: If you think he is going to pull his foot away in five seconds, put it down after only four seconds.

6   **Desensitize and hold the back legs.**
    Following the same exact steps as above, desensitize his back legs, first with the lead rope, then with your hands. If he starts to really kick and thrash at any point and you feel unsafe, just stop what you're doing, and then start again when he is calm. Be patient and don't get in a hurry. As long as you make sure to keep the horse's nose tipped toward you (this forces his hindquarters away from you), he can't kick you.

Back-foot handling tip: When holding a back foot, place your hand under your horse's hoof, more toward the horse's toe, and curl the toe backward. This hold is more comfortable for him and less likely to cause panic. Try not to squeeze the pastern with your hand.

7   Tap his feet
Now that you can cue your horse to lift any foot, and you can hold it while rubbing his leg all over, it's time to use the "approach and retreat" process to desensitize him to the tapping sensations of being shod. Start with your hand, just patting him on the sole of the foot. Keep the same motion, speed, and intensity until he relaxes. If he resists, try to let the horse's leg move back and forth, but gently keep tapping. As soon as he stops moving around and starts to relax, continue tapping for a few seconds, then release the foot and rub him to show that the quickest way to get rid of the tapping is to ignore it.

When he tolerates this well (stands relaxed for 15 seconds), use a small shoeing hammer, a stick, a rock, or anything that has some weight to it, and gently tap on the horse's hoof. As your horse becomes calmer, start tapping harder to simulate and desensitize him to what actually being shod will feel like.

Not only will these steps make the whole trimming and shoeing experience easier on your horse (and on you), your farrier will sincerely appreciate your preparation.

▥ Your place in all this hoof-talk

So, you've found a great farrier, and you get your horse trimmed and/ or shod regularly, but where do you fit into this whole plan for keeping your horse sound, literally from the ground up? Shocked by my lack of knowledge in this fundamental area of horsekeeping, I did a little research—the results of which are included here to help you (not to mention me!) hold up our end of the healthy-hoof bargain.

⦀ How to clean *and inspect* a horse's hoof

1   Before and after each ride, and before you turn a horse out and after you bring him in, use a hoof pick to pry away the packed dirt, manure, and debris from the bottom of each foot.

2   Remove any rocks, sticks, or debris lodged in the crevices of his foot around the frog.

3   Use the tip of the pick to scrape any remaining dirt or gunk from the sole of his foot.

4   Use a small stiff brush (you can get a hoofpick with one on the reverse side) to "sweep" the bottom of each foot, exposing the entire surface of the sole.

5   If your horse is shod, check the condition of his shoes. Look for "risen clinches" (those nail ends your farrier trimmed and clinched that may now have worked their way through the hoof), and a "sprung" or "lifted" shoe (one that has pulled away, bent, is no longer sitting flat, or has moved to one side or another). Ask your farrier to show you how to remove a shoe that has sprung or shifted (yes, you can do it!) to save your horse unnecessary pain and hoof damage. (For a great online shoe-pulling primer, go to www.fairhillforge.com/pullashoe. html and let Matt Taimuty, CJF, show you how.)

6   Check the temperature of each foot by putting the pads of your fingers on the sole. They'll probably feel slightly warm, but should not feel hot—and they should all feel the same.

7   Check your horse's digital pulse by pressing two fingers against the back of each pastern. You're not interested in the rate of the pulse, but merely its strength. You'll get to know what's normal and what is not for your horse.

8   Check the frog by pressing gently with the pads of your fingers. It should have the texture and firmness of a new rubber eraser. (If you're like me, you may have to stop by an art supply aisle to remember exactly what this feels like!) Don't be alarmed if the frog seems to be peeling off—most horses shed their frogs at least twice a year.

9   Be alert for signs of thrush: stinky, oozy dark gunk around the cleft of the frog. It's important to catch this issue—caused by too much moisture or unhygienic conditions—early because it can cause big problems if left untreated. Make sure your horse is not standing in mud, water, or soiled, wet bedding.

10 Look carefully for any sign of a puncture. This will be hard to see unless the object that caused it is still in the horse's foot. If this is the case DO NOT PULL IT OUT. Because the details of entry, exit, angle, and depth will be of special interest to your vet, it is really best to leave the object in and let him remove it.

11 Check for cracks. With hoof cracks, it's sometimes hard to know which are superficial and can wait until the next farrier visit and which need immediate attention. If in doubt, call your farrier and describe the crack, or take a picture with your cell phone or digital camera and email it to him so he can decide if it's a now or later thing.

12 Watch for signs of abscess or laminitis. If when you check it, that digital pulse seems stronger than usual (imagine your own "throbbing" tooth) and you feel increased heat in the foot, your horse may have an abscess. Call your vet immediately. If both front feet seem hot and have a stronger-than-usual digital pulse, and your horse is shifting uncomfortably from side to side, he may have laminitis (an inflammatory hoof condition that can cause severe hoof damage and can even be fatal) and must be seen immediately.

Grow good hooves

The following elements are integral to strong, healthy hooves and a sound horse:

> **Diet** Fine tune your horse's diet to ensure he's getting plenty of the right nutrients, and add a biotin supplement if your vet or farrier agrees he needs one (see sidebar below).

> **Exercise** Consistent exercise on good surfaces, especially at the walk and trot, increase circulation in your horse's feet.

> **Maintain moisture** If your horse is shod, try to minimize the fluctuation between "wet" and "dry" hoof environments by cutting back on summer turnout time, using a moisture reducing agent on the lower two-thirds of your horse's hooves before evening turnout, and avoiding unnecessary baths.

> **Consistent care** Be sure to schedule farrier visits every four to six weeks (or at whatever interval seems right for your horse and his hoof growth rate) and stay on schedule.

- -

Battling bad hooves?

Are supplements the answer to dry, brittle feet or soft, overly tender ones? "If your horse has good solid feet," says Certified Journeyman Farrier Matt Taimuty, "there is no need to waste your money on hoof supplements. However, if you are sure your horse is getting good farrier care and food, and he still has bad feet, then it's time to look into feed supplements."

Taimuty points to biotin supplements, vitamin supplements, and combinations of both, and emphasizes that a horse needs more than biotin and "if you feed a supplement that has only biotin in it you will get iffy results." And, even with supplements, genes, overall diet, and hoof care all play major roles in hoof composition.

Above all, improving bad feet takes time. In fact, it takes at least three shoeings (about 18 weeks) for any results to show. Just be patient and stick with a program for six months before evaluating its effectiveness.

Wait, there's more...

In the space of a few months and more worry than I would care to admit, my midlife horse Trace had his diet overhauled, cleared several vet checkups, had his teeth floated, got a pedicure, and even had a massage (but that's another story). There's a certain amount of irony in that, I thought, staring down at my own gnarly toes, still unable to figure out why he didn't want me on his back. "You know," said a friend, "Maybe his saddle pinches..."

So off we go, midlife sisters, into yet another area of necessary horsekeeping know-how. Keep reading.

9

Let's get tacky

Without guidance, stepping into the worldwide tack shop can be an overwhelming, confusing, and downright dizzying experience. But, if like me, your eyes glaze over and your brain locks up when too much advice starts flowing, here's just enough basic information to help you get tacky enough to ride while keeping you safe and your horse comfortable.

I HAVE A CONFESSION TO MAKE. I own three saddles (and have access to two more) and none of them fit my horses. Or maybe all of them fit my horses just fine. I really don't know.

Now, before you start rolling your eyes, let me explain. I was using one of my dad's saddles, but it killed my knees after long trail rides. Then I borrowed his custom cutting saddle to sort cows. Shortly after that I made my first rookie blunder. I fell in love with a saddle— without seeing how it fit my horses. It was pretty, and it was comfortable (like the living room sofa I didn't buy in its stead—this saddle made me happier when I was sitting in it than any sofa ever could). It's something called a "balanced ride" saddle, designed to be easy on the knees on long trail rides and to provide a deep, secure seat for working cattle. With an unexpected cash windfall burning a hole in my wallet, I plunked down my money without a second thought.

The next saddle in my personal collection was the one that came with Rio. I was delighted with this particular saddle—a Billy Cook Barrel Saddle—not because I'm a barrel racer (nor have I ever been) but because I liked the way it fit my butt, plain and simple. And finally, the latest saddle purchase was work-related (or so I told myself, whipping out that plastic without hesitation). I had just gone to work for horse trainer and clinician Clinton Anderson, and of course I had to be able to write knowledgeably about all his tack and equipment, right? But more than that, I loved the security I felt in this pretty Aussie-style saddle he designed with Martin Saddlery. It positioned my body just right and made it much easier to really move with the horse.

Each of these saddles give me a totally different feel when I ride, all are well made, and if it is extravagant and goofy for a woman my age to own three saddles (and regularly use two others) while living in a house full of hand-me-down furniture, then so be it. The problem with my personal saddle ideology surfaced a few months later: This wasn't about me. To my great disappointment, every time I got on Trace, he crowhopped. At a clinic, on the trails, in the arena.

As I shared early in the last chapter (see p. 168), I didn't immediately pinpoint the saddle as the culprit. Part of this was because I switched saddles, and got the same response. Pretty soon I could barely get a saddle on him at all. I looked at his diet, his teeth, and his feet all as potential contributors to the problem. But Trace continued to regress at breakneck speed, and I was getting worried that the neck about to be broken was mine.

I enlisted the help of my friend Emily, an equine massage therapist well known for her knowledge of saddle fit, and I drug-on-out my three saddles and watched Emily settle my expensive-but-worth-it McDaniel "balanced ride" saddle on Trace's bare back (she said this would give the clearest picture of what was going on), and hoped for the best.

Although my saddle had "Quarter Horse bars" and was supposed to fit "any Quarter Horse," Trace's short back and "mutton withers," made his build unlike most Quarter Horses. "There looks like there might be a little bit of Arab in there," Emily said as she stuck her hand under the front and back of the saddle and all along underneath the sides.

"This saddle doesn't fit him," she pronounced. "It's pinching him in the withers and digging into his hips."

My barrel-racing "good butt" saddle was better, but not great, and the Aussie-style saddle was the best fit of the three. "You know, she said, I think what might fit him better is an Arab saddle."

Did I mention I already had three saddles?

When it comes to the subject of horse tack, especially saddles, you're stepping into yet another great big horsey world rife with differences in opinion. And it gets even more heated when you start to consider bridles and bits, halters and lead ropes, and the myriad other items of horse "clothing" that will—surprise, surprise—make a difference in your day-to-day handling, riding, and training of your horse.

"Fitting" a moving target

When it comes to picking and purchasing a saddle, three things that seemed to hold steady, in all the conversations I had, and in everything I read on the subject, were:

1   Your horse has to be comfortable and able to move freely without pain.

2   You need to be comfortable and well balanced in the saddle.

3   The saddle must be designed and suited to the purpose you intend to use it for.

It's not that you can't sort cattle in an English saddle (I've seen it done quite well!), and there are many people that consider reining nothing more than "Western dressage," but by and large, especially if you show, there are just some things you're going to need or want in terms of saddle appearance and feel when you're using it for a specific purpose.

It was a line in *The Revolution in Horsemanship* by Dr. Robert Miller and Rick Lamb that put everything into perspective for me. "We can now build a saddle that reflects the exact topography of a particular horse's back," Miller writes. "What we have yet to account for, however, is the most perplexing part of the puzzle: The fact that the horse's back constantly changes shape. Making a saddle fit a horse is rather like trying to hit a moving target."

What he means by this is not just the moment-to-moment changes in the shape of a horse's back that occur with his movement, which master saddle maker David Genadek calls "a river of energy that rises, falls, twists, and turns." He is also referring to the more gradual changes that occur over time with age, body condition, diet, and exercise. The fact is, in some ways you can actually change a horse's conformation with proper work. (Theoretically, I could change mine, too...)

▥ Let's consider how a horse is put together

It appears that first order of business in achieving good saddle fit is to consider the horse's basic shape (his conformation). In terms of saddle fit, this includes his rib cage, his "ring of muscles" (see below), and his front legs and shoulders. If you can bear with me through one more "here's how a horse works" summary, I think it will help you understand what you're really looking for in a saddle—and why.

>) **Ribs** Rib cages on horses come in four basic shapes, Genadek says. There are the flat-backed, then somewhat bowed ribs typical of Morgans, Arabs, and Warmbloods; the somewhat more angled rib cages with a little less bow in Quarter Horses and Thoroughbreds; the steeply angled ribs with very little bow you see in

Paso Finos, Tennessee Walkers, and some mules; and the "onion shape," which also describes some mules and many gaited breeds.

) **Ring of muscles** When you hear speak of the horse's "ring of muscles," it is referring to the connected sets of muscles and ligaments that run along a horse's back, neck, croup, and abdomen to "regulate coiling and uncoiling of the loins, the key locomotory movement in horses," according to Dr. Deb Bennett, a noted vertebrate paleontologist with an active interest in the biomechanics of living animals. (Check out Dr. Bennett's downloadable "Ring of Muscles" PDF at www.equinestudies.org.) Calling upon the expertise of Dr. Bennett, Genadek explains that the "ring of muscles" sends signals from the back to the front of the horse, and the object is to encourage the topline to relax and the muscles underneath the horse to contract in order to make it more comfortable for the horse to carry a rider.

) **Shoulders and front legs** Unlike humans, horses don't have collar bones that hold their shoulders firmly fixed into place. Instead, their shoulders are attached by tendons and muscles that act as a big "sling" into which their ribcage fits, and their front legs are more like pillars. This allows significant movement in the shoulder area.

Fundamental parts of the saddle

There are two "bases" and three primary "systems" to a saddle, whether it is English or Western—as Genadek describes quite well in his informative and detailed DVD *About Saddle Fit* (About the Horse, Inc, 1999).

Tree
This is the saddle's foundation upon which everything is built. The bottom part of the tree typically anchors the rigging system to create the

"fit" with the horse; the top part of the tree serves as a base for the seating system.

Saddle trees are made of all kinds of things, but traditional thinking is that hardwood provides the greatest stability, durability, and strength, according to Ron McDaniel, master saddle maker and owner of McDaniel Saddlery in Alvarado, Texas. McDaniel says saddle makers seeking to cut weight have tried other materials such as fiberglass, pine, or synthetics, but for structural soundness, his saddles will always use hardwood.

The trouble is, he adds, since it's "all covered up" when you buy it, you can't really know for sure what your tree is made of, how well it's made, or (in the case of a used saddle) if it isn't cracked or broken. (This reminds me of a recent story in the press about foreign-made saddles discovered to have trees made of cardboard held together with staples instead of screws.) Your best bet is to buy from a reputable saddle maker whose quality can be trusted. A used saddle from a good saddle maker is far better than a new one of questionable origin.

Bars/panels

In a Western saddle, the bars are two "rails" that run more or less parallel on either side of a horse' spine, resting evenly on the big band of muscles horses have along their topline. In an English saddle, the panels are two leather or wool "sacks"—which like the bars rest on either side of the horse's spine—stuffed with "flocking" to form a soft interface between the tree and the horse's back. It is the job of the bars or panels to distribute the saddle's—and rider's—weight evenly.

What features make bars and panels more likely to fit the contours of your horse's back? And more important, what do we need to understand about them in order to ask smart questions of salespeople and make a reasonably informed and intelligent decision when acquiring a saddle? Genadek provides a few enlightening definitions when examining this area of a prospective saddle:

) **Twist** The change of angle from the front of the wither area to the ribs. It affects the angle of the bars and panels against the horse's back, and the width of the saddle between your legs.

) **Rock(er)** The slight "sleigh-runner-like" shaping, or curve from back to front of the bars or panels.

) **Flare** The sideways curve at the front and rear that accommodates the motion of the shoulders and withers and makes room for the legs to move freely.

) **Gullet** The spread, or distance between the bars at the front of a Western saddle, and between the panels from front to back on an English saddle.

When you first look at a saddle for fit, you have to look at ALL these elements—twist, rock, flare, and the gullet. All of these things, combined, determine the shape of the saddle where it comes into contact with the horse's back, and it needs to mirror the back's shape both at a standstill and in motion for it to be a good fit for your horse.

Rigging/billet system

The rigging (Western) and billet (English) system is the "harness" that holds the saddle on the horse's back. Although construction varies from English to Western, its job is the same.

When you consider the rigging or billet system of a saddle, Genadek suggests we imagine a rocking chair—only instead of the chair doing the rocking, it's the floor beneath it. In this example, the rocking chair is the saddle, and the floor is the motion of the horse's back. The object of any good rigging or billet system is to harness the saddle to the horse, keeping the pressure coming from the center, regardless of the movement below. To accomplish this, there are a variety of rigging and billet systems to work with different conformations and different sports. Check out Genadek's DVD or the excellent saddle-fitting books and DVDs by noted saddle-fitting expert Dr. Joyce Harman (see Resources, p. 311) for specific information.

Seating system

This provides a level platform for your pelvis and positions your legs properly to help keep you balanced. Again, what this looks like varies with discipline, but the function is the same.

There are many philosophies about seating systems, depending on the type of riding you do and the type of horse you ride. Different kinds of "seats" can put your body and legs in different positions on the horse, either for the purpose of rider comfort or sometimes to encourage specific movement from the horse (for example, the saddle seat tradition of riding further back on the horse to allow for more shoulder freedom and more expression with the front legs).

Traditionally, regardless of the type of saddle you ride in, the "classic" equitation position places the rider in a state of balance with her ear, shoulder, hip, and heel in a straight line when viewed from the side. According to Genadek, this position is also best for the horse. "When you're braced against the stirrups [for any reason], you keep the horse's weight on his forehand," he explains, "and this makes it more difficult for him to move his shoulders and legs."

Genadek tells us to think of a saddle's seat as a level bowl for our pelvis to rest in. And, because the human pelvis is also like a bowl, getting the right fit is a matter of nesting a "bowl within a bowl." (As a veteran dishwasher unloader and creative dish stacker, this practical explanation makes more sense than I'd like to admit.) "We want the low point of our bowl to rest in the center of the low point of the saddle seat's bowl," Genadek elaborates.

And how big should that "bowl" be? For lots of us, seat size has always been a guess (and usually, a sore subject). Guessing (or relying on the guesses of others, especially those trying to sell you a saddle) it turns out, is not a very good way to get the right fit. The seat size you see on the hangtags of saddles is a measurement based on specific points of the seat for that discipline. Looks can be deceiving here, so the best way to determine the size seat you need in a specific saddle is to ride in several different sizes and styles and measure the seats (between the same exact points) of the ones that feel right to you. The average of these measurements will most likely be a good average seat size for you.

Skirting system/sweat flap

This is the leather or other material meant to protect the horse from the motion of the stirrup leathers and help distribute the weight of the saddle and rider over as large an area as possible. Good skirts on a Western saddle and good flaps on an English saddle (with or without knee rolls) add stability.

▥ How to evaluate (Western) saddle fit

With the help of David Genadek's DVD, along with tips from Stacy Westfall in the January 2010 issue of *Horse&Rider*, I got a crash course in how to evaluate Western saddle fit. It seems only fair that I now pass them along to you!

1   Begin by resting the saddle on your horse's back (swing it over, settle it, and then slide it back till it naturally stops) without any sort of pad so you can clearly see exactly what's going on.

2   First, experts agree, you should be able to slide your hand easily between the saddle and the withers. Check this from both sides, as just like us, horses are sometimes unevenly built. You can have a friend pick up each of your horse's front legs and pull it slightly forward while your hand is under the front of the saddle to see if it pinches.

3   Next, run your hand along the base of each bar, along the length of your horse's back. There should be good, even contact with no gaps or spaces. Genadek says that the average Western bar is 22 inches long, and the average amount of space between the horse's point of shoulder and last rib is 20 inches. If there is a gap in contact, pressure points are created at the withers and loins. When you put your weight in the saddle, this pressure will intensify and make the horse drop his back, put him on his forehand, and make it harder for him to move. It may even be bad enough to make him strive to remove the cause of the pressure (somewhere, I hear a bell going off).

4   The back of the saddle should lift slightly off the back of the horse, just enough for you to slide your hand underneath the back of the saddle skirt.

5   Now stand back, facing the side of the horse, about 10 or 15 feet away. Is the seat level?

Although we're probably never going to get a perfect fit for every horse, this evaluation can help you get pretty close.

▥ How to evaluate (English) saddle fit

On the English side, saddle fit is an elaborate science, and depending upon the discipline, there are many factors to consider (who would have known that little bit o' leather could be so complicated?) But it stands to reason, when you think about it, because the smaller surface area makes the "load" (you) more concentrated, and therefore magnifies a bad fit in a much worse pinch.

To evaluate the fit of an English saddle, you basically follow the same steps as those outlined for the Western saddle.

1   Place the saddle directly on the horse's back without a pad.

2   Check pommel clearance (you should be able to run your hand all the way to the back of the withers).

3   Slide your hand between the points of the saddle tree and either side of the withers. You should feel even contact.

4   Run your hand up under each panel, all the way to the front, and then all the way to the back, looking for any gaps or tight spots. "There can be a small gap," says Andrea Barnett, the English saddle fitter at Teskeys Saddle Shop, a large tack and equine supply store in Texas, "but there shouldn't be a lot of pressure at the edges." She reminds us to be sure to check both sides on the English saddle because of differences in a horse's shape from side to side.

5   When it comes to the gullet on an English saddle (the space between the panels that allows room for the spine), Barnett tells us to remember that it's the panel spread, not the size of the gullet that makes the biggest difference in fit.

What does an English saddle fitter look for? Barnett says the slope of the horse's shoulders, the width of the horse's back, and the width across the withers are key factors that help determine the right English saddle. (She agreed that Trace has "mutton withers" and would fit best in a dressage saddle made for warmbloods. Fat chance. I'm not even going to speculate how long I could stay on his back in an English saddle.)

Because of significant variations in manufacturer measurements, if you are going shopping for an English saddle and you can't hire a professional saddle fitter to evaluate your horse, the next best thing to do is to measure your horse yourself. All you need is a flexible curve ruler (sold at office supply or art supply stores), a large sheet of paper or cardboard, a black marker, and a pair of scissors.

1   Find the spot two fingers' width behind your horse's shoulder blade
    (You can do this by picking up his front leg and moving it up and
    down; at the top of this leg movement is his shoulder blade). This is
    also where you would place the saddle.

2   Mold the flexible curve ruler across your horse's back in this spot.
    Make sure that it is lying flat on both sides and against the horse's
    coat all the way around the length of the curve.

3   Lift it gently off the horse, taking care to retain its shape, and lay it
    flat down on the paper or cardboard.

4   Trace around the inside of the curve, and be sure to note which side
    is the horse's left and which is the right, as some horses are very
    different from side to side.

Cut out your tracing, and bring it with you to the tack shop. You
should be able to hold your paper model up "inside" a saddle to see if it
might fit your horse. You'll still need to try any saddle you find on your
horse, of course, but this should get you in the ballpark.

▌ The telltale dry spot

"Saddle fit is a science, but it isn't rocket science," says Jill Logan, the
Western saddle fitter at Teskeys. Logan says that people come in every
day asking about saddle fit problems and trying to figure out, in the
vast sea of saddles, which saddle they need. She feels it is very important for us all to be able to assess our saddle's fit, and she reminds
us that another good way to do this is to check for dry spots on our
horse's back after every ride.

Dry spots in the saddle area (i.e. distinctly sweatless areas on an
otherwise sweaty horse) can mean one of two problems:

1   They can indicate a gap in contact where the saddle is "bridging" over a low spot in the horse's back.

2   They can indicate an area of tightness or pinching where the pressure on the horse's back actually compresses the sweat glands enough to keep them from producing. Left too long, the horse's back muscles can atrophy from this kind of pressure, and this loss of tissue can be permanent.

▥ More pad ain't better

Whether riding in a Western or an English saddle, it is important to understand that a thicker saddle pad is not the answer to a bad fit. "Too much pad" takes away a saddle's fit (remember, we've been evaluating saddle fit on the horse's bare back). Logan says she commonly sees people trying to correct poor saddle fit by simply adding more pad. "One lady came in just the other day and said that all her horses were so big she didn't have a saddle that really fit any of them, so she just added more pads," she relates. "Now let's just think about this for a minute. If you have a pair of boots that are too tight, do you just add more socks? Does that help at all? Of course not! But that's what we do to our horses when we 'overpad.'"

That's not to say that you can't improve a less than perfect fit with certain kinds of pads—or more specifically—with "shims" (wedges of foam) placed strategically to alleviate pressure.

"Filling the hole"
When you are stuck with a saddle that's fit isn't ideal, sometimes a little work on the pad side of the equation can make all the difference in the world. One English trainer I talked to always buys her saddles extra wide and custom shims for every horse, just to make sure they have plenty of room to move and that their own individual conformation issues are accommodated. So how do you know if you have a fit problem that can be solved with a pad and/or shims?

"If you have an 'air pocket'—a place where the bar or panel is not making contact with the horse's back, that means you have pressure points around it," says Ron McDaniel, owner of McDaniel Saddlery. "It's like laying a two-by-four across a hole."

I took my midlife horses Trace and Rio, and my friend Susan and her barrel horse Shawnee, to visit Ron McDaniel and show him my "issues" with the "balance ride" saddle I had bought from his company about a year before. McDaniel scolded me a little for waiting so long to get my horses and the saddle over there so they could take a look, explaining that they could shorten the skirt, make other adjustments, or even take it back in trade for one that fit my horses better, if necessary.

We started by taking a look at the saddle on Trace. Sure enough, there was a large "air pocket" where the bars of the saddle didn't come close to touching him. ("See?" Trace seemed to say. "I told you it hurt.")

"A perfect fit is going to be hard to get with a back like this horse's," McDaniel said. "But if you can get the pressure off the edges of the hole, you can then encourage him to straighten up his own back."

There were two things we needed to do. First, we had to relieve those pressure points, and then, if necessary, we might have to shim, or raise up, the surface of Trace's back to eliminate the space. "You've been trying to fit the hole," McDaniel observed, looking at my saddles all lined up like soldiers in his driveway. "What we need to do instead is fill the hole—and eliminate the pressure points."

Huh?

"Lie down on your side on the concrete," he said. I didn't but my trusty pal, Susan did. Pointing to where her shoulders and her hips rested on the concrete, McDaniel explained that those were where pressure points would start to make themselves known if she stayed in that position for a while. If we put pillows under those contact points, she would still feel the pressure, even though it was padded, and eventually it would get uncomfortable again. This, he explained, is like the orthopedic pads we can use under our saddles. They are great for absorbing shock, but they don't eliminate the pressure points created by less than ideal saddle fit.

EXERCISE

Create Your Saddle Wish List

1   Think about a saddle you enjoyed riding in, and list all the things you liked about it.

2   Think about a saddle you didn't like very much and list what bothered you about it.

3   How important is weight and ease of handling? What's your ideal range?

4   If there's a specific vendor you like, or a shop that is convenient for repairs or adjustments? (Buying online is fine, as long as you remember the cost of shipping can negate a good deal.)

5   Where is your ideal saddle made? What materials? Color? Accents?

6   What kind of saddle tends to fit your horse's breed/shape best?

7   What kind of saddle do you need for your discipline?

8   What is your ideal price range?

9   What would you accept in a used saddle, and what would make you pass? (Experts agree that there are a lot of barely used saddles for sale out there—once you know what you're looking for, look on eBay or Craig's List. Just be sure the seller will let you return it if it doesn't fit.)

   Like making a list of the characteristics of your ideal mate, just the act of thinking through all these issues and committing your answers to writing not only clarifies your intent, but it helps you realize where you need to acquire more information before you buy. Sometimes it's okay to settle for less-than-ideal, but it's also a good idea to know what your personal deal-breakers are. (Yep, that's hard won life advice, across the board.)

"To eliminate the pressure points," McDaniel went on, "and to keep them from happening in the first place, we are going to put a pillow (think "shim") underneath Susan's waist where the gap is. The idea is to get this shim thick enough to raise her shoulders and hips up off the pavement just enough to equalize the pressure the length of her body— and thus eliminate the points of pressure at the two edges of the gap."

Wow. This meant that if we put a shim in the gap where the saddle wasn't meeting Trace's back solidly, it would take the pressure off the places where the saddle pinched, poked, and pissed him off.

Commercial shims can be bought, or Genadek and Dr. Joyce Harman tell you how to make your own in their DVDs and books (see Resources, p. 311).

The subject of saddle fit and correct padding is a big one, so as in all these horsey subjects, it's a good idea to learn what's out there and be as well informed as you can be before plunking down the credit card. A little knowledge can go a long way to keeping both you and your horse as comfortable and safe as possible.

▥ A final note on saddle fit

At some point during this section, you probably asked, "If all this is such a big deal, how is it that people for centuries have ridden horses without analyzing or examining or mitigating anything? They just saddled up and rode. They survived, their horses did fine. What's so wrong with the way things have always worked?"

The answer is, sometimes, nothing. Horses, after all, are individuals, and some horses don't seem to care what you do, within reason. Depending on your horse's threshold of discomfort (Trace doesn't have one) you can get away with a horribly fitting saddle for years upon years, never even realize it's been hurting your horse every time you get on.

Physiologically, poor saddle fit (and those pressure points we've been talking about) constricts blood flow to the muscles in the horse's back. This affects his sweat glands, as well as coat and skin (hair loss, pigment loss, and saddle sores). Left untended, muscle atrophy develops, then skeletal problems, scar tissue, and chronic pain. Some horses accept this as part of the deal, others buck, rear, bolt, and bite. Unfortunately, unless a knowledgeable someone fixes the problem, the latter often get sold as "problem horses," and unless luck is on their side, this can ultimately lead to years of unhappiness, ill health, and bad relationships with the humans around them.

So, yeah, you can ride some horses just fine with a saddle that doesn't fit right. You can use whatever pad happens to be in the barn. Or, you can do the right thing by this animal you've pledged yourself to protect and take care of.

Bridles, bits, and other "tacky" stuff

While saddles and pads are the main things you need to be concerned about when it comes to outfitting your midlife horse for midlife riding, this chapter would not be complete without at least a question or two raised (and an answer or two given) in the areas of bridles (and their many variations); bits (worlds of controversy waiting for you there); cinches/girths; halters and lead ropes; and blankets and sheets.

▥ "Headgear"

What you put on your horse's head—the bridle headstall and bit(s)—is largely a matter of riding discipline and personal preference. Within these areas, however, exist a few consistent principles. Usually, new horse owners just keep riding their horse in whatever tack he was ridden in when they bought him. If they do try something different, it is usually because a knowledgeable friend, horse trainer, or instructor advises that it might help their horse perform better and/or be more comfortable. Nevertheless, needs change, situations change, training advances, and at some point you may need to be able to figure it out on your own. So here we are.

I like to think that today's choices in horse headgear reflect a dramatic shift in thinking. Or, as Dr. Robert Miller and Rick Lamb write in *The Revolution in Horsemanship*, "Today...we see the function of headgear differently. It is no longer to impose our will on an unwilling servant. It is now to communicate the wishes of a benevolent leader to an eager and willing follower." Doesn't this mirror the kind of authentic and willing partnership we were looking for when we started this midlife horse journey?

How does the bit and bridle work?

Before choosing a bit, or any other headgear, for that matter, the folks at Myler Bits—one of the world's leading bit companies owned by third-generation horsemen in Marshfield, Missouri (www.mylerbitsusa. com)—recommend taking a few minutes to get to know your horse's mouth so you'll understand the action and reaction involved in communicating with him from your hands via a set of reins.

Before you make any new decisions about headgear, have your horse's dental health evaluated. Your vet or equine dentist should take care of any issues prior to a bit or bridle change. Then, perhaps with the aid of your vet or equine dentist, have a look inside your horse's mouth and familiarize yourself with the following areas that a bit affects:

) **Bars** The gaps where there are no teeth on either side of the horse's mouth.

) **Palate** The roof of the horse's mouth.

) **Tongue** Note how thick and wide it is. The tongue is important, according to Myler Bits experts, because it is where the actions of "pressure" and "relief of pressure" give the bit its main means of control.

Two other places of importance because they, too, are affected by the bit and bridle, are the horse's chin (the groove behind it where the curb strap or chain on many bits goes) and the poll (the spot at the top of his head just behind his ears, which the headstall crosses, exerting pressure in many kinds of bridles).

Legendary Australian horse trainer and clinician Ian Francis describes the communication between the rider, headgear, and horse as "ringing the telephone": Your hands on the reins send the signal, the reins are your "telephone lines," and pressure on the headstall and/ or bit is the receiver at the other end. When you ask your horse to do something, your hands "dial the phone," the reins "carry the signal," and with any luck, your horse answers. If he doesn't, Francis quips, you just keep calling him back until he does!

A little bit about bits

According to representatives at Myler Bits, "Every horse-and-rider combination has specific needs." These needs are based on a horse's training level, the rider's ability and experience, and the discipline they are pursuing. There are hundreds of bit types, and because they have the potential to cause the horse pain and distress if mischosen or misused, I urge you to study up and ask for guidance before trying something new.

As a very basic foundation, there are two main types of bits:

) **Snaffles** The snaffle, long used in early training of young horses, is often now the bit of choice for all kinds of riders, in every discipline, from beginners just learning the concept of "feel," to trainers and clinicians (and their students) at all levels, to those at the top echelons of competition. Snaffle mouthpieces are usually "broken" (hinged) once or twice in the middle and are designed for two-handed riding (direct reining). They are direct pressure bits that affect the horse's tongue, bars, and occasionally the palate.

) **Curbs** are "shanked" bits that use leverage to exert indirect pressure on the horse's poll, chin groove, bars, tongue and palate (especially in the case of those with a "port," or inverted "U" in the middle of the mouthpiece). A curb can have a solid or broken mouthpiece, and depending on the discipline and shape of the mouthpiece, can be used with one hand (neck-reining) or two hands.

Parts of the bridle

Although all bridles are definitely not created equal, most are created similarly enough that knowing the names of the basic parts and functions will enable you to speak intelligently about bridle issues to your trainer and tack shop sales people.

) **Browband** The strap across the forehead that holds the crown-piece (the strap behind the ears) in position and keeps the bridle from being pulled back over the ears and down the neck. (Some Western bridles have ear loops instead—one or two.) It should rest just beneath the base of the ears, snug without being tight.

) **Noseband/cavesson** This piece goes across the horse's nose, usually about two fingers' width below the horse's cheekbones (exact placement depends on the style and discipline). Traditional fit requires two fingers space between the noseband buckle and your horse's lower jaw when the noseband is secured.

) **Cheekpiece** These two pieces on either side of the bridle connect the bit to the crownpiece. They determine the level of "communication" between your hands and reins and the bit. The cheekpieces should be adjusted so the bit rests appropriately in the horse's mouth—not too loose and not too tight (you may need your trainer's help to determine appropriate height).

) **Throatlatch** This runs underneath the horse's jaw. Its function is to prevent the bridle from slipping over the horse's head. This should not be tight—that would constrict both the horse's breathing and movement at the poll—but it should be in proper position to be effective, about three fingers' width between the strap and the jaw. Too loose is better than too tight on this one.

Three good habits that save tack time, wear, and tear

Margaret and Michael Korda give us a few good ideas in their book *Horse House-keeping*. Here's some of their advice I've found indispensable:

1   Clean and inspect your tack after every time you use it. That's right, every time. Don't roll your eyes—it really only takes a few minutes to make sure everything is as it should be before you put it away. This kind of frequent inspection helps keep you ahead of any problems that need to be addressed (such as a frayed rein that could lead to a big wreck out on the trail!)

2   Keep an old toothbrush in your grooming box and use it to give your bit a quick scrub every time you take it out of your horse's mouth. Run it under clear water for a few seconds and then brush the crevices with the brush. Dip the brush in a little Canola oil give the bit a light coating, then wipe it clean with a soft cloth.

3   Fluff your pad. After unsaddling, always examine your pad for dry spots (could warn you of improper fit). Then, using a rubber curry comb, brush away loose hair and fluff up the pad, then hang it "inside up" to air out or dry.

I admit that when I started writing this chapter on tacky information, I was skeptical. Is it all just a bunch of marketing hype geared mostly toward separating us from our money? Yes, some suppliers see how many things they can make us think we need with dire threats and ridiculous promises. It's up to us to educate ourselves well enough to know whether an item qualifies as a want or a need.

10

Getting there

Whether you board or keep your horse at home, whether you trail ride or compete, the day will come when you'll face the big "truck-and-trailer" quandary. With shows any number of miles away and veterinary hospitals sometimes across town (and countryside), there's a certain peace-of-mind that comes with having a rig of your own parked out back. Even when that's not the case, you still need to be able to get your horse ON a trailer from time to time. Here's what you need to "get there" safely.

IT SEEMS LIKE REGARDLESS OF WHAT you want to do with your horse, you're going to (eventually) need a truck and trailer. It's intimidating, and more than a little scary, but the only way to blaze new trails in our psyche is to forge on forward, so let's work through this complicated issue one step at a time.

Most people, it turns out, learn to pull a trailer by trial and error. More acquaintances than I can count have relayed stories of how they drove their truck to the dealership to pick up their new trailer and, after a quick lesson in the parking lot with the sales rep, hauled on home with absolutely no idea what they were really doing. Even scarier, they then loaded their horses and took off for the trails. "Oh I don't even know it's back there," chirped one friend about her ease at learning this new skill. (This prompted my mental note to NEVER let her haul my horse, no matter how desperate I was to get somewhere.)

What I tried to explain to my friend Susan—and to the post-pubescent sales boy at the trailer place I visited with related questions—is that while I know the ability to pull a trailer, like driving a car, is very easy once you've learned how to do it, there's got to be some basic stuff you need to learn if you haven't done it all your life.

What is this vital information? I wonder. And why does no one seem that concerned about it? People who know how to pull a trailer don't know either, because, like they say in that popular spaghetti sauce commercial, "It's just in there." When I asked the trailer-boy if there's a course I could take on hauling horses and trailer safety, he just snickered. "No, but I can take you out back and show you how to do it."

"Why is this so funny?" I pressed, notebook poised.

"Oh I don't know, he said. "It's just that nobody ever asked me before."

Why the hell not? I couldn't help but wonder. Instead, I summoned my patience and said, "Okay, let's say I'm going down the road, 70 miles an hour, with two tons of weight behind me. The life and safety of my family, my little dog, and my four horses are in my hands. I am not used to driving a truck, and I have never pulled a trailer in my life."

I could tell by his expression he was starting to get the picture, but still had no answer. So I continued. "I have had a driver's license for many years, and I do remember there were some very specific skills involved in learning to drive a plain old car that were unfamiliar to me when I started. Of course, now that I've driven for so long, I do these things—use these skills—quite automatically, without even thinking about them or being able to isolate exactly what they are." I paused, to let this sensible argument sink in. "I expect there are some skills like that involved with pulling a trailer full of horses, and I would like the opportunity to learn—and practice—them before I actually do it."

"Like what?" he asked.

"Dealing with the size, for one thing," I replied, hiding my exasperation. "And weight. And the time it takes to get going and stop. How

The Smart Woman's Guide to Midlife Horses

much distance to allow when turning a corner and changing lanes. When I leave here with my new trailer, I'm probably going to have to negotiate city traffic: People are going pull out in front of me, and there will be corners that I don't realize are too tight to turn, or cars pulled out too far in intersections. And God forbid, I may get in a position, despite my best efforts, that requires I back up."

"I can show you how to back up," he said, clearly defensive. "I don't know about the rest of it—people just do it. And they do it all the time."

But I want a course! I thought on the way home from this exhausting experience. I want a simulator, an instructor sitting beside me. A test that shows I know what I need to know. I understand that experience is the best teacher, but I want a basic competency level before I get behind the wheel! Am I crazy? Maybe. I shudder to think how many people are on the road today who have no idea how to pull a trailer except what they learned in the back lot of the trailer dealership.

Happy trailering

"Take a CDL course," my brother advised. He had just gotten a commercial driver's license to drive a school bus.

So, I went online and courtesy of the California Department of Motor Vehicles and the July 2010 Issue of *Horse&Rider* magazine (in which Gavin Ehringer weighed in with "Truckin' & Trailerin'"), I pulled together a few primary pointers for smart truck-and-trailer purchasing and safe trailering.

Besides the load of "probably" that comes with the half-ton and SUV options, it is always advisable to buy more truck than you think you need, and if you don't have experience pulling a trailer, a "gooseneck" (hitched to a ball-and-socket above-and-forward of the rearmost axle of the towing vehicle—usually in the bed of a pickup) is easier and safer than a "bumper pull" (a ball hitch on or under the rear bumper of the tow vehicle).

Word on the street has it that if you have any choice at all in the matter, a half-ton pickup or SUV—even with a "towing package"—is not the wisest course for pulling a horse trailer. Apparently it is not the towing capacity that is the most important thing, as I (and most people) assumed was key. The axiom I kept hearing, "It's not what it will pull—but what it will stop," made no sense to me until I had it explained in graphic detail by a guy who hauls horses for a living.

"It's in that small percentage of time," he said, "emergencies, bad weather, you know, when you need to get that trailer stopped quick, that you realize that the towing capacity is really not the important thing. In that instant, you're gonna wish you had more truck."

Without exception, according to everyone I talked to (dozens of men and women), since I had no experience pulling a trailer of any kind, the opinion was that a three-quarter-ton truck would be safest and a gooseneck trailer would be easiest to pull.

Of course, it goes without saying that horses have been pulled successfully, over countless miles, in whatever someone could manage to hitch a trailer to, for as long as anyone can remember. As always, you have to use your own judgment, based on your own abilities.

▓ Seven commandments of safe trailering

1   **Know thy vehicle.** Pulling a trailer, regardless of its size or shape, requires several important things of us. First, we must know our vehicles well, including the towing capacity (never exceed 85 percent of a vehicle's maximum towing weight), clearance height (ground to the top of anything attached to the top of the trailer—think about low bridges, car washes, and tunnels), and condition. Before heading out the first time you have everything loaded for a long trip, make a quick stop at a weigh station to make sure you're still under that 85 percent once the grain, hay, horses, tack, and miscellaneous items are on board. Your vehicle should have a towing package, preferably a manufacturer-installed one. And, follow the manufacturer's prescribed maintenance schedules for both your truck and trailer, and make a habit of regularly checking air

and condition of tires (spare, too!), fluid levels (coolant, engine oil, transmission oil, brake fluid, transmission fluid, and windshield washer fluid), and floor (wash out after each trip and be sure to raise the mats inside and look underneath the exterior floor for anything loose or hanging.

2   **Check thy connections.** In addition to your regular inspections of all parts of your hitching mechanism, check it for rust, corrosion, or other damage. Make sure the locking mechanism snaps firmly in place (test it by pulling on it) and if it's a bumper pull, make sure your two safety chains are in good shape and are crisscrossed in an X between truck and trailer. Plug in your electrical connections and check to make sure brake lights, turn signals, parking lights, running lights, and hazard lights/flashers are working. (Also make sure you have spare bulbs and fuses for these in case they go kaput on the road.)

3   **Double-check thy details.** Give the braking systems a quick check, (including emergency brakes), and make sure your wheel chocks are on board and secured. In fact, make sure everything is secured on the inside, including stall mats and partitions, butt bars, tack, and other objects. Check for anything loose or protruding that could hurt or scare a horse, and remove any old feed or hay. Make sure horses are tied high and securely, but with quick release snaps or rings in case of emergency. Check windows and vents— there should be good airflow and ventilation, even in the winter, but never leave the window panel open where a horse can stick his head out as you go down the road (bugs and road debris could really hurt him at speed). And speaking of bugs, be sure to check the inside of the trailer for spider webs, hornet and wasp nests, and bee hives (before you load) to avoid road hysteria.

4   **Though shalt practice thy tricky trailer maneuvers in advance.** It is a good idea to get familiar with how your trailer handles in a

parking lot or other open space before you attempt to make a trip with cargo on board. This should be done more than the one time on the day you buy your trailer, though. Practice turning; changing "lanes" by crossing in front of cones or objects to learn to estimate distance and spacing; parking; pulling out and turning across "traffic" to see how much acceleration it takes to do it quickly and safely; and be sure you know how to back that "thang" up.

Hand at the Bottom for Good Backing

I don't know about you, but that old "turn-in-the-opposite-direction-you-want-the-back-end-of-the-trailer-to-go" advice muddles my brain. A better go-to for me is, "Put your hand on the bottom of the steering wheel. The direction your hand moves is the direction the back of the trailer will go."

5   **Know thy letters.** Particularly the difference between "V" and "L" to avoid "jackknifing," or getting your truck and trailer stuck in a "V" that will damage the hitch and trailer. Just pay attention to this angle and be sure the trailer never gets beyond the 90-degree "L" shape in relation to the truck. This happens most commonly when you're backing up, and sometimes when making too sharp a turn. Take it slowly, keep the movement of the steering wheel to a minimum, and always remember that if you start to get into trouble, just pull forward, straighten out a bit, and try again. It takes a lot longer to get a truck and trailer "un-jackknifed" (not to mention repair to the damage caused) than it does to just take it slow and easy the first time. Ignore hecklers. You can do this.

6   **Keep thy distance.** Once on the road, there are many important things to remember, but the main one is to stay an extra-safe distance from the cars in front of you, and above all, slow down.

Breakdown Tips

Here are a few tips for preventing or handling a breakdown from US Rider (www.usrider.org), a consistent source of valuable trailering advice and an organization with a membership plan that includes roadside assistance, towing, and other travel-related benefits.

▸ **Replace tires often** You should replace tires on your truck and trailer every three to five years. Be sure to buy from a high volume tire dealer to make sure you're not getting tires that have been sitting on the shelves. "The number one reason for trailer disablement is a tire issue," says Mark Cole, managing member for US Rider.

▸ **Balance the load** In the case of a "straight load" trailer (horses are parallel to the trailer walls), place the heaviest horse—or if you're just hauling one, the only horse—on the left (driver's) side.

▸ **Carry a spare spare** That's right, not just one, but two spare tires, because of the high incidence of two simultaneous flat tires.

▸ **Use reflective material** Secure reflective tape on the back of your trailer to make sure it's visible if your breakdown includes a loss of power (i.e. flashers).

▸ **Protect your horse** Use shipping boots and a head bumper, and DO NOT unload him if you break down.

▸ **Keep your headlights on** Unless your breakdown includes a loss of power, this increases visibility.

7 **Keep thy judgment sound.** Never drive when you're too tired, injured, or taking medication that can alter your judgment or reaction time. As someone who enjoys a cold beer or margarita after

a ride as much as anyone, even I am among the first to say losing even a fraction of your reaction time before you hit the road in control of a trailer is just not worth it. Wait till you get home and have two to make up for the wait (make one of them for me!). And above all, stay off the phone. If you need to call someone for directions, read and/or answer a text message, or take an urgent call, PLEASE find a safe place and pull over.

▥ A system for maintaining a trailer that's ready to go when you are

Traveling with horses adds a whole new layer of things to think about and stuff to gather. People who travel a lot with their horses more than likely have a system, a routine, or a method of getting ready. They probably keep their trailers stocked with certain things, and a bag or two packed with items that always go along on the road. But if you haven't done this before—or if you don't do it often—it can be harrowing. And, when you find yourself going where you're going without your reins or saddle pad, it can be expensive, too.

I have a friend who created a "vacation spreadsheet" for her family with a column for each kid. In the far left column she made a horizontal entry for each day, special activity, and planned event. The corresponding daily squares in each person's column listed necessary clothing, accessories, and reminders—what each person might need for the planned activity, as well as any changes in wardrobe and equipment (including sunscreen, insect repellent, and medication).

Sure, it took her an entire afternoon to build this spreadsheet, but from that day forward, packing for trips and vacations was largely cut and paste. More importantly, she and her family rarely forgot anything, as everyone had a packing list that she could use as a checklist before loading the car, both going and coming back home.

I stole this idea for horse camping, and my competitive friends said it would work even better for shows. By creating a column for each human and each animal traveling with you, you force yourself to think all the way through each day and activity on the itinerary. Things come up, plans change, and sometimes we still have to switch things around on the fly and make do with what we have, but this approach saves an amazing amount of packing time, virtually eliminates the grief of forgotten necessities, minimizes yelling (at family members or at yourself), and promises a much more relaxed departure because you will have a very good idea of "what's in your trailer."

Always work from a fresh spreadsheet and be sure to include a column for checking off items as they are accounted for. When packing, be sure to make visual contact with the item in your trailer before checking it off. Many a person has thought a crucial item was in there (and checked it off), only to remember when they get to where they're going that they took it out (for just a minute) and forgot to put it back.

Oh yeah...and then there's loading your horse...

After being in the unique position to watch many kinds of (frustrated) people handle many kinds of "he-won't-get-in" trailer-loading scenarios, and after studying many kinds of trailer-loading demonstrations from many kinds of horse trainers and clinicians, I have to say that Clinton Anderson's techniques still speak most clearly to me. With his permission, I've included the key points of his trailer-loading method, and I encourage you to watch the demonstration he does on the second day of every Walkabout Tour (entertaining as well as educational) or take a look at his DVDs (see Resources, p. 311). Although I won't say you'll never have another loading problem again (these are horses we're talking about, after all), if you follow Anderson's principles, I can almost guarantee you won't have a loading problem you can't solve.

"People sometimes remark that it's my patience that makes this trailer loading technique work," says Anderson. "It's not that at all. I'm really not that patient—I just know that no matter how long it takes, that horse is going to go willingly into the trailer. It's not a matter of if, but when."

Horse Show Trailer Parking Tips

‣ Don't park near the entrance or exit gate—it's one of the dustiest spots on the show grounds.

‣ Try to park with your tie rings in the morning sun so the trailer will provide shade in the hotter afternoon sun.

‣ Leave 30 feet between your trailer and your neighbors to give tied horses on each trailer ample room.

‣ Set up your water, hay, and muck bucket before you unload your horse. Also be sure to police the area before you unload for sharp objects, broken glass, holes, and the like.

‣ If your trailer doesn't have a dressing room, create one! Once your horse is unloaded, sweep out the trailer (remember that muck bucket) and lay down a clean plastic tarp. Secure it with folding chairs and move your cooler between them to use as a table. You now have a shady, comfortable place to relax. (Coolers, by the way, in addition to keeping food and beverages cold, make a great place to store anything that melts—like makeup!) Make use of a portable fan, magnetic mirror, spring loaded closet rods, a bucket for a trash can, and use bungee cords and clamps to secure doors to add privacy.

▦ Clinton Anderson's do-it-yourself trailer-loading tips

❭ When your horse refuses to get into your trailer, don't force, pull, beg, cajole, bribe with food, tap, spank, or put a rope behind his butt. Instead, just move his feet. It's that simple. You're going to make getting in the trailer easy, and staying outside the trailer just plain old hard work.

❭ Starting as far away from the trailer as you need to, get him hustling those feet on the lunge line, either around you in a circle or back and forth in front of the trailer door. Keep him moving at a brisk pace for five minutes or so, and then ask him to load.

> If he moves even one step closer, let him rest for a few seconds and give him a rub. Horses don't learn what you want them to do from the pressure you put on them (in this case, moving his feet), but from the release of pressure (letting him rest). Now ask again. If he refuses—and every time he refuses or takes a step in any direction other than closer to/further into the trailer, back him up and start moving those feet again.

> As he starts to get tired, he'll eventually figure out that outside the trailer means work, and inside the trailer means rest. Once he makes that connection, you're almost there. However, don't stop too soon. Lots of people, with their horse half-way in and half-way out, go back to pulling, coaxing, and forcing. Resist this temptation, even if you're getting tired yourself or are in a hurry. You are setting the stage not just for getting this horse loaded now, but for making him easier to load from now on. Stay with it.

> Remember, each time you ask your horse to get in the trailer, wait a few seconds to give him a chance to do the right thing, then, without making a big deal of it, just back him up from wherever he stopped and hustle those feet for at least five minutes (this will start to seem like a long time to you, too, believe me!), and then ask again. Don't stop until the horse goes all the way into the trailer and stands there without being tied. Rub him, pat him, and let him rest. If he runs backward when you try to tie him, it means you're not done. Follow him out of the trailer and start again.

> This technique also works for the horse that unloads too fast (shoots out of the back of the trailer the minute you untie him).

Don't try to stop him when he does this; follow him out, move his feet, then put him back in. Pretty soon—again when he associates ouside the trailer means work and inside means rest—he'll want to take his time getting out!

A road to somewhere

If you can get your horse on your trailer, and you can drive your truck and trailer in a safe and appropriate manner, there is no end to the midlife adventures ahead of you. Where will your road take you? Let's consider some of ways you can grow as a horsewoman and continue to experience the rich variety of activities and relationships (both human and horse) a "midlife horsis" can lead to...read on!

11

Picking up the correct lead

When it comes to matters of the horse, is everyone you talk to a know-it-all? Are you confused by conflicting advice? Have you ever felt worse instead of better after a riding lesson? In the pages ahead, successful midlife horse owners share why it's crucial to align with the training information and approach that makes sense to you, and find riding buddies and teachers that have your best interests at heart.

THE FIRST TIME I TRIED TO LUNGE ONE of my midlife horses I stood facing his side, just like my friend said to, the flat, blue, web lunge line stretched between us with the "proper" amount of slack. I held onto the black rubber disk at the end and clucked. Nothing happened. I waved my free arm. Nada.

"You need a buggy whip," someone said. So I got one of those and that did get my horse moving—albeit backward. The more I tapped his butt to get him to go forward (another piece of advice I got), the faster he went backward. I wondered how many backward laps around the round pen would qualify for the latest edition of Guinness World Records.

Thinking the round pen was inhibiting my horse's forward movement, I tried lungeing in the pasture. There, no longer contained by the walls of the round pen, he just had a much larger playground. He dragged me all over the place as I imagined I was flying a great big kite shaped like a horse—it wasn't a good visual, trust me.

Clearly, I needed help.

When I'd last had horses as a youngster, we "didn't do no stinkin' groundwork." We just saddled up and rode—sometimes on horses that had been turned out on 500 acres for several weeks—with nary a circle. In fact, I didn't even know what "groundwork" was until I "found my lead," which as you know by now is a foundation of basic horse handling skills as taught by Australian horse trainer and clinician Clinton Anderson. His explanations made sense to me, his step-by-step instructions and exercises were things I could actually do, and because I could "work with him" via his books and DVDs on my own timetable, I'd found a way to fit in and afford professional instruction that helped me work productively with my horses and vastly improve my relationship with them. That's not to say that there aren't other programs out there that could have done the same thing, but this is the way it worked out for me.

Where do I begin the search?

How do you know when you're on the right lead when it comes to instruction? The same way you know when you're riding a horse. You feel it. It's comfortable. You experience the kind of elation you imagined when you first dreamed of owning a horse. Anything else feels choppy, awkward, and ineffective.

Informational "cross-firing" happens all the time with the bounty of information and advice out there these days. From those know-it-all horsey friends and acquaintances, to books, articles, and television shows dedicated to training and working with horses, to Youtube, to the scores of websites built to fill our mind with an unprecedented plethora of horsemanship how-to and equine-related self help. What's worse, sometimes it's hard to tell who really knows what they're talking about, and who's just good at talking.

Ah, midlife sisters, this is where we start to come back to our quest. By tuning in to the voice of our authentic self (see p. 4 for when we figured out how to find it!), we can start to discern what rings true for us and our purposes—and when we are better off just smiling, nodding, and "walking on by." Regardless of our level of accomplishment, this is the time to listen for a different voice—one that resonates with the same quality that brought us to (or back to) horses in the first place.

Begin by opening yourself up to all that is out there. Sample the buffet of wonderful learning options for all levels, disciplines, and breeds. Watch, listen, and read everything you can, and then subject it all to the "sniff test" of your inner lead mare (see p. 12). She'll know.

▥ Choosing from the many

There are, for the first time in history (and some would say, to our great detriment), lots and lots of clinicians, horse trainers, and riding instructors out there. The "revolution in horsemanship" that Dr. Robert Miller and Rick Lamb describe in their book by the same name has brought about amazing changes in not only how we deal with and train our horses, but in the learning opportunities that now exist for everyone from the average horse owner to elite competitors across all disciplines. And what's more, technology can now bring people we used to travel many miles to see or ride with right into our living room, office, or barn via the Internet and television. Now as never before, everyone has the opportunity to learn directly from the biggest names in the horse world, just by clicking a mouse or turning on the television.

The challenge to us now is one of discernment—we have many choices where only a few used to exist. The responsibility falls on us to educate ourselves enough going in to develop a reliable measuring stick.

So, just as you did when choosing the right horse (see p. 119), ask yourself which "lead" is good for you, right now? Even though I do believe that you can learn something from everyone, what we're looking for here is the one person or program that can give you the most of what you need to learn right now, without breaking your bank or destroying your self-confidence along the way. That's your correct lead. It might be an instructor at a local barn whose abilities you will soon outgrow, but she's just right for helping you get your seat back (or finding it in the first place!). It might be an Olympic rider with a great blog and a series of training articles in your favorite magazine who gets you pumped. Or maybe one of the horsemanship clinicians will inspire you the way Clinton Anderson's method inspired me.

Beware Gimmicks, Gadgets, and Shortcuts

There are some folks out there who give training horses and teaching riding a black eye with gimmicks, gadgets, and "shortcuts" that are just plain dangerous to both people and their horses. Horse trainer and clinician Liz Graves (we'll hear more from her later in this chapter) says (with a laugh, but I don't think she's kidding) that whenever she hears the terms "natural horsemanship" or "classical dressage" she takes out a can of disinfectant and gives it a good spray before getting any closer to it. I think that's very good advice for all of us to follow, whichever discipline you're pursuing.

Many paths, one destination

Horsemanship is like religion to some people (and believe me, the zeal and fervor surrounding it can be quite similar). We need to remember that whichever saddle we ride in, and whosever theories we believe in, it's the same center we're all seeking. Like the spokes of a wheel connecting "where the rubber hits the road" to the "hub" of solid horsemanship, there are many "true" paths to follow. As long as we all end up in the center, that place legendary horseman Tom Dorrance refers to as "true unity" with our horse, can we please just agree to disagree on which spoke is the most "pure"?

What do we need to learn from the right equestrian or equestrian program at this point in our journey? In my estimation, must-have skills include:

> ❭ The ability to listen, feel, and read our horse.

> ❭ The ability to communicate exactly what we want him to do in a way he understands it.

> ❭ Sharpened self-preservation instincts (ours may have slipped a little during years of motherly nurturing) so we can be as safe as we possibly can when interacting with a 1,000-pound animal.

The real challenge to all instructors and clinicians is that you just can't explain or teach "feel." That comes only with experience—plain, old-fashioned hard work and time in the saddle. This goes double for learning to "read a horse's insides." But what can be taught—and learned—in step-by-step fashion are the basic horse handling tools and techniques, riding skills, and horse management expertise that will help you lay a solid foundation on which you can build upon in pursuit of your ultimate midlife horse-related goal (whatever it may be).

▓ Look for full circles and common threads

For the purposes of an example I decided to go all the way to the top of the horsemanship tree in my personal midlife horse world. Tom Dorrance is a legendary horseman who was, without question, the "lead" for the natural horsemanship clinicians of today. And , after studying Dorrance's work and words, I could see some common threads among the top programs in the "natural horsemanship movement." It also parallels what horsewomen Linda Kohanov and Deborah McCormick describe from their "softer," more feminine point of view, and echoes ancient Celtic horse wisdom and the early writings of Xenophon.

The most significant common thread here is the importance of establishing a sincere connection with your horse based on respect that honors both the needs of the horse and the needs of the human. The key to this connection is communication—being able to, as Dorrance puts it, "present yourself to the horse in a way that he will understand what you're asking him to do" and at the same time, "Listen to the horse. Try to find out what the horse is trying to tell you."

Another thread that is important in my eyes is (as Clinton Anderson says), "making the right things easy and the wrong things difficult, and always rewarding the slightest try." A jumper trainer, a dressage instructor, and a top reining clinician may all use different words to describe this tenet, but if you can (no matter what) see that this is the same big picture of communication you're working toward, you are on the right track. You're establishing a connection with your horse that allows subsequent learning to flow.

The fact remains that whether we're talking about diet, fitness, religion, or horsemanship, the Great Truths (caps intentional) are the threads that run common to all, even in those that appear to disagree on the surface. Look for these common threads of truth and follow them whenever and wherever you find them.

⦚ Self-paced study: books, DVDs and sideline auditing

Compared to the price of riding lessons and clinics, horse training books and DVDs are cheap. Plus, they give you the singular advantage going back over and over them until you suck out every bit of knowledge you can. When you go back and read the same material a year later when you're in a different place, and your horse is in a different place, you can see and understand things you never "got" before.

Friends ask me, "How in the world do you just sit and watch hours and hours of horse training DVDs? Isn't it information overload? How can you remember anything?" Well, first of all, you don't just sit and watch a horse training DVD like a feature-length movie, beginning to end, with popcorn and Slim Jims on a Friday night. Nor do you read a serious manual on developing equitation in a single sitting like you might a romance or mystery. The key is to take one exercise at a time, watching or reading at most for 30 minutes (and sometimes, not even that long), and then spending however many days it takes to teach it to yourself, teach it to your horse, perfect it, and practice it a few times before coming back and gleaning something new from your study material.

EXERCISE

How to Get the Most from a Training Book, Article, or DVD

Have you ever read a horse training book or article, or watched a great instructional DVD, and thought you understood what the author was saying, but when face-to-face with your horse, couldn't remember exactly how it went? Here's help.

If you have had kids in school, you are probably familiar with the educational science that says the more you can combine/overlap the three basic kinds of learning in a short space of time: visual (seeing), auditory (hearing), and kinesthetic (hands-on doing), the better the retention.

When you watch a DVD, for example, you see and hear instructions, but most of us rely on doing the actual exercise (later, with our horse) as the kinesthetic element. And it is. However, writing down what you're seeing and hearing (just like taking notes in school) forces your brain to process it. Writing is not only also kinesthetic, it "loads" the information you're recording into your subconscious, as well. And, unless you have a big ol' flat-screen in your arena (if you do, can I come over?), writing instruction down just after you see and hear it is the most immediate way to reinforce what you just learned kinesthetically. (Note: It has been shown that for some reason, typing doesn't do the same job of getting the information into your brain as writing does—so break out the old notebook and pen.)

Here, in six easy steps, are my recommendations for making the most out of the masses of affordable horse-related reading and viewing material out there.

1   **Get a lay of the land.** To do this, skim the whole book, or watch the whole DVD, beginning to end, straight through, without giving much thought to application. Just let the information enter your brain and get a good idea of what's there, how it unfolds, and how you're supposed to get from Point A (where you are now) to Point B (what the book, article, or DVD is supposed to teach you to do).

2   **Write down the "learning steps."** Most trainers and instructors outline steps for you; just copy them down. I try to stay with their steps as closely as possible at first, and definitely in the same order. (They've figured out the sequence that works best, after all—that's why they've published a book about it!)

3   **Break "big" steps into "mini-steps."** This can help with retention and is especially useful when fear or anxiety is involved (more on this later). I like to use a plain, spiral notebook with holes already punched to record all these steps. That way I can keep each "log book" in a giant loose leaf binder to refer back to as needed. (You'll be surprised at how many times this personal "reference library" will come in handy.)

4   **Crib your notes.** For whatever reason, the very process of boiling information down to its barest bones forces our brain to understand it well enough to summarize it. I like to make a plain white index card for each lesson I plan on using in the ring, but whatever fits in your pocket works just fine. (Note: Used envelopes are my second favorite, but napkins tend to disintegrate.) The drill here is to make your brain process the information that you wrote down in steps yet again, this time reducing it to the key point of each part that will prompt your brain to recall the rest. Think of it as adding a pathway in your brain—the more you use it, the clearer it gets. Use only the front side of the card, and be as concise as possible (so you can

read your writing in the glaring sun with sweat dripping into your eyes).

5 **Lather, rinse, repeat.** Try the exercise or lesson or tip and see how it goes. Remember two things here to keep your expectations reasonable: 1) The first time you try to teach yourself or your horse something new it may not be pretty, and that is okay. You're really just exposing yourself and the horse to the idea of what you're trying to learn. 2) Your crib notes may need to be redone. Sometimes what you thought would be important or difficult turns out to be no big deal, while some little detail you barely noticed kicks your butt. Just roll with it. After each lesson, making a few notes about it your log book—how it went and what you want to do differently next time.

6 **Refine.** Once you think you've got it, go back and watch the segment or read the article or chapter again. I guarantee you'll see things you'll swear weren't there before. They were, they just mean something to you now that you've tried the lesson or exercise for yourself. Make yourself a new index card (the other one's probably getting pretty ratty anyway) and incorporate whatever new reminders you need to with each step. Keep practicing. Another good way to refine your technique is to splurge on a lesson from someone who knows what it is you are trying to learn. Another set of knowledgeable eyes can help pinpoint small adjustments that can make big differences.

7 **Practice "perfect"—then quit.** As the saying goes, "Practice doesn't make perfect; perfect practice makes perfect." This means don't drill until you're sure you have a move right. It also means don't let yourself (or your horse) get sloppy when you practice. What does that mean? Don't reward half-hearted attempts; insist on the "right way," with careful attention to every detail, every single time—or don't practice at all. There's another important corollary to this rule. Practice something only until you and the horse get it right, then STOP right there. That's right. STOP. Take a nice break, give your horse some love

and yourself a pat on the back, and then, if you must, go on to something completely different.

Dial says this last point is one of the hardest things to do when teaching your horse reining maneuvers. "When your horse does a really great spin, what do you want to do?" he asks. "You want to do it again, because it was fun!" Resist this urge with all your might, and make your self-training and horse-training efforts stick by practicing "perfect," getting it right, and then getting out.

A REAL-LIFE, MIDLIFE HORSE STORY *MANDY*

One of the most dramatic stories I've ever heard about turning a horse around "via DVD" (and part of the impetus for this book) is that of Mandy of Doniphan, Nebraska, and her midlife horse, Peter.

When Mandy first got him, Peter was a stallion and he had terrible ground manners. He'd run over her, pin her against walls, bare his teeth, and just generally be as pushy and aggressive as a horse could be—it approached downright dangerous behavior. Under saddle he was worse, but Mandy actually felt safer on his back.

Mandy was about to give up when a friend loaned her some of trainer Clinton Anderson's DVDs. Feeling a flicker of new understanding, Mandy worked through the exercises on the ground, one by one. She worked with Peter for at least a little while every day, even when that meant doing it under a streetlamp on freezing Nebraskan winter nights.

It didn't happen overnight, but Peter began to improve. Encouraged, Mandy decided to take him to one of Anderson's clinics to see how her self-study measured up. Peter was so out of control at the clinic, Anderson advised she "get rid of that horse before he hurts somebody." But Mandy knew how far Peter had actually come and was encouraged enough by his progress to continue, so she went back home and resumed her DVD study.

Fast-forward nearly six months, and Mandy took Peter to another of Anderson's clinics. This time, it was a different story. Peter was well mannered, would pivot 360-degree turns on cue without Mandy even touching him, side-pass away and toward her, and lie down when asked. Even Anderson couldn't believe the change.

What was the key to this transformation in both horse and owner—and the relationship between them? As important as the training method Mandy chose to use was her willingness to really go out there every day, no excuses and no shortcuts, and just work with her horse. By the light of a streetlamp, she forged a new path for Peter to follow.

Ready to audit or ride in a clinic?

Clinics are a great way to fill holes in your knowledge, take what you do know to the next level, expose yourself to a whole new discipline, ride with those at the top of their discipline, and get out of a rut or off a plateau in your horsemanship journey. When you acquire and practice new skills under the supervision of a clinician who can correct problems before they are ingrained, you have a better chance of success when you're back on your own in the arena.

In addition, since clinic settings generally involve multiple riders and an audience, you get the bonus of seeing how the same knowledge can be reflected and applied differently within variations in temperament, personality, and individual experience—in both people and in horses. I believe it is wise to try auditing a few clinics before you participate on a horse. Not only is it usually much cheaper (and sometimes free!) to be part of the audience than one of the riders, you also learn differently from a clinic by watching how others learn than you do when you're doing the learning yourself.

Clinics are intense, plain and simple. Whether it's one day, three days, seven days or ten, it's information overload—and usually physically and mentally exhausting. But if you choose the right one (that is, it is right for you right now), prepare well, and have a specific strategy for capturing all the information flying at you and storing it in a way you can review and retain it, it's so, SO worth the time, energy, and expense.

▓ Choosing the right clinic

To maximize your clinic experience and learn all you can, you have to be in good physical shape, your horse has to be in good physical shape, and you have to do your homework and choose the clinic that's right for you and your horse for where you really are, not where you wish you were. Can you go to a clinic that's a little over your head? Sure. Can you opt out of activities that are beyond your capability or that of your horse? Usually. Most clinicians respect the edge of your comfort zone and even though some may push you a little, only you can decide when to stay within your range and when—and how much—to push the envelope.

Clinicians often travel region to region, providing a single, multi-day event for a broad area. Watch postings at local barns and show-grounds. Ask around. Information is everywhere, just get in the habit of looking for it. Check with your breed or discipline association (they may have an events calendar online), do an Internet search for the specific type of clinic you're looking for, call local trainers, boarding facilities, and riding instructors, and ask your horsey friends. (Everybody, it seems, knows somebody who went to a clinic last weekend.) Check your favorite rider or clinician's website—clinic schedules are usually public and registration available online.

EXERCISE

finding Your "Dream Clinic"

As with everything else, make a list of what your "dream clinic" would look like, set your intent, clarify your purpose, and open the door to the information you need. Who will teach at this clinic? Where will it be held? What will you learn? You may be amazed by the opportunities that flow your way! (A little "woo-woo," I know, but nevertheless, try it. What have you got to lose besides a piece of paper, a little ink, and about 10 minutes?)

If you don't know what you're looking for, how will you know when you find it? And worse, when you're not clear on what you want out of a clinic experience you can waste a lot of money on the wrong ones! Costs vary, so be sure to shop around, and remember that you usually get what you pay for.

How to make the most of a clinic

Of course, you can just pay your money and show up with your horse, but as I discovered in interviewing both clinicians and participants (and in attending and observing quite a few myself), the secret to getting the most out of a clinic involves good advance preparation, a plan for capturing as much information as possible, and a strategy for processing what you learned and putting it to use when you get back home.

> **Practice at home.** While rider requirements vary from clinic to clinic, be sure to read the fine print on this and, if you can, ask someone who has ridden in the clinic before. You don't want to be overfaced by the height of the jumps or humiliated when the dressage instructor tells you to perform a movement you've

never heard of. Once you are certain the clinic is right for your riding level, ride consistently running up to the clinic dates, for both your sake and your horse's.

This reminds me of a "beginning reining" clinic I took my midlife horse Rio to—I had watched a little reining and thought it was pretty. I had heard it called "Western Dresssage, and that intrigued me. Other than that, I knew absolutely nothing about reining when I had a chance to attend a private clinic taught by reiner, trainer, and clinician, Greg Dial. In this clinic, Dial was going to break down each of the basic reining maneuvers, one by one. I had never considered reining maneuvers

10 Questions to Ask when Considering a Clinic

There are a few questions—other than those related to directions, hotel information, and discounts—when choosing a clinic:

1   What is the scope of this clinic (what will I learn)?
2   What are the rider requirements?
3   What are the horse requirements?
4   What is the physical difficulty of this clinic?
5   What is the ratio of participants to instructors?
6   Will there be help sessions at the beginning or end of each day if I'm having trouble?
7   What tack or equipment is required? What will be provided (or available for sale) if I need it? What are the costs of these items?
8   What health papers and immunizations are required for my horse?
9   What accommodations are provided for my horse?
10 Are there any extra fees or is everything (including horse accommodation) included in the price of the clinic?

as separate entities, because when you watch reining, it all sort of flows together into a beautiful, seamless pattern.

We did a little bit of bending, a little bit of collecting, and all that seemed pretty straightforward. Then we started talking about two kinds of circles, and it was soon our turn to try a "big, fast circle." (How hard could it be, right? I had cantered plenty of circles before.) It was during the first few seconds of our first frenetic attempt at this that I realized I had no idea how to control the size of the circle and the speed of it—and neither did Rio. What we did was about the farthest thing from any circle I've ever seen. "Y'all don't do much of this at home, do you?" Dial asked in his wry drawl, trying very hard not to smile. Funny man.

) **Desensitize, desensitize, desensitize.** Try to ride in a few group scenarios before the clinic, but if that's not possible—or if your horse is especially jumpy and sensitive—it still pays to spend a little time desensitizing him to things he is likely to encounter so you get your money's worth of education at the clinic, instead of spending hours calming a manic mount. This can include flappy signs and banners, loud noises, groups of people, strange obstacles, a PA system, and unusual cues and touches from you. Use your imagination and try to think about what you'll be seeing and experiencing at the clinic from the horse's point of view.

) **Build your endurance (and your horse's, too!)** The other thing I never realized about a clinic is how gruelingly hard it is. Most of us midlife horsewomen do horse chores, most of us ride, occasionally for pretty long stretches. But there's something about the combined intensities of physically participating in a clinic, while mentally trying to learn and absorb all you can, and then sustaining this combination of physical and mental effort all day long, for several days straight, sometimes in extreme temperatures. The experience can take you to a whole new level of fatigue.

Processing New Information in a Learning-Intensive Environment

At the end of each clinic day, after you've unsaddled, fed, watered, and tucked your horse in for the night, take a few minutes (before dinner and that glass of wine) to jot down the things you want to remember from the day. Use your spiral notebook or your laptop—just do it.

Remembering the details about clinics, I've noticed, is like remembering those funny things your kids used to say when they were little. You think you will remember special moments forever because they are so important to you, but after lots and lots of these moments get layered, some of them tend to fade away or get muddled. Write them down (summarized in just a few words—you can fill in details later) before you relive the day with other clinic attendees. If you talk about your experiences first, and write about them later, you may get your impressions mixed up with those of others.

At a writer's workshop, of all places, I learned that studies show that when we tell a story verbally first, before we write it down, our writing of it is weaker, somehow diluted, because we've processed it into expression once before. Apparently, the first time information flows out of your brain, it's in its purest form; after that, any repetition of it is censored or "reprocessed."

With your "clinic notes" neatly organized on paper or computer, you'll have a source of visual "cues" to remind you of other things you learned. When you get home, the details will come back to you, and the important lessons from your clinic will be there waiting to be incorporated into your riding or training "action plan," whenever you're ready for them. Don't leave important insights, discoveries, and ideas in the dirt of a faraway arena—you did pay for them, after all!

In the weeks running up to a clinic, build a little extra personal fitness time into your day (go back to chapter 4 for ideas on how to do this), and gradually increase your horse's endurance, too. Try to spend longer and longer stretches in the saddle to get your own body acclimated to extended riding workouts. Think of how marathoners train—alternate short, intense rides with longer, more leisurely mileage.

Working with instructors, coaches, and trainers

Since one of the recommendations prior to getting a midlife horse was to taking a few (at least) riding lessons, you are likely already familiar with private instruction. Lessons with an instructor, coach, or trainer can provide remedial help when you're stuck, refinement of technique for competitive purposes, or specific help when you need to work through a particular problem.

Private instruction in this context can vary greatly. For you, it can come from an elite, certified riding instructor in your discipline, someone accomplished in his or her own right and who has a knack for breaking things down and a gift for teaching. There are also "coaches" who are combinations of personal fitness trainers and equestrians, or psychologists and equestrians. For your horse, you might find a trainer with expertise in "finishing" a nice riding horse, or perhaps one who specializes in dealing with "problem horses." Sometimes, a fantastic rider can teach your horse a whole heck of a lot. The key to this "someone" is that he or she has solid experience (and plenty of glowing referrals), and his or her training and riding philosophy aligns with your own.

Instructors, coaches, and trainers are valuable at all levels and in all disciplines, because they can see what we can't see in our own riding or in our horse's behavior. Therefore, they can be the magic ingredient that leads to your ultimate success. "Private instructors and trainers give us the tools we need to make good decisions when we are alone with our horse," says Emily Kutz, dressage rider and equine massage therapist. Even periodic work with an instructor or trainer keeps us moving forward, she adds.

How do you find a good instructor, coach, or trainer? The answer is, it really depends on what you're trying to do. Nevertheless, here is some basic guidance to help you get started:

Instructors

These individuals help riders develop skills at all levels, from basic, general horsemanship skills to the most advanced maneuvers and applications. Asking for recommendations from riding friends and boarders at your barn is a good way to start. There are also several US organizations that certify instructors: The Certified Horsemanship Association (CHA), American Association of Horsemanship Safety (AAHS), and American Riding Instructor Association (ARIA). Instructors can be members of these associations without being certified by them, and certification requirements differ by organization. Check out all three and see which includes the kind of instructor you're looking for. Certification means they have been exposed to rules and procedures and have passed an exam that reflects competence as measured by the standards set by an organization—and that this level of competence has been verified by a reputable source. Note: There are plenty of great instructors who have never been certified by anyone.

Trainers

Horse trainers vary widely in their skill, experience, philosophy, and background. Generally, a "trainer" is going to be more focused on the horse side of the equation than an instructor (although in some geographic regions and disciplines, it is common to say you "train with so-and-so," and thus your "instructor" is considered your "trainer").

Sometimes, especially when you're trying to solve a specific problem or you're working toward a specific goal, finding a trainer for your horse who is willing to work with you on your horse is a great advantage. Often, this means putting your horse in training with someone

Certified Horsemanship Association (CHA) Instructor Levels

While this example of instructor levels by no means indicates a preference of one organization over another (I just happen to be more familiar with this one), the CHA certifies instructors at eight levels, and describes them as follows on their website www.cha-ahse.org:

> **Assistant** English and/or Western, qualified to assist in a lesson or trail ride, under the supervision of a certified instructor.

> **Level One** Qualified to provide foundational instruction to beginners, with a strong emphasis on safety and group control; candidates must demonstrate ability in ground handling, mounting, correct position, and control at walk-trot.

> **Level Two** English and/or Western, qualified to improve all aspects of the first level, and progressing through canter/lope, including diagonals, balance of horse and rider, pre-jumping exercises, Western patterns, and trail riding.

> **Level Three** English and/or Western, qualified to coach students in improving form, style, and understanding of the natural aids, including basic jumping, school figures, and leads with a greater emphasis on horsemanship theory and horse care.

> **Level Four** English and/or Western, qualified to improve the performance of advanced riders and their horses, including jumping courses, dressage movements, reining, and other performance events, advanced horse management and horsemanship theory.

> **Master** Qualified in Level 4, both English and Western; highly experienced in a variety of teaching and management situations; recommended to direct horsemanship programs.

> **Assistant clinic instructor** Minimum age 21; qualified to assist in certifying instructors.

> **Clinic instructor** Minimum age 25; qualified to conduct CHA certification clinics and certify instructors with assistance from another CHA clinician.

full time, then traveling to the trainer's barn to take lessons on your own horse.

If you have more than one horse, having the same trainer working with each one has the added benefit of quickly finding any weaknesses in your own riding or training technique—because usually, each of your horses will have an issue related to your weakness.

When it comes to finding a trainer for your horse, the people I talked to agreed: Referral is king. And, if you are a competitor, find a trainer competent in the discipline and at the level you want to show, and who works with the breed of horse you're showing. Here are the best tips I heard for finding the best fit for you and your horse:

> **Referrals** Without a doubt this is the most important piece of the "find-a-trainer" puzzle. What constitutes "good," beyond a few basics, will vary with your purpose, and some trainers are better at some things than others. It is, therefore, largely up to you and depends on your ability to pinpoint exactly what kind of help you're looking for—as well as an honest assessment of where you are and what you're ready for as a rider. Ask around your peer group, canvas horse shows, riding stables, horse expos and trade fairs, breed associations, and often, tapping your vet, farrier, and feed rep for information isn't a bad idea. The horse community—as global as it is in one sense—is still a small world, and a good trainer's reputation is usually well-known, as is a bad one's.

> **Experience** Often, quantity of experience isn't nearly as important as quality. Do your homework, make your list of what's important to you, and be sure to ask a prospective trainer:

How long has he/she been training horses?

How many horses has he/she trained?

What's his/her specialty? Colt-starting? Problem horses?

What is his/her training process/philosophy? Where did it come from?

Did he/she work in a professional capacity prior to training horses in your discipline (as a cowboy, jockey, or judge, for example)?

) **Way with horses** Watch a prospective trainer interact with your horse. (Some trainers provide a free evaluation.) Ask yourself:

Does his/her manner seem compatible with how you deal with your horse?

Are you comfortable around him/her?

Does your horse seem comfortable?

Do you agree with his/her approach and philosophy?

Does he/she seem to be accountable and have integrity?

Does what he says about your horse ring true? Are his stories consistent?

) **Instruction** If the trainer will also be working with you, it is a good idea to take a lesson with him/her. As you ride, consider:

Are his/her explanations easy to understand?

Is he/she willing to answer all your questions fully and patiently?

Is he/she competent at the level you're aspiring to, and can or will he/she give you visual demonstrations as needed?

Does he/she provide the type and level of correction you're look-ing for? (Some people respond better to "strokes" while others thrive on "tough love.")

Do you leave a lesson inspired and eager for the next one—or at least with a full understanding of what you need to work on for next time?

Trainer Agreements—What You Need to Put on Paper

It's a good idea to sit down with your prospective trainer and iron-out a written agreement that stipulates each of your expectations. This can be as simple as a single sheet of notebook paper with points written by hand, or it can be a bonafide legal contract. The goal is to prevent misunder-standings that could later undermine your relationship. Points to cover in this agreement include:

> **Price and terms of training fees** Know what the trainer will charge you, what is included in his fee, and what is potentially bill-able (feed, accommodations for your horse, equipment and sup-plies, travel and other expenses). It's a good idea to agree on a not-to-exceed limit for any expenses without prior approval from you in writing. As examples of "terms," several common ways to break payment down include: half up front and half at the end; one month up front, with monthly installments thereafter; or a third up front, a third at the training period "midpoint," and a third at the end.)

> **Training schedule and frequency** Indicate the number of times a week your horse will be ridden by the trainer, as well as the num-ber of times a week/month you will work with the trainer on your horse (if applicable).

> **Goals of training** What is the hoped-for result? What do you want for your horse? For you? For the two of you together?

> **Duration** What is the expected time it will take for the trainer to accomplish your training goals?

> **Checkpoints** These are dates when progress notes/verbal reports will be provided. Will you be allowed to watch training sessions?

> **Transition plan** It is important to have a transition plan in place for bringing your horse "home," as well as instructions for maintaining his progress on your own.

> **Follow up** To maintain progress and address any questions or problems, it is a good idea to arrange for a series of lessons with the trainer once your horse comes home. You may also want to stipulate that the trainer be available for phone or e-mail consultation for a certain number of months following his work with your horse.

> **Exit clause** Create a provision for early termination by either party if things don't work out. Writing this in now while you're both still happy makes it much easier if things happen to go south over the course of training.

On students and teachers and schools of thought

As with most things, "becoming a student of the horse" has many facets. First, there is theoretical knowledge, which is what you get by reading, watching, listening, and asking questions. Then there's practical knowledge, which is what you gain from actual experience, or "butt-in-the-saddle" time. Finally, there's transferal knowledge, the two-way learning that comes from teaching what you know to others, and deepening your understanding through their process of learning. This, it seems, creates a circle of learning in which the student perpetually becomes the teacher and the teacher perpetually becomes the student. This, my midlife horse friends, is one elite circle you want to be invited to join. But as with all elite circles, you first have to be invited, and then you have to pay your dues.

When the Doctors McCormick advised me and the other attendees at her Equine Experience Retreat (see p. 12) to "become a student of the horse," I thought that meant to read all the items on the list she handed out (see the Resources—p. 311—for this list), and to maybe take some classes and study the considerable theory that lurks behind every dressage and equitation maneuver. However, it turns out that, as I discovered with my midlife horse Trace, theoretical knowledge will only take you so far. To develop the "muscle memory" that makes you effective in the saddle, your muscles have to actually remember doing it, not just reading about it (or writing about it, for that matter). And this is where good teachers—those clinicians, instructors, coaches, and trainers—come into play.

Learning to learn

Although Everett Mrakava, a Canadian horse trainer, is not a woman in the middle of her life, the story I am about to share reflects an important lesson on the difference finding the right teacher can make to even the most experienced of riders.

Mrakava grew up on a ranch in South Alberta, Canada. As the youngest son and only child still at home with older parents, he learned everything he knew about horses and cattle from hands-on experience. At age six he became his father's only hired hand; he was little more than ten when he started his first colt. When Mrakava was just 16, his father was badly injured in an explosion, so he singlehandedly calved their 200-head herd while doctoring, feeding, and caring for the horses, and keeping the ranch in working order. It goes without saying, then, that when Mrakava took his first clinic at age 20 with Peter Campbell, a horse trainer and clinician who learned from Tom Dorrance and worked with Ray Hunt, Mrakava felt like his practical knowledge was pretty solid.

"Trying to teach him something new was like trying to drive a nail through an anvil," Campbell relates. "I guess I was pretty full of myself," Mrakava admits. "I knew what I knew from doing it, and I wasn't interested in listening to all that stuff about basics."

For whatever reason, Mrakava stayed at the clinic, and he says that a week later, when he saw how much difference Campbell's exercises were making in his horse and in others, he understood the value of finding the right teacher. Six months later, he participated in another clinic, and he has been a dedicated student of Campbell's ever since.

"I always felt safe with Peter," Mrakava says of Campbell. "When things got tight, he told me what to do, and I learned to do it without question. Who he is and what he does with horses changes people's life. He changed the insides of me so I could start thinking about the insides of a horse."

The only way to really own what you learn about horses and riding is to do it, Mrakava emphasizes, and then to go back to your teacher from time to time to learn more. "As long as Peter is in this world, I know that there is always more I can learn from him," he adds.

When the teacher becomes a student

She was pretty far along by anyone's standards on her horseman-ship journey when horse trainer and clinician Liz Graves encountered a frustration that is familiar to many, if not most of us. "I have engaged for several years now with a deep-seated frustration in my own riding skills," Liz wrote on her blog. "I kept trying to find the feeling in my own seat I remember having as a child." This feeling of the horse "giving himself over to her" 100 percent and "working within the same energy and gravity in perfect timing and harmony," was something only Graves knew she was missing. "Most people never knew there was more than what I was getting, but I knew," she says. "It was not complete for me yet."

Graves went through a period of mourning this loss—wondering if her body structure had simply changed or if the wear-and-tear of years in the saddle had somehow made it impossible to find that place again. She says she could see what she wanted happening in others, but the feeling still eluded her. Then the door opened for Graves when her friend, rider and trainer Peggy Cummings (www.connectedriding.com) came to the ranch for a visit.

When Graves shared her private frustration, Cummings—who founded Connected Riding® and Connected Groundwork®, a method of helping riders and horses regain their elasticity, and learn what it's like to move without bracing patterns, compression, and counterbalancing—knew just what to do. "So to work on me she went, and my heart was singing," Graves writes. "I felt what I had been seeking again."

"The single biggest gift we can give our horses is becoming 'live weight' whether on the ground or in the saddle," says Cummings. "When we can learn to rebalance our bodies in motion while remaining upright over ourselves with our joints moving freely without bracing or clamping on the horse, we can truly be 'in sync' with his motion."

In the months that followed Cummings' visit, Graves followed the instructions for the exercises they had practiced together, then flew out to Cummings' place in Washington for more help. "I had to know if I was getting it just right," Graves recounts, "What an experience it was; one I will take with me forever."

In finding just the piece of instruction she was seeking Graves once again became part of horsemanship's never-ending circle of learning, from teachers, students, and horses. She says the experience impacted her as a teacher, reminding her of what it takes to be a good student.

As a teacher of both humans and horses, Liz Graves encourages students to explore every nook and cranny of each solid, hard-earned experience by "working on themselves, for their horses and through their horses, as part of their lifelong journey as a student." She says that this piece of the horsemanship puzzle is achieved by working hard, not only in the physical realm, but in the emotional realm of finding "emotional maturity" and "emotional wisdom" to help those that follow us in seeking the same path. These are the teachers we want to find—and the teachers we want to become.

⦀ Finding the teacher

Above all, when you're choosing a teacher, learn to discern. "Please don't be one of those who walks around with 'eyes wide shut' as the saying goes," Graves implores. It is very easy to be confused and misled in the world of marketing, and the uneducated consumer's demands tend to motivate manufacturers and retailers to step up and provide what is asked for. "It's sad so many folks have been led astray due to unethical teachers looking to keep the public confused for their own personal gain or reasons," Graves says. "It's up to us to open our eyes and really learn how to see with them."

In an effort to help us as we set off on this part of our midlife journey, whether searching for or waiting for our "teacher to appear," Graves offers us 10 signs that an individual is an ethical teacher of humans and horses. An ethical teacher:

1   First looks out for the safety and well-being of their students.

2   Is in touch with both truth and reality so horse and human can experience success.

3   Helps horse and rider become the best they can be within their abilities without physical or emotional harm.

4   Teaches with truth and honesty, never holding a student hostage to his or her own limits or desires.

5   Is honest in telling students when they have reached the limits of his or her teaching abilities and directs them to the best teacher to take them to the next level.

6   Offers the simple reality that any true success is about correct work done in a reasonable amount of time.

7 Recommends proper supportive aids if need be but never allows the student to fall victim to the belief that shortcuts, gadgets, or gimmicks can bring them to the highest level of quality horsemanship.

8 Is a listener of the student and the horse, firm if need be, but never a bully.

9 Knows themselves to also be a student.

10 Always strives to improve him- or herself and his or her abilities.

Horse Trainer Liz Graves: "What I've Learned As a Teacher of Horses"

> The horse will tell you how well you are doing by his actions.
> Making mistakes is part of learning; never deny when you make them, the horse knows anyway.
> Don't miss seeing willingness in the horse and rewarding it.
> Reward any amount of "try" a horse presents, and he will want to try some more.
> Show the horse simple acknowledgement that he matters.
> You will come to a place where you no longer care what other humans think or how they may try to influence you; it will only matter what the horse thinks.

Discovering That Journey Called Horsemanship
By Elizabeth Graves

Break free from the traps, those of others and our own.
Seeing the reality before us, then trying it and finally living it.
Honesty to one's self first, present honesty to the horse,
this is when the door opens, and when a horse truly gives itself over to you.
One never really finds this place until we enter the place of self-discovery,
of what we are in our strengths and weaknesses,
admitting them, accepting them and working on them.
It is a place one starts to discover, learn, grow,
it's a place with no end.
In this place, horse and human are both teacher and both student,
showing, giving and sharing with each other.
Each respects and reflects what the other has to offer.
True horsemanship is not of power or of control but of just being,
allowing, learning to let happen in its own time,
when communication between two different species is clear, understood
and reasonable to both.
True horsemanship has no place for trickery, hiding, or games,
but opens up curiosities in each other, horse and human.
It brings understanding, while finding comfort in their own skins and with
each other,
rewarding with enjoyment in their time together.
It is in thinking WE, not me, that we find that working relationship
with a horse.
More is not always better, but less can be more.

Starting at ground zero

Although there is no "one right way" or "single path" to good horse-manship, regardless of which "lead" we choose, the basic steps we all take are very similar. In learning how to deal with a horse at midlife, you kind of have to start from ground zero. You need to be able to work independently, study books, articles, and DVDs, and strive diligently to acquire a solid set of fundamental horse handling skills. You need to go to clinics, and seek out instructors and trainers so you can learn more, hone those basic skills, and acquire new ones. You need to be both patient and ambitious, both student and teacher. You need to step up to your place in the circle—go ahead, you've earned it.

12

Plateaus and ruts— and FEAR...Oh My!

When we start out on this midlife journey, we might imagine it's all exhilarating gallops on grassy fields and sandy beaches, but the reality is, having horses in your life is just as likely to challenge you at times as it is to fulfill you in ways you desperately need. It's easy to get stuck, and there's a good chance that something, somewhere along the way may scare you back OUT of the saddle. Here are a few useful tools for conquering the fears that having horses may bring to light.

SOMETIMES, DESPITE OUR MOST diligent and disciplined study and conscientious effort, and sometimes even after attending clinics and working with instructors and trainers on an individual basis, we can still find ourselves "stuck."

Sometimes we encounter things with our midlife horse that just require us to, as they say, "put on our big girl panties and ride." Horses are always testing and challenging the pecking order in their herd. If, in your own little herd of two, you seem to be the one "getting pecked," it may be time to lay down the law. Sometimes—no, wait, make that ALWAYS—this is much easier said than done.

At one of the Clinton Anderson clinics I attended, my midlife horse, Trace, really let loose and gave his "hell pony" exhibition. Every time I mounted, he started prancing and bunching up his back the minute my butt touched the saddle. I immediately responded with a one-rein flex to pull his head around before he could get going (and possibly launch me), but when I released his head, he started right back into his hop-kick-hop-kick dance.

In the long version of this story, I'd tell you all about the previous day's antics and how Anderson's assistant trainer solved the problem by getting on him and getting his feet moving. And how today, she sat on the fence and helped me gain the upper hand, turn by turn. The problem was, we followed this display with work at the lope in the group, and I couldn't help but notice a whole lot more "hump" in his back as he cantered. The ceiling suddenly seemed lower, and I had the uncomfortable sensation that I was riding on the back of a jackrabbit. This was not his usual canter.

But the clinic was over, and I was about to head home, where I didn't have a trainer who would sit on my arena fence and prevent the situation from spinning out of control with sensible solutions to Trace's behavior. I was more than a little bit nervous about getting on my horse by myself. Was I afraid? You betcha. In no way could I justify taking the chance of getting hurt. Was it time, like my dad advised, to get rid of my "problem horse" before he hurt me?

In her book *For the Good of the Rider*, author and instructor Mary Wanless describes the two opposing forces in a frightened rider: the desire to ride, and the fear of falling. "Bold riders can rarely understand how the nervous rider is caught between these two cohabitating forces," she writes, "They expect her to ride and be brave, or not to ride at all."

Yeah, that was pretty much it. I knew I was plenty capable of riding Trace. I knew how much I wanted to ride him or I wouldn't still have him. But all of a sudden, I couldn't make myself get on him and just ride through this place we had somehow gotten ourselves to.

Wanless describes what she calls "a catastrophe curve," in which at lower levels of stress (such as riding a giant jackrabbit while being supported by a knowledgeable someone, telling you what to do and when to do it), performance increases up to a certain threshold. But at the point where the performer perceives a mismatch between the demands of the situation and her ability to match them (riding a giant jackrabbit alone in an arena back home), there is an onset of anxiety in which performance drops. Once the performer falls off this curve (and performance drops), this "catastrophe theory" (proposed by Dr. Lew Hardy and Dr. John Fazey, who borrowed it from French mathematician Rene Thom) says that it requires a large reduction in stress before even the original skill level can be found.

Clearly, even though nothing really bad had happened at that clinic with Trace, I had somehow fallen off "the catastrophe curve." As a rider, I was regressing, and it was all in my head. What was it going to take to climb back on the curve? And more importantly, back on my horse? What had taken root in me that was "stealing my bliss"?

"If you're not fallin' off, you're not ridin'," the old saying goes. And it's not like I haven't fallen off plenty in my life. What was the big deal now? How could I incite my love for my horse to grow greater than this suddenly towering fear of riding?

Putting fear in its place

Let's just say it. Sometimes, we're just plain afraid. Sometimes there's a good reason; sometimes it's just that vague awareness of what could happen. To help us all learn to stop the fear snowball before it rolls right over us, I talked with Dr. Matt Johnson, a certified sport psychology consultant and licensed professional counselor in private practice in Fort Worth, Texas. Johnson frequently works with members of the Texas Christian University equestrian team (as well as other TCU athletes) on performance-based issues, anxiety, and fear. Dr. Johnson agreed to help dissect the very real fear many of us will encounter when we start riding horses in midlife so we can put the potentially debilitating struggle in its proper place and get back in the saddle with newfound confidence (leaving white knuckles in the dust!)

The function of fear

Fear, as much as we dread the feeling, is not a bad thing in and of itself. Often, it's the very thing that keeps us safe. When it gets out of proportion to actual danger, however, it can be, at worst, debilitating, and at best, a big damper on your fun with your horse.

"Fear is a natural part of being human," Johnson says. "Our job is to separate the productive fear that helps keep us safe from the non-productive fear that hinders our performance."

Because fear is such a powerful emotion, he goes on to explain, the more we think about it and try to force ourselves through it, the bigger and more powerful it gets. Because anxiety is related to our perception of our skills and knowledge, fear can distort these perceptions and make everything seem much worse than it actually is.

A REAL-LIFE, MIDLIFE HORSE STORY *BARBARA*

When Barbara (whom we first met when she gave up city life and moved to the country—see p. 142). While out riding with friends one day, a freak, ill-timed hop over a stream caused a tumble that was later determined to have fractured a vertebra in her back. After six long weeks in a back brace and complete disruption to her life, Barbara discovered something she had never had before when it came to horses. Fear.

Her injury healed and she rode again, but there was a new uneasiness where her bravado used to be. She wondered if she would ever be truly comfortable riding again. Were her carefree riding days over? As her enthusiasm for riding waned, but her love for her horses continued, she sought help from a young instructor, an eventer (which, I think, by definition means "without fear") who proved to be wise beyond her years. Barbara's first lesson began with a very important question: "What exactly are you afraid of?"

"I'm afraid that something weird will happen and I will come off, and I will be hurt so badly I won't be able to take care of myself and my family, and the rest of my life will be ruined," Barbara replied.

The young instructor was silent for a moment. "Okay," she said, "then we'll go back to the very beginning and rebuild your confidence, step by step."

Over the next six months, they worked together several times a week, taking one little step at a time, leading Barbara right up to the edge of anxiety, staying there as long as possible, then going back to something she felt really confident about. Gradually, as she grew stronger and more accomplished—her riding skills improved dramatically—her confidence came bounding right back. She has since gone on to do many remarkable things with horses, and although no longer debilitated by a fear of being injured, she has a new regard for safety that, the truth being told, will probably do more to keep her safe in the saddle now than if the accident had never happened.

Sometimes fear comes not from something that actually happened, but from the idea that something bad might happen. I have to assume that this has something to do with our mothering gene, which has been on high alert for signs of danger since the moment our babies were first born and began to move around on their own. We've been scanning the "horizon" for potential hazards for years, so it only makes sense that it can play a factor in our midlife horse journey.

Six exercises for conquering fear

In order to put fear, whatever its cause, in its proper place, and work through our "fear distortions," Dr. Johnson offers the process—made up of six exercises—that he has found to be successful at all levels of endeavor. You'll need one of the good ol' spiral notebooks you've used for earlier exercises, and a pen or pencil.

EXERCISE I: WHY DO YOU RIDE?

To help us remember our passion for riding horses in the first place, Johnson first asks us why we want to ride, and what we want to get out of it. Writing as fast as you can without censoring, jot down anything that comes mind about riding a horse that makes you want to do it.

"The simple act of writing (and reviewing) this list will help keep you in touch with your passion," Johnson says. "I want you to remember what you love about riding horses in the first place."

EXERCISE II: WHAT ARE YOUR GOALS?

If fear were not an issue for you, what would you want to do with your horse? Trail ride? Compete? Liberty work?

1 Make a list of specific goals you have—or would like to have (your "horsey dreams," if you will).

2 After completing this list, rank your goals in order of importance.

3 Now set aside some time over the next several days (as many days as there are dreams on your list) and each day, for about 15 or 20 minutes, go to a quiet place and imagine yourself fulfilling one of your goals. Don't just picture yourself doing these things, imagine how it would feel. Engage as many senses as possible and imagine the sensation of:

That sliding stop underneath you, followed by applause and whistles from the crowd.

The motion of your cutting horse as he "gets after" a cow.

The grace and strength of the horse lifting you up and over a fence, followed by the splash of water as you head out toward a wide expanse of green on a cross-country course.

Moving in perfect sync with your horse as he completes flying changes in a dressage test, then standing before the judges as you make your final salute.

Trotting down a beautiful trail on a perfect spring day.

Sleeping under the stars while camping out with your horse, then waking up at sunrise for a beautiful ride before breakfast.

Swimming your horse in a lake.

Obviously these "visions" could go on forever, but you get the idea. Since our brain and subconscious cannot tell the difference between an actual event and one vividly imagined, a good bout of multisensory imagination can store a memory as well as an actual event can!

EXERCISE III: WHAT CAN YOU DO? HOW WELL CAN YOU DO IT?
To help you work through a specific fear, such as fear of cantering, Johnson now asks that you make a list of everything you can do related to the horse, starting from the second you get to the barn or pasture, all the way up to whatever you're afraid of. To make this even simpler, I've provided some prompts—can you:

- Catch the horse?
- Pet the horse?
- Lead the horse?
- Tie the horse?
- Groom the horse?
- Saddle and bridle him?
- Get on the horse?

❭ Walk and trot the horse?

❭ Do a one-rein stop at the walk and trot?

❭ Canter a few steps?

❭ Canter on a loose rein?

1 **What can you do?** In your journal, rewrite each of the above questions in the affirmative and personal (i.e., I can catch my horse). If cantering isn't the thing you fear, create your own list.

2 **How well do you do it?** Rate your comfort level with the items on your list, from "1" to "10," ("1" being "No way, Jose!" and "10" being "Piece of cake!")

Johnson says that more often than not, when he asks people to read their list of competencies aloud, they are surprised at how much they do know, how many things they are confident about, and what a small part of the "big picture" the fearful thing really is. "Fear can make a lack of confidence in 20 percent of the competency required to canter a horse feel like 80 percent," he adds. "It's only by breaking it down in this way that we can put fear into its proper perspective."

3 **What's it going to take?** Now, choose any number on your rating scale that is less than "10" and ask yourself why you chose that rating. Write your explanations in your journal, followed by your initial thoughts on what you think it might take to move the rating to the next number down. (Think: Baby Steps!)

EXERCISE IV: WHAT ARE YOU AFRAID OF?

Johnson says that it's important to identify exactly what you are afraid will happen, starting with the biggest, baddest fear and working down to the smaller more annoying ones. So get out that journal and let's delve into the dark place.

1   Write down your fear. Write down each of your fears in as much
    detail as possible. Leave space beneath each entry, because you'll
    be coming back to them.

2   Write how you currently respond to each fear. Under each entry,
    write down everything you can think of that you might do in
    response to the particular fear. (Note: Squealing, wetting your
    pants, and running away are all respectable answers here.)

3   Write down what skills you'd like to have to address this issue. For
    example, if you're afraid your horse will start bucking when you
    ask him to canter, you might want to learn to recognize when he's
    about to buck. Or you might want to learn how to ride through a
    buck. Maybe both.

4   Assess where you are now. Rate your ability (from "1" to "10") right
    now to do the skill(s) you identified in Step 3.

5   Map your path to a "10." Make a list of all the possible ways you
    could acquire or improve the skills you need to respond effectively
    to the fearful situation you identified in Step 1.

EXERCISE V: VISUALIZE SUCCESS—WITH ALL YOUR SENSES

1   Imagine the fearful situation as if it's occurring right now. In this
    powerful multisensory visualization exercise, you not only mentally
    see yourself in the fearful situation (such as a horse that's kicking up
    or starting to buck), but you imagine hearing the sound of his hoof-
    beats, smelling the sweat on his flanks and neck, and feeling his back
    rise underneath you as the dreaded hump appears in his back.

2   Imagine yourself responding effectively with impressive skill. See
    yourself remaining calm during this exchange. Feel that hump dis-
    appearing as you get your horse's feet moving forward. Hear his

feet come to a stop and his sigh as he relaxes underneath you. Smell the sweat you generated (on him!) when you made his feet move.

Being able to visualize in this way—using all your senses—is a skill that sometimes takes a little practice. The better you are at multi-sensory visualizing, however, the more powerful its effect will be. As I mentioned earlier, Johnson explains (and science confirms) that our brain and subconscious really can't tell the difference between a vividly imagined event and one that actually occurred. "The more you can use your imagination to engage all your senses," Johnson reiterates, "the more powerful your visualization will be and the more it will take root in your brain." So if you can visualize vividly enough to make your brain think you've done something before (and your subconscious has that memory), it will know that you can do it again! If you can't do it at all, it is important to move back down the list of competencies you made in Exercise II (see p. 274) and find something you can visualize yourself doing well.

Johnson says that another way to visualize success is to find a model that is as much like you as possible, and watch that person negotiate the situation you see as fearful, with ease. Although this is no substitute for your own visualizations of yourself doing these things, it does augment that image.

EXERCISE VI: CREATE AN ACTION PLAN OF SMALL, ACCOMPLISHABLE STEPS

This is where the process becomes very individual, Johnson says. Each person must determine exactly where her starting point is and which steps will take her from that place to the place where she'd like to be.

Once you find your starting point—that place where your confidence starts to wear thin and your fear begins to gain momentum, go back to chapter 11 (see p. 258) and determine the type of instruction or learning experience that will help you improve your competency.

Breathe Into Your Belly to Avert a "Spook"

Here is an extremely powerful technique borrowed from the yoga world. When you feel that old familiar stab of fear in your gut, take a deep breath and imagine that you are pushing it down through your belly, down into the ground, like coffee in a French press. This action grounds that feeling of fear (kind of like a lightning rod).

Several experts agree that in order for this to work when you're on the back of a horse, you have to first feel the fear and acknowledge it (the horse knows you're afraid and you earn his respect by being present with it rather than denying it), then breathe it down into the ground. As you do, you will "sweep" the fear from your horse's body along with your own.

Nipping fear in the bud—keys to a safe horse

For many of us, it is a random act (or a habitual one) on the part of our horse that first awakens our fear or fears. Such a reminder that our horse is an independent being with a mind (and fears) of his own, and therefore not entirely under our control, can really "kill the joy" our midlife horse experience was meant to instill.

Is there really any such thing as a "safe" horse? While there is no foolproof system for keeping you safe when you're dealing with a 1,000-pound animal that has a mind and will of his own, here are a few tips for building maximum safety into your midlife horse experience. This comes down to consciously creating safe habits and practices, as well as remembering a few important safety tips from the experts.

▓ Safe habits

Creating safe habits means learning what you need to do to be safe on the ground and in the saddle, and then doing those things the same way every time you work with your horse until they are as automatic as the safety habits you use when driving a car. It does take some effort at first, however, especially if you haven't been around horses before or in a long time. Even experienced horse handlers can unwittingly grow careless over the years, so it never hurts to take a good look at your habits to make sure you're doing everything you can to keep yourself safe to ride another day.

> **Teach your horse to respect your space.** This is not something you teach once and forget, but like holding the line when raising a teenager, you must "patrol this fence" regularly. Let me share a short story that tells you why: My midlife horse, Trace, knows that the way to get out of doing anything he isn't enjoying is to lower his head and come put his face up against me. We both know that melts my heart, and on the surface it appears as submissiveness. It's not. That's because he knows that when he does this I will immediately stop asking him to do the disagreeable thing and rub his face. Now you tell me, who has trained who?
>
> After a time, I unknowingly let this habit slip. A trainer who happened to be giving a lesson at my boarding facility noticed this and commented, "That horse is always getting into your space and you're not doing anything about it. That's why he doesn't respect you." Wow. If she could see that just from watching us work in the round pen for a few minutes, it suddenly became breathtakingly clear to me that this little problem I had let develop wasn't so little at all. In fact, it just might be at the root of the Big Problems we were having.

> **Insist on two eyes.** This is akin to the personal space thing, but relates more to when you have the horse on a lead or lunge line and he's either not cooperating or completely ignoring you. As horse trainer Clinton Anderson often says, "A horse cannot kick you or run away from you if he's got both eyes on you." So bump on that lead rope to keep both eyes on you at all times.

) **Pay attention to where you're standing.** This is a big one that's easy to let slip. Most of us know not to walk right up behind a horse (even one who knows and loves us) without announcing ourselves. Horses have a blind spot back there and sometimes—not always—they'll kick first and ask what it was they hit later. Where's the safest place to be? At a 45-degree angle to your horse's front shoulder, most experts agree. There you're out of kicking range, you can't be run over or clobbered by a pawing front foot, and you can easily get out of the way if the horse starts to come toward you.

) **Tack and untack the same way every time.** This may sound a little obsessive-compulsive, but in this case, it doesn't hurt. A few years ago renowned horse trainer John Lyons wrote an article that recommended we always groom, saddle, and bridle in the same order so we will never skip a step. I've stuck by this since then. The routine ensures every snap is snapped, every buckle is buckled, and there aren't any burrs, bumps, or wrinkles waiting in hiding for you to clamber aboard so they can give your horse a surprise pinch.

) **Tighten your girth/cinch three times.** This tip from Clinton Anderson is near the top of my list of safe habits, especially for horses that tend to "puff up" (hold their breath/distend their belly) when you first saddle up, as one of mine does. This is also easier on the horse than yanking that girth or cinch tight the first time (something Anderson compares to having someone yank your underpants up over your head). The first time you tighten the cinch, get it just barely snug. Walk your horse or do a little groundwork (five minutes or so) and snug it up again. Then, just before you get on, tighten the cinch the rest of the way. If you've ever had a saddle slip to the side of a horse (or even underneath as I once did) you'll understand the value of this tip.

▥ Safe practices

) **Mess up your hair, not your head—wear a helmet.** The English-riding midlife horsewomen have it easier in this department, since helmets are traditionally part of the attire (although less so in the dressage world, so future DQs, heed this advice). For those of us who ride Western, helmets are just not cool. And, while lots and lots of people ride—and even fall off horses every day without wearing helmets and escape permanent injury, the inflexible reality remains. As my riding friend Margie once put it, "it doesn't take much of a bump on the head to ruin the rest of your life."

The good news is helmets are getting better, even a little more stylish (they now have some covers for these things that are downright fun! Check them out at www.equestriancollections. com and www.helmetcovers.com). They are becoming more commonplace, even in groups where you would have never seen them before, and the United States Dressage Federation recently passed new rules that extended mandatory helmets to higher levels of competition.

The even better news is that at this point in our lives, we are beginning to care less and less what other people think, and if we happen to look a little bit dorky while protecting our noggins, we don't really give a rat's behind. Putting up with a little bit of "helmet head" means that if you do happen to take a tumble off your horse and slam your head on a rock, you will most likely be able to ride again—and enjoy the rest of your life in a non-vegetative state.

) **Install an emergency handbrake—practice the one-rein stop.** A true one-rein stop, the kind that gives you a real emergency brake, has to be taught to your horse and practiced a LOT to be effective. It is more than simply hauling your horse's head around to one side. It should be practiced at EACH gait, EVERY time you ride, so when you have a problem, the one-rein stop is your automatic response, and your horse's automatic response is to obey it. (See recommendations for learning the one-rein stop in the Resources, p. 311.)

) **Get control of nervous feet**—teach your horse to bend in a circle. This is another deceptively simple exercise that can be a lifesaver when you need to get control of a horse that is nervous or panicked. Bending your horse first this way and that can take his attention away from something he finds scary and put it on you, where it belongs (see sidebar, p. 284).

) **Shut off the power**—teach your horse to disengage his hindquarters. Every time a horse does something dangerous—like bucking, bolting, or rearing—it requires power from his hindquarters. So when you feel things starting to head in the "danger" direction, the very best thing you can do is to take away that power. Apply heel pressure right behind the girth or cinch until your horse's back leg on that side crosses in front of the opposite hind leg. This move needs to become as automatic to you and your horse as the one-rein stop.

) **Bail out safely**—learn and practice the emergency dismount. In the April 2008 issue of *Horse&Rider* magazine, reining champion and horse trainer Stacy Westfall provided five steps to practicing a safe emergency dismount. They require a quiet horse, a (patient) friend to lead him, and a good amount of upper body strength. Begin at the walk before trying it at other gaits.

1 Sit on the horse with your feet out of the stirrups, looking straight ahead, and holding onto a hunk of mane with both hands.

2 Lean forward, pressing down on your horse's neck (keeping hold of that mane) and shifting your weight onto your hands.

3 Supporting yourself on your hands, swing your right leg up and over the horse's back until your legs are parallel and hanging straight down off the near side of the horse

4 Controlling the speed of your slide down with your arms, prepare to push yourself away from the horse.

5 As you push away from the horse, twist your body counterclockwise so that you land with your feet facing forward and moving at the same speed as your horse's.

Believe me, when it comes to protecting your safety, any time it takes to prepare your horse is time well spent. And honestly, once you get used to horses that know how to do these things, you really don't feel safe on one that doesn't! As far as I'm concerned, it's a good way to be spoiled.

Bend It Like Francis

Australian horse trainer Ian Francis offers this method of asking your horse to go forward and bend in a circle at the same time:

1 Press with your inside leg (closest to the inside of the arena) on the middle of the horse's side in order to push the rib cage to the outside and get a little bend in your horse.

2 Use a direct rein (the inside rein) to bend him laterally to the inside.

3 Press with your outside leg behind the girth to create forward motion or impulsion.

This combination of pressures urge him to go forward and shape his body around your leg. Practice at all three gaits. (See Resources, p. 311, for information on Ian Francis' training DVDs.)

Safe Outfits: Protective Gear Worth Considering

Besides the good ol' helmet, which I mentioned already as being number-one important when staying safe on horseback, here are a few other riding accoutrements that can help keep you safe (and make you feel safer) while in the saddle:

> Always wear boots with a 1-inch heel to prevent your foot sliding through the stirrup and getting caught.

> Consider safety stirrups or putting safety cages on your stirrups, intended to prevent a foot getting caught in the stirrup in the case of a fall (check out www.sidestepsafetystirrups.com, www.breakawaystirrups.com, and www.smartrider.net for more about these).

> Wear gloves when you ride for a better grip on the reins and to protect your hands from rope or rein burn, or blisters.

> Consider a protective vest when you are in the saddle. Protective vests are commonly used by eventers, and several models are now being marketed for recreational use. Lightweight, breathable, allowing complete range of motion, yet protecting our necks, torsos, tailbones, and even shoulders and collar bones when we fall (that is, if we fall), they may be just enough added insurance to get many of us Nervous Nellies back in the saddle. (Check out www.smartpakequine.com and www.crazyhorsetack.com to learn more.)

Remembering what this is all about

Even though this midlife horse journey had romantic beginnings, it is only to be expected the hard truths of having and riding horses will rise up and challenge us along the way. In other words, "the road ain't paved the whole way." But when it is fear that is keeping you from truly enjoying your horse and all he has to offer you, do not lose heart. Fear is a conquerable thing, and being safe around horses is something we can be proactive about. Forge on, midlife sisters. Don't forget that our horses are mirrors—if we're afraid, it is likely pervasive in other parts of our lives, and dealing with it in the saddle helps us deal with it elsewhere.

13

From the horse's mouth

Trouble with a horse, the great horsemen of our time will tell you, almost always comes down to some kind of breakdown in communication— and more often than not, the breakdown is on our end. Here are some surprising insights on taking your horsemanship to a whole new level by learning to listen to your horse.

AS WE HAVE TRAVERSED THE PAGES of this book together, I've shared some of the trials I have experienced with my midlife horse, Trace. By now you know that his general distaste for anything on his back, and the resultant bucking, had led me to veterinarians, nutritionists, farriers, masseuses, and saddle fitters (not to mention trainers and clinicians). Some things helped, some things didn't, but still, the problem remained: I couldn't ride my horse the way I wanted to.

Here is where I admit I called an animal communicator. That's right. Sure, in a certain sense I was grasping at straws. However, I had the name and phone number of a woman that a friend of a friend had called (initially sort of as a joke) and gained some surprisingly accurate insights about what was going on with her show horse. I figured neither I nor Trace had much to lose at this point.

"Oh dear, you have a real problem on your hands," was the woman's summation of the situation. "He's telling me that nobody is ever going to ride him again. He hates it, has always hated it, and he just isn't going to put up with it anymore." The animal communicator recommended I get rid of Trace and get a horse that was more agreeable. I asked her to check in with Rio, and she said, "Oh he's a sweet one, and he really loves you. He is wondering where you've gone. Is he turned out somewhere else?"

Well, he was. I had been so busy working I had turned him out at my parents' place and hadn't really even seen him more than few times in the last couple of months. Every spare minute had been spent working with Trace.

"If you keep this other horse, you're going to need professional help to get him past this resistance," she said, adding that she couldn't imagine why I would want to keep a horse that felt the way he did about being ridden. I was starting to wonder myself. And yet, something in me still didn't want to let go.

Take out your "inner garbage"

As if in answer to my silent "Now what?" plea, Canadian horse trainer Everett Mrakava (we met him in chapter 11—see p. 262) appeared in my life a couple of weeks after I called the animal communicator, and I took him up on his offer of a "free evaluation."

"Easy, easy," Mrakava said to me as I loped Trace—not happily, I might add—around the smallest round pen at my boarding facility.

"Easy, easy," I echoed, trying to reassure away the "knots" I felt in Trace's formerly smooth (remember my first ride on him, when I defied better judgement and bought him?) forward motion. Oddly, his "knots" were not unlike the knots in my own stomach.

"I was talking to YOU," Mrakava said. "The horse is doing just fine."

Oh. I thought, slightly embarrassed. Whose side is he on?

With Trace behaving more and more like a complete ninny, Mrakava got on him, and loped him around the round pen.

"He just feels really lost and bothered," Mrakava told me. "He's all tied up in knots on his insides and he needs to learn how to get all that worked out and let down on the inside. He's a good horse."

Well wasn't that interesting—and a little bit embarrassing. Suddenly I felt exposed. Of all the money I'd spent on therapists trying to make sense of my own emotions and responses to life's ups and downs, no inkblot could have been more revealing of my own psyche. Remember all that "mirroring" mumbo-jumbo we talked about in chapter 2. In the process of imagining himself inside my horse's skin and feeling what he was feeling, Everett Mrakava had hit the nail on the head—and me between the eyes with the Great Truth of this midlife horse experience I had been searching for all along.

"Solving problems with your horse is so often not as much about training the horse as it is dealing with your own inner garbage," says Mrakava. "When you get rid of your own baggage, you'll free up your horse—and that is when you'll start to get good with your horses."

Horses are prey animals, Mrakava reminds us. Their very survival depends upon their ability to read the emotions of others in their herd. "Your relationship with your horse is a 51/49 partnership," he says. "A horse will test you every day to make sure you're still the most qualified to be in charge. Sometimes this doesn't take but a few seconds, but you still have to earn your 51-percent majority seat every single day."

Well, okay. But how best to earn that majority seat? If we can take anything from the great horsemen of our time, you can do this by learning how to communicate with your horse, how to read him like he reads you, and how to understand the lessons his actions teach you about yourself.

How to communicate with your horse

I've always known that there are people who can communicate on different frequencies than the rest of us. One of them explained to me a while back that for her, it's like a radio dial (remember those?), where you can turn the knob and hear lots of signals in varying strengths all the way across the dial, you just have to slow down and move back and forth until you find just the right spot where the signal comes in clearly. When it comes to "psychic" communication, she continued the analogy, saying some people's brains are simply "wired" to receive more signals than others, and they can pick up some "stations" clearly that others can't hear at all.

Science has known for a long time that we only use a small percentage of our brain's capacity. It is also starting to understand how light, energy, and information travel and connect all kinds of things from the tiniest particles of light to living, breathing organisms. This is actually plain old quantum physics, and trying to get my mind fully around it sort of makes my brain hurt.

So, when you consider that science certainly doesn't rule out the possibility, and when you think about how dramatic our other differences from one another can be—in terms of mental, physical, and emotional development and capabilities—why, does it really seem so farfetched that some of us might be able to communicate on different frequencies, and even on the frequencies of animals?

A REAL-LIFE, MIDLIFE HORSE STORY *KENDRA*

Kendra, a law student, was worried about her very successful Western pleasure horse. He was not performing well and had, in fact, begun misbehaving rather badly.

An acquaintance suggested Kendra call an "animal communicator" that she knew of, to see what was going on.

Skeptical, but willing to spend $35 on a phone consult to see what the animal communicator had to say, Kendra made the call.

Law students, by definition, need solid proof in order to believe something. Kendra got it.

"He prefers to be called Topper," the animal communicator told her. Although Kendra shrugged at the time, she went back through her horse's papers a little later, and sure enough, the name Topper was very prevalent.

"He really likes Kimmy because she has long fingernails, and he likes it when she scratches him," the woman went on.

"Kimmy" was actually a friend of Kendra's from childhood—and no one else but Kendra called her Kimmy. Kim did have long nails, she did come to the barn occasionally to see Kendra, and she did scratch this horse with her nails while she was there.

"He's a little worried because he heard you tell Kimmy you were thinking about selling him," said the animal communicator. Sure enough, that conversation had occurred the last time Kim visited.

The clincher came when the woman told Kendra that her horse was really, really warm. "Well, yeah," Kendra replied. "It's August in Texas, and we're all 'really really warm.'"

"No, he's exceptionally warm and he is getting very worried about it," the woman insisted. "It's really, really getting hot in there where he is."

Immediately after the phone call, Kendra went out to check on her horse in his air-conditioned barn, chiding herself for calling this "crackpot" in the first place. When she got to the barn, she discovered that the air conditioning was, in fact, off in his stall and he was drenched in sweat.

From that day on Kendra called her horse "Topper," and he returned to his good-natured and high-performing self.

⦀ Dolittle demystified

Julie Dicker and Anna Clemence Mews explain the kind of communication between animals and humans that I just dared allude to in their
book *What Horses Say* (Trafalgar Square Books, 2004). Dicker, an animal communicator and healer who helped hundreds of horses and
their handlers over the course of her lifetime, described what she did
as "working with the invisible energy that surrounds all living creatures,
defined loosely as 'energetic material.'"

"This vast sea of energy in which we all swim," write Mews and
Dicker, "whether we actively perceive it or not, connects us to every
form of life from an earwig to an elephant, from a snail to a stallion.
Some individuals are able to make this 'connection' more easily than
others, although it is almost certainly a dormant talent within all of us."

Dicker, for her part, said that horses communicated with her in pictures—visible images as well as sensations or feelings in her own body.
"If I don't get a kind of inner voice or a picture, then I get a feeling of
where it's hurting in the horse, reflected in my own body," she said.
It was Dicker's fervent belief that by opening oneself up to the possible connection to "universal energy," it is indeed possible for anyone to
give and receive information from a horse—or any animal, really.

"If you want to improve communication with your horse," Mews
and Dicker share in *What Horses Say*, "love is the first and most important factor...Then you need time. Plenty of it. Don't rush, be patient.
Keep things very simple. Have no expectations. Place no judgments. Be
an observer looking in. Just look and see things as they are. Watch."

⦀ Learn to "read" your horse without interruption

Whether you dare flirt with the idea of touching down on the field of
"universal energy," the fact remains that across the board, the majority
of talented horse trainers today list *observation* as the first step to
developing honest and meaningful communication with your horse.

In the bestselling book he wrote with his wife—and fellow founding star of the hit show *Cavalia*—Magali Delgado, renowned liberty trainer Frédéric Pignon says that he has to learn to "read" a horse's "thoughts" by watching the movements of the nostrils, ears, eyes, and through them decipher the horse's overall attitude. A horse is always telling you, through subtle signs, how he is feeling.

"I always watch the horse with every fiber of my being," writes Pignon in *Gallop to Freedom* (Trafalgar Square Books, 2009). "I not only try to read him with my senses of sight, hearing, and smell, I concentrate my mind on communicating my own thoughts and listening to his. I concentrate so hard that other thoughts are excluded."

Pignon goes on to say that when you work with horses and ask them to pay complete and total attention to you and your wants or needs, without giving them the same uninterrupted attention in return (he uses the example of answering a phone call while in midst of a lesson), you risk ever regaining the horse's full attention again. So *watch* your horse, *read* the subtleties of his equine language, and *concentrate* while doing so, and you're well on your way to forming a reciprocal "conversation" with him.

Where your horse's personality comes into the picture

Renowned animal communicator and trainer Linda Tellington-Jones founded the Tellington Method® in the 1970s, and since then has traveled the world teaching others how to better communicate and work with their horses (and other animals, too) via her unique form of body-work (TTouch) and ground and under-saddle training (TTEAM). By understanding who your horse really is, you will better know how to approach him when it comes to training him, whether on the ground or from the saddle, and the greater the likelihood you will communicate clearly with him, and he with you.

"It seems clear to me," Tellington-Jones writes in *Getting in TTouch with Your Horse* (Trafalgar Square Books, 2009), "that the individual personality of any creature isn't a fixed 'thing' at all, but more like a kind of continuous dance of communication that goes on between an individual and the surrounding world."

In other words, your horse certainly brings some character traits to the table, but his environment, his health, and his interactions with—yes—you, all impact the sum total of what we might refer to as his "personality." And it is this personality that we are trying to read, decipher, and get in tune with in order to better transmit what it is we are asking (or emphatically not asking) on a day-to-day and moment-to-moment basis.

Learning how to evaluate your horse's personality can help you determine whether he is the right match for you, for your discipline, for your trainer, for the herd he hangs out with (or doesn't), and perhaps how to deal with related problems should they be apparent. (Tellington-Jones insists you'd be amazed at the issues that can seemingly melt away once the root cause is understood—I believe her! With Trace, however, it just seems I'm still mining for that darned "root.") Most importantly, "knowing your horse's innate tendencies allows you to correctly evaluate and even predict behavior under a variety of circumstances," and then adjust your reactions accordingly. And this, in many ways, is the very basis of horse-human communication—it's not so much about "seeing pictures" as it is about plain old knowing your horse and developing "feel."

How to analyze your horse's personality

Tellington-Jones uses a form of personality analysis based on the ancient tradition of measuring the type and number of swirls (or "whorls") on the horse's head as indicators of character type (hair swirls on horses are the equivalent of fingerprints on humans, she says). Her technique combines observation of a horse's physical features and conformation—specifically, the head—with the swirls on the horse's body to provide a framework for "reading" your horse's personality at a glance. I should add that much of the work she's done in this area has the backing of statistical surveys and studies.

EXERCISE

Mind Your Body Manners

"All horses, whether domestic or wild, tell the truth," writes Ryan Gingerich, *The Behaviorist*, in his book *Beyond a Whisper* (Trafalgar Square Books, 2010). "Nothing a horse does is wasted motion or mis-communication...We, on the other hand, are not tuned in to our movements, our body language, or our posture...We aimlessly swish our arms around. We make funny faces that have no purpose and carry no meaning...Most concerning of all, we are never consistent."

The danger here, which Gingerich mentions in his book, is that we are unknowingly but quite often "lying" to our horse. If you ask your horse to halt next to a riding friend, but then in the course of having an animated discussion tighten your seat slightly or grip just a bit with your legs, your horse may likely move off, in response to what he believes is the cue to go forward. And you will just as likely correct him—perhaps even sternly with bit pressure and a loud, "Whoa!" But was he really disobeying?

The next time you work with your horse, whether on the ground or in the saddle, pay extra attention to your body language, vocal habits, and barn or arena "rituals." Take note of where you wave a fly away from your face—an instinctual reaction on your part, but a motion that your horse may "read" as he would the flick of the ear of a herdmate. Does he raise his head in surprise? Do you "correct" this reaction?

Remember, horses primarily communicate with each other via body language, and they are sensitive enough to touch to feel the smallest of flies that lands upon their flank. Every time you rub your nose, shake your hair from your eyes, scratch your thigh, or even shift your shoulders back when you feel your end-of-the-day slouch coming on, you are telling your horse something. Do your best to become aware of this constant flow of unintentional messages, control it, and you'll clear the airwaves for some far more valuable conversation.

I'll refer you to Tellington-Jones' excellent book *Getting in TTouch with Your Horse* for a complete description of her technique, specific instructions, and fascinating photographic examples and case studies, but in a nutshell, here are some of the physical characteristics that can point to specific personality traits, and thus dictate how you should "speak" to your horse, how you should "listen" to him, when to reach out, and when to leave him alone, when to chalk it up to a bad day, and when to get worried that something may be amiss. Believe it or not, according to Tellington-Jones' form of personality analysis, "good communication" can all boil down to the shape of your horse's head and understanding what that means:

) Is your horse's profile straight, dished, or roman-nosed?

) Are his jowels large, medium, or small?

) Is his muzzle sloping, square, refined, or rounded?

) Is his mouth long or short?

) Is his upper lip stiff or extended?

) Is his lower lip flapping or drooping?

) Are his nostrils narrow and inflexible, large and open, or shapely and well-defined?

) Is his chin pointed and hard or long and flat?

) Are his eyes, large, soft, hard, small, or almond-shaped?

) Are his ears long, short, or lopped?

> How many swirls does he have on his head? What do they look like?

▥ A teacher appears

Clear, consistent communication is precisely what legendary Amercian horseman Tom Dorrance was most likely referring to when he said, "The best thing I try to do for myself is to listen to the horse . . .I try to feel what the horse is feeling and operate from where he is." Dorrance says that to understand what is taking place inside a horse, people need to be able to picture what he is seeing and experiencing and then to be able to get themselves into that picture. What's more, he recommends picturing your training commands: "When a horse is standing—before you ask him to go forward, back, left, or right—have a picture in your mind of what you are going to ask him to do, and how you expect him to respond, before you start."

This surprising common thread between animal communicators like Julie Dicker and Dorrance is some of that gold we've been mining for all this time. And, when you start to weave this thread into how you deal with your own horse, you just may find yourself on the path to the meaning, magic, and mastery you've been looking for since the beginning of this quest.

By going all the way back to the teachings of Dorrance, I found a new understanding of the gentle wisdom that spanned more than eight decades and brought to the world of horsemanship to a kinder, gentler way to look at horses. Dorrance was truly the "granddaddy of them all" when it came to understanding the inside of a horse, and thanks to his book *True Unity*, and Maravilla Productions' *A Day with Tom Dorrance* DVD, I had him right in my own living room where he sat and patiently explained everything I needed to know to try to get "unstuck" with my horse. (You can invite Tom Dorrance to your house, too. Go to www.tomdorrance.com.)

Did he give me the magic incantation? The secret handshake? The decoder ring? Well, sort of, but it's gonna take a lot of brain rewiring, soul searching, time, sweat, and elbow grease to make it work. More than that, it will take my slowing down, listening to and watching my horse, and then digging deep inside myself to find "a better way of presenting myself to him." It will take examining exactly what I am doing—from Trace's point of view—to feel what he is feeling and operate from where he is—not where I think he should be. With that understanding as my backdrop, I was ready to start the work of figuring out how to set boundaries with him that honor his needs and feelings, even as they made what I want him to do the priority.

In doing all the talking and very little listening, not only had I ensured our communication was somewhat lopsided, but in operating completely from my own needs (and fears!) rather than his, I was not only missing the point, but I was actually making matters worse. This shift in focus made it very clear that while the more mechanical learning I hade done up to that point was necessary to get to this place, the new part of the climb was suddenly a very different one—like a hike when it reaches the timber line. Granted, the way before me was rocky, steep, and unfamiliar, but I could see the summit and an occasional glimpse of the magnificent panorama that lay beyond.

Of his legendary work with horses, Tom Dorrance wrote, "The part that has meant the most to the horse and me is the communication between us. This is the part where I really had to devote a lot of thought...by studying their actions and reactions I have been helped to understand how to present myself in such a way that the horses will respond to what I may ask of them...this is something I have had to develop in myself, for myself, by myself. The 'True Unity' and 'Willing Communication' between the horse and me is not something that can be handed to someone, it has to be learned, it has to come from the inside of a person and inside of the horse."

An immovable object

Our assignment now is to "find a way to present ourselves to the horse in a way that's understandable to the horse."

"What exactly does that mean?" we might wail. In this world of how-to, self-help, quick-fix, and spoon-fed instant gratification, and with all the black-and-white thinking and acting we've worked on earlier in this book, isn't this just one big, fat grey area? Yes. And no. Using the tools, the mechanics, the techniques we've acquired via instruction and study, we can now start to discover for ourselves how to apply this knowledge on the fly, working with our horse's response to what we're asking and adjusting our request (or, as Dorrance says, "how we present ourselves to him") until what we're asking him to do aligns with what makes sense and is more comfortable to him.

A great example of this appears in *A Day with Tom Dorrance*, as Dorrance and fellow horseman Larry Mahan taught a problem horse to back up. Mahan simply held pressure on the horse's bit steady—not tight, not pulling, yanking or sawing, just solid, even contact that created an Immovable Object (caps intended). Mahan waited for the horse to figure it out.

At first, of course, the horse tried to push through the bit pressure. Then he tried to shake his head and get rid of it. Finally he realized (you could almost see the light bulb come on over his head) that the only way to get away from this Immovable Object was to back up. Voila.

The object, then, of everything we want to teach our horse to comes down to figuring out how to safely create an Immovable Object, and then wait for the horse to figure out the answer that puts his idea in line with our own. "Then instead of turmoil, we find a way to work things out so that the horse is happy and [you're] happy," Dorrance explains. "When you can work things out that way, horses will work their hearts out for you."

"Pet your horse"

Another important lesson from Tom Dorrance that will make our nurturing middle-aged hearts sing is that it's not only okay to pet our horse, but it's exactly what we should be doing. "I've always spent a lot of time petting my horses," Dorrance says. "Lots of people had things to say about that—they told me to 'quit that or you'll spoil that horse.' I never paid much attention."

One thing I noticed about my problem child Trace early on was that for all his high-headed stinkiness and independence, he loves to be "loved on." Some horses, Dorrance says, are not really trying to be bad—but like a child, they are craving "their person's" attention. Most people don't recognize this or know how to present themselves to the horse in a way that satisfies the horse's need for attention but still allows them to keep the "majority seat" (see p. 289). Instead, they may punish the horse, thinking they're doing the right thing by "sending him away" and not letting him "get away with it."

"This is not a good situation," Dorrance reflects in his interview with Mahan. "Then, pretty soon, [the horse is] just lost. I always try to set things up so that the horse would rather be with me than any place else on earth."

How to read your horse like he reads you

Dorrance's idea of "presenting yourself to your horse" seemed odd to me, at first. Sure, I know all about body language and nonverbal communication—that is part of what we learned from Deborah McCormick and "moving a horse from the inside" and from finding our "inner lead mare" (see p. 12). But how does this all tie together?

"Presenting yourself to your horse," as Dorrance tells us, is where the variation comes into your training. If a horse is "tight and tense and buggy-eyed" (it felt a little like Dorrance was talking directly to me and Trace with this description), you need to "present yourself" in a relaxed manner in order to bring him down to your own energy level. It is apparent, then, that "reading your horse" is a significant part of this equation.

▥ Learn to recognize your horse's expression

So how do we do this? What exactly are we looking for? If you've seen that cutsey little "This is what sad looks like..." photo series of cats depicting emotions that circulated the Internet for a while, apply this oddly accurate unit of measurement to your horse. Take some time to just study your horse and become familiar with his mannerisms.

> ⟩ **What does "normal" look like?** Spend a lot of "down time" with your horse, just watching him, learning his usual mannerisms. It is important to establish a baseline of comparison so you can pick up anything different in his actions and expressions.

> ⟩ **What does "let down" look like?** Learn specific signs in his demeanor that tell you when he's relaxed or "let down" on the inside. And, by the same token, learn what the first signal is that he's starting to feel anxious or "tight."

> ⟩ **What does "I get it!" look like?** When a horse understands what you're asking him to do and willingly responds to your request, you know you've presenting the idea correctly. Learn what in his demeanor says "I understand!" so you can recognize the signs that you're doing your part right.

> ⟩ **What does "I'm humoring you" look like?** Sometimes a horse just goes along with something we ask him to do, but he's not that happy about it. Learn how to recognize the signs of this feeling in him so you can be ready to respond the split second this reluctance turns to tightness or refusal.

> ⟩ **What does "I'm outta here" look like.** Okay, this is the most important one—and with some practice, you may not have to see it very often. When you notice the signs your horse is "so over"

whatever it is you are doing, it is time for a quick response to redirect his negative energy and get his mind on something new.

How to understand the lessons your horse's actions teach you about yourself

"I believe that horses naturally have tremendous faith in the human being," writes Tom Dorrance. "It is their natural instinct of self preservation that the person needs to understand in order to gain the confidence of the horse." And, it appears, vice versa.

After the utterly exposing "evaluation" I'd had with Everett Mrakava that I told you about at the beginning of this chapter, I'd decided to have him work with Trace for a while. I had a lesson on Trace after Mrakava had been riding him for about three weeks. I was on the lunge line and Mrakava was walking beside us, asking me to relax my "insides" and feel the horse moving underneath me. He asked me to tell him when each of Trace's feet touched the ground. In a few laps around the arena, this assignment went from completely impossible, to kind of hard, to almost doable.

I didn't really "get" the exercise until the end of the lesson, however. After walking, trotting, a little bit of cantering, and changing directions, all on the end of that line, Mrakava asked me to exhale— let all the air out of my body and look down at the saddle horn. Trace stopped. Then he lowered his head. Then he sighed, too. And just that suddenly and simply, I felt a connection with my horse I had never experienced before. I now realize that moment was the turning point in the tumultuous relationship between Trace and me, and the true beginning of our journey together.

full circles and half-passes

Sometimes the midlife horse journey is a jagged path to success, where progress just doesn't always follow a straight line. In fact, sometimes it looks a little bit like going backward. And sideways. And occasionally, in circles. But if you examine these experiences closely, chances are good you'll find the lesson you came looking for, disguised as a horse problem that you must solve to continue your journey. Bless these things—they're your pot of gold at the end of a long, colorful rainbow.

"YOU KNOW, THIS IS LIKE TRAINING A 60-year-old man," horse trainer Denise Barrows said, heaving herself up and across Trace's back, belly flopping into the saddle and reaching across to slap his opposite side. "There are certain things we're going to be able to change about how he reacts to things that annoy him, and there are just some things we are going to have to accept. He's pretty much who he's going to be." She rubbed his neck, all the way up to his ears, and then waved her hand over his head. Trace's head shot up, giraffe style, and even though his eyes were still soft, he was clearly annoyed.

What was even more interesting to me, however, was that instead of coming completely unglued, as he had so often in the past, he didn't move. Head still straight up, he started licking his lips. Barrows and I laughed at the same time, clearly sharing the same thought. Clinton Anderson and many other horse trainers agree that, in horses, licking the lips is a sign of submission, or as Monty Roberts calls it, "Join Up." This horse was clearly neither submissive nor "joined up." He was, however, tolerating Barrows' unending silliness and seemed mildly interested in seeing what she was going to come up with next.

"Ah, there we go," she said, sliding all the way to the ground and patting his shoulder. That's right where we want him to be: okay with whatever crazy thing we're doing, not reacting to it, but paying attention because he can't figure out what's coming next." She handed me the reins.

"This is never going to be a bombproof, jump on, put-the-reins-down-and-go kind of horse. You're always going to have to stay one step ahead of him mentally—keep him guessing by being a lot less predictable so he can't take control." She laughed. "He's just a control freak and he's always going to try to outguess you so he can be in charge."

What a funny thing to say about a horse, I thought. I wished I could say she was wrong, but I knew she was right. For some reason, I have always been drawn to control freaks. And I think I might be one myself.

Barrows continued, "He's gotten so good at groundwork and at reading your body language, he knows what you're going to do before you do it. You feel like you're in charge, but you're really not. That's how he takes the control away from you. He's not being bad, right? He's doing everything correctly, right? So what's wrong with that?" She paused. "He's calling the shots and you don't even know it!"

How in the heck did that happen? How could I not see it?

How many trainers does it take to change an older horse? What about an older rider?

For me and for my midlife horse Trace, at least one more, apparently. In the book I wrote with him, *Lessons Well Learned,* Clinton Anderson says that retraining older horses can be done, but it takes a lot more time and energy. Comparing it to the grooves of an old vinyl record album, he said that new ideas and training take a while to get as deep in the horse's brain as the things the horse has been doing the same way for years upon years. For many people, this is rarely worth it. For me, however, it had become a calling. A personal challenge. Somewhere, I think, I knew there was an important life lesson (and it turned out to be several) in this struggle, so I pressed on.

When my friend Margie told me about Denise Barrows, a trainer she found and really liked, I nodded politely. I was done with trainers. I was done with spending money. I was done with new points of view. But in making my list of all the things I was done with, I realized I had backed myself into a corner. If I didn't want to have a 1,000-pound dog, and I didn't want to get on him myself, I was going to have to find some help. By then Barrows was riding horses for several other people I knew, and she was highly recommended by everyone she worked with. Her company, Practical Equine Solutions, was largely devoted to helping people solve problems they were having either with their riding or with their horses. Or, as was usually the case, some combination of both.

Watching her ride one morning, I noticed the quiet way she rode, slow and deliberate at times, energetic at others, but all the while relaxed and easy with the horses she rode, and they all seemed to be performing well and having a good time doing it. When I spoke with her about Trace, she said she'd take a look and see if she could help.

She could. I realized she was the perfect fit for Trace's quirkiness, with just enough sympathy for his issues laid over a resolve of steel and zero tolerance for his antics. Over the next few months, starting in the round pen, we worked together, under Barrows' direction, to teach Trace that bucking was the incorrect response to ANYTHING. Once Barrows was satisfied he had learned that lesson, and we had him thinking, we started making real progress—even under saddle.

With an older, been-there-done-that kind of horse like Trace, Barrows told me, you have to push him harder, but in smaller steps. "Eventually he won't need to be pushed as much," she said, "but for a long time (possibly years) he will need to know that he *does* have a job—paying attention to you every second you're with him. He needs to know you expect him to work hard, and he needs to save his energy and focus for it."

My horse, she explained to me, is very driven, athletic, and needs a lot of rules and reasons. Like an older person, he feels entitled to his opinions and he doesn't mind making us mad. Like a teenager, he's going to push the envelope to see if boundaries are real and still in place. And, like a child, he needs small steps, rewards, and discipline. The bottom line is that in dealing with Trace, I have to constantly challenge him and make him think—not about what he wants, but about what *I* want.

Now, after nearly four months of working twice a week with Barrows, I'm back on my horse at last. I'm finally learning to ask clearly for exactly what I want (left rear foot cross under, bend around my inside leg, shoulder in, shoulder out), and accept nothing less than what I ask for. What all of this boils down to, Barrows tells me, is focusing on exactly what I want, being very clear in how I communicate that, and refusing to accept anything less.

In considering her last point, I have to wonder if this is maybe exactly what brought Trace to me—and me to him—at this point in my life in the first place.

Are you being "chumped" and don't even know it?

Clinton Anderson calls the kind of trouble I'd run into with Trace "chumping you in a thousand little ways." I've heard him say it, clinic after clinic, to shocked women who thought their horses were doing everything just right. Now I knew exactly what he meant. When I asked Barrows what to do about it, she said, "You're going to have to be a whole lot pickier with him."

Here's what that "being pickier" means in short form. (And of course, like so many things in this horse world, it's all very easy to say, much harder to do.)

) **Be clear in your own head first.** Know exactly what you want and stay two or three steps ahead of your horse at all times. No room here for muddled thoughts, multitasking, or wandering focus. (I quickly realized how namby-pamby I'd been—in many areas of my life—sort of knowing what I want, but not locking down on the specifics. Was the clarity I'd been looking for in my life directly related to the clarity Trace was forcing me to find in the arena?)

) **Follow through.** When you ask for something your horse already knows how to do give him one chance to do it and then get after him in a big way. "There can never be any wiggle room for a horse like Trace," Barrows admonished. "Ask clearly one time and he either does it or he gets in trouble. The good news is he really doesn't like to get in trouble, and after two or three times of getting in trouble for the same thing, he usually decides it just isn't worth it." (I'm thinking this is advice I can also apply in raising my teenager.)

) **Be consistently inconsistent.** This one is a little murkier, but the bottom line is to keep your horse guessing. According to Barrows, in groundwork, riding, and even grooming—being unpredictable is the key to keeping his attention. "Don't ever do things the same way twice," she elaborates. "If he thinks you're going to trot next, walk. If he wants to go left, go right. If he speeds up and you didn't ask for it, slow him down; if he slows down and you didn't tell him to, pick his speed back up. Every time there's any choice at all, make SURE you are the one who made the choice." For me, a "go with the flow" kind of person who's just happy to be riding her horse again, this is maybe the hardest thing. Why upset my riding buddy when things are otherwise going so well?

"That's how he does it," Barrows said when I mumbled something to this effect.

"Does what?" I replied.

"Gets back in control of things," she said. "It's one little sloppy response here. Another one there. Then a pattern starts to emerge. Next thing you know, he thinks about bucking. To stay ahead of that curve you have to keep him thinking, keep him guessing, challenge his mind to figure out what you want. Anytime he gets to the point of bucking, you need to remember that it means he's been calling the shots for a long time and you didn't realize it."

Older horses have layers

Of course, the prospect of eternal vigilance outlined by Barrows seemed tiresome, if not completely daunting. Was this a battle I want to fight for the rest of my horse life? Do I really want a teenager that will never grow up? Would the situation with Trace ever change?

Not for a long, long time, Barrows told me. "Remember, he's been this way for 15 years, and it has worked well for him. But just like he builds up to being in control one little disobedience at a time, you can re-establish control in a similar way."

Barrows explains that we can push an older horse harder, because he has had more years of surviving scary things but with an older horse you have to break things down into much smaller steps. Take things very slowly, one at a time and enjoy little successes. This is all about the journey, anyway, isn't it?

Now where have I heard that before? The long-term goal, Barrows explained, is not a horse that is simply compliant—just putting up with being ridden—but one that is fully committed to accepting a rider on his back. In the past, Trace had just been pretending. Now we wanted him to do everything we asked, and not just the parts he chose. "It's a process," Barrows said. Because Trace IS older, this kind of commitment will only come in baby steps, layer upon layer, over time...and only if I meet his commitment with one of my own. (Will this horse *ever* stop airing my personal issues in front of the horse trainers I hire?)

My part in this, Barrows told me, is the commitment to do what needs to be done consistently, give my horse the time it takes, and understand that with his age it's not going to be easy—some days are going to be tough and I'll never be able to force it. (Reinventing yourself midlife is *never* easy, apparently—whether you're a horse or a "woman of a certain age.")

"If you're clear about what you want, consistent in doing whatever work it takes, and always honest and authentic with the emotions involved," Barrows said, "it's going to be worth the struggle in the end. He's a good horse, and if you don't give up on him, he's not going to give up on you."

To quote Dr. Sheldon Cooper (and there is a strange resemblance, come to think about it) when he puts one over on an "unsuspecting someone" on television's *The Big Bang Theory*, as I come to this realization in the last pages of this book, I imagine Trace in his stall 7 miles away saying, "Bazinga."

Afterword

The transformation I experienced at the hooves of a horse had a profound effect on my life, connecting me to people, events, and opportunities (like writing this book) I never would have imagined. This is yours to have, as well, midlife sisters. In accepting this call of our authentic souls we open ourselves to adventure designed to stretch our minds, ignite our spirits, and shore up our strength for whatever lies ahead. In reclaiming the horse dreams of our past, we can move forward with the confidence and wisdom our "inner lead mare" awakens within us.

I was out lunging Trace the morning I finished this book, and I sensed the oppressive Texas summer heat might have a small crack in it. Was that the first faint breeze of fall sneaking through?

At my signal, Trace moved around me in a quiet, gentle trot, wearing his saddle (but more important to me, wearing a happy look on his face and a new softness in his eyes, with one ear cocked toward me, waiting to see what we were going to do next), and I realized how far we had come. What's more, as I reflected on the journey my midlife horses had taken me on, I felt a surge of gratitude. From the people I'd met, to the conversations I'd had, to the things I'd learned, I never would have seen any of it from the back of a different horse. As I dug for answers to the many questions Rio and Trace raised, not only in my horsemanship, but also in my life and self, I was suddenly aware of all they had taught me.

When I put my foot in the stirrup for this ride to midlife authenticity, it's probably best that I had no idea what the journey would entail. But I can say without question that it's been a path worth taking, and it's far from over yet.

Resources &
Selected Bibliography

Products, services, and sources mentioned in this book were simply the result of my own research—and so the resources I've included here are in no way exhaustive. Mostly, I just want to share what I found and give you some ideas of how and where to look for your own answers. In fact, if you know of additional resources that you find indispensable in any of these areas, I'll gladly add them to the resources section of the Midlife Horses online community (www.smartwomansguidetomidlifehorses.com).

Resources in this list include those used in the creation of this book (note I have not listed them in traditional bibliographic format for ease of use—instead, you'll find contact and purchasing information where applicable) as well as related materials for further exploration and those recommend by experts I consulted. I've listed them by topic in order of appearance in the book. Please remember that listing here neither specifically endorses nor assumes liability, on the part of the author or the publisher, for the use or outcomes involved with any of these products, ideas, or services.

BOOKS

Finding Your Soul's Calling
Age Is Just a Number by Dara Torres with Elizabeth Weil (Crown Archetype, 2009)
The Age of Miracles by Marianne Williamson (Hay House, 2008)
Finding Your Own North Star by Martha Beck (Crown Publishers, 2001)
The Joy Diet by Martha Beck (Crown Archetype, 2003)
Simple Abundance by Sarah Ban Breathnach (Grand Central Publishing, 2009)
Steering by Starlight by Martha Beck (Rodale Books, 2008)

Understanding Communication between Horses and Humans
The Book of Creation: An Introduction to Celtic Spirituality by J. Philip Newell (Paulist Press, 1999)
The Highly Sensitive Person by Elaine Aron, PhD (Broadway Books, 1997)
Horse Sense and the Human Heart by Adele von Rust McCormick, PhD and Marlena Deborah McCormick, PhD (HCI, 1997)
Horses and the Mystical Path by Adele von Rust McCormick, PhD, Marlena Deborah McCormick, PhD, and Thomas E McCormick, MD (New World Library, 2004)
Horses Never Lie by Mark Rashid (Skyhorse Publishing, 2011)
The Language of Emotions by Karla McLaren (Sounds True, Inc, 2010)
Listening for the Heartbeat of God by J. Philip Newell (Paulist Press, 1997)
On Horsemanship by Xenophon (Book Jungle, 2007)
Reflections on Equestrian Art by Nuno Oliveira (J.A. Allen, 1988)
Riding Between the Worlds by Linda Kohanov (New World Library, 2007)
The Royal Horse of Europe by Sylvia Loch (J.A. Allen, 1986)
She Flies Without Wings by Mary Midkiff (Delta, 2002)
Sometimes a Woman Needs a Horse by Betsy Talcott Kelleher (Pleasant Word, 2004)
Talking with Horses by Henry Blake (Souvenir Press, 2007)
The TAO of Equus by Linda Kohanov (New World Library, 2001)
Thinking with Horses by Henry Blake (Souvenir Press, 2007)
Waking the Tiger by Peter Levine, PhD (North Atlantic Books, 1997)
The Way of the Horse by Linda Kohanov (New World Library, 2007)
What Horses Say by Anna Clemence Mews and Julie Dicker (Trafalgar Square Books, 2004)
When the Heart Waits by Sue Monk Kidd (HarperOne, 2006)
Why We Ride by Verna Dreisbach (Seal Press, 2010)
Of Women and Horses by GaWaNi PonyBoy (BowTie Press, 2000)

Equine-Assisted Therapies & Learning
The 5 Dysfunctions of a Team by Patrick Lencioni (Jossey-Bass, 2002)
Chosen by a Horse by Susan Richards (Mariner Books, 2007)
Connecting with Horses by Margrit Coates and Linda Kohanov (Ulysses Press, 2008)
Considering the Horse by Mark Rashid (Skyhorse Publishing, 2010)
The Horse Boy by Rupert Isaacson (Little, Brown and Company, 2009)
Horses Don't Lie by Chris Irwin and Bob Weber (Marlow & Co., 2001)
Horsemanship through Life by Mark Rashid (Spring Creek Press, 2005)
Planning Your Business in the 'Horse as Healer/Teacher' Professions by Ariana Strozzi (BookSurge Publishing, 2009)

Making Time & Making Choices
The 4-Hour Workweek by Timothy Ferriss (Crown Archetype, 2009)
10-10-10: A LifeTransforming Idea by Suzy Welch (Scribner, 2009)
Making Choices by Alexandra Stoddard (Harper Paperbacks, 1995)
Making It All Work by David Allen (Penguin, 2009)
Stand Up for Your Life by Cheryl Richardson (Free Press, 2003)

Health & Fitness
Fitness, Performance, and the Female Equestrian by Mary Midkiff (Howell Book House, 1996)
Flexibility and Fitness for Riders by Richenda van Laun and Sylvia Loch (J.A. Allen, 2000)
Learning to Ride as an Adult by Erika Prockl (Cadmos Books, 2003)
Riding for Life by Rallie McAllister (Eclipse Press, 2007)
Yoga for Equestrians by Linda Benedik and Veronica Wirth (Trafalgar Square Books, 2000)

Horse Care & Health
All Horse Systems Go by Nancy Loving, DVM (Trafalgar Square Books, 2006)
Eco-Horsekeeping by Lucinda Dyer (Trafalgar Square Books, 2009)
Feed Your Horse Like a Horse by Juliet Getty, PhD (Dog Ear Publishing, 2009)
The Horse by J. Warren Evans, Anthony Borton, Harold Hintz, and L. Dale Van Vleck (W.H. Freeman, 1990)
Horse Economics by Catherine O'Brien, CPA (Trafalgar Square Books, 2005)
Horse Housekeeping by Margaret and Michael Korda (William Morrow, 2005)
Making Natural Hoof Care Work for You by Pete Ramey (Star Ridge Publishers, 2005)

Tack & Equipment
The Horse's Pain-Free Back and Saddle-Fit Book by Joyce Harman, DVM, MRCVS (Trafalgar Square Books, 2004)
The Western Horse's Pain-Free Back and Saddle-Fit Book by Joyce Harman, DVM, MRCVS (Trafalgar Square Books, 2008)

Horse Training & Riding
The Art of Horsemanship by Xenophon (CreateSpace 2009)
Beyond a Whisper by Ryan Gingerich (Trafalgar Square Books, 2010)
The Cavalry Manual of Horsemanship and Horsemastership by Gordon Wright (Doubleday Books, 1962)
Centered Riding by Sally Swift (Trafalgar Square Books, 1987)
Clinton Anderson's Downunder Horsemanship by Clinton Anderson with Ami Hendrickson (Trafalgar Square Books, 2004)
Clinton Anderson's Ground Manners Short Course by Clinton Anderson with Jennifer Forsberg Meyer (Primedia Equine Network)
Clinton Anderson's Lessons Well Learned by Clinton Anderson with Melinda (Kaitcer) Folse (Trafalgar Square Books, 2009)
For the Good of the Rider by Mary Wanless (Trafalgar Square Books, 1999)
Gallop to Freedom by Magali Delgado and Frédéric Pignon with David Walser (Trafalgar Square Books, 2009)
Getting in TTouch with Your Horse by Linda Tellington-Jones with Sybil Taylor (Trafalgar Square Books, 2009)
In the Company of Horses by Kathleen Lindley (Johnson Books, 2006)
Lyons on Horses by John Lyons with Sinclair Browning (Skyhorse Publishing, 2009)
Natural Horse-Man-Ship by Pat Parelli (Western Horseman, 2003)
The Revolution in Horsemanship by Dr. Robert Miller and Rick Lamb (Lyons Press, 2005)
Ride the Journey by Chris Cox with Cynthia McFarland (Western Horseman, 2008)
Think Harmony with Horses by Ray Hunt, Millie Hunt, and Roy Hunt (Pioneer Publishing Company, 1995)
True Unity by Tom Dorrance (Give-It-a-Go Enterprises, 1987)
The Ultimate Horse Behavior and Training Book by Linda Tellington-Jones with Bobbie Lieberman (Trafalgar Square Books, 2006)
The United States Pony Club Manual(s) of Horsemanship (Beginning, Intermediate, Advanced) by Susan E. Harris (Howell Book House, 1994–1996)
Whole Heart, Whole Horse by Mark Rashid (Skyhorse Publishing, 2009)

DVDS

Amy Bento
NRG Fitness DVDs
www.nrgfitness.net

Clinton Anderson
Fundamentals series
Horsemanship 101 series
Trouble-Free Trailering
www.downunderhorsemanship.com

David Genedek
About Saddle Fit
www.aboutthehorse.com

Ian Francis
Foundation Training series
www.downunderhorsemanhip.com

Joyce Harman, DVM, MRCVS
English Saddles and *Western Saddles*
www.harmanyequine.com

Linda Tellington-Jones
Hit It Off with Your Horse!
www.horseandriderbooks.com

Peter Campbell
Horsemanship—The Art of Being a Rider
Horsemanship—Everyday Basics
www.petercampbellhorsemanship.com

Ray Hunt
Colt Starting with Ray Hunt
Ray Hunt Appreciation Clinic
Back to the Beginning with Ray Hunt
www.rayhunt.com

Tom Dorrance
A Day with Tom Dorrance
Visits with Tom
Feel, Balance, and Timing
www.tomdorrance.com

LIFE COACHES, SEMINARS, INSTITUTES, & RETREATS

Equine Studies Institute
Deb Bennett, PhD
Classes, clinics, seminars
www.equinestudies.org

Hacienda Tres Aquilas
Drs. Deborah, Tom, and Adele McCormick, of the
Institute for Conscious Awareness, a non-profit organization for human development and transformation
www.therapyhorsesandhealing.com

Kathleen Ingram
Life coach, consultant, holistic counselor, equine-
assisted therapist
www.sacredplaceofpossibility.com

Koelle Simpson
Workshops, personal coaching, equus coaching
www.koelleinc.com

Linda Kohanov
Epona Equestrian Services
Workshops, leadership programs, team-building,
horse training
www.taoofequus.com

Marianne Williamson
Life coach, workshops
www.marianne.com

Martha Beck
Creating Your Right Life
Life coach, workshops
www.marthabeck.com

Mary Midkiff
AWARE (A Woman's Approach to Riding
Effectively) Clinics
www.womenandhorses.com

TRAINERS & CLINICIANS

Clinton Anderson
Downunder Horsemanship
Stephenville, Texas
www.downunderhorsemanship.com

Denise Barrows
Practical Equine Solutions
Fort Worth, Texas
www.practicalequinesolutons.com

Everett Mrakava
Alberta, Canada
Email: mrakavaranches@yahoo.com

Kathleen Lindley
Cheyenne, Wyoming
www.kathleenlindley.com

Linda Tellington-Jones
The Tellington Method
Santa Fe, NM
www.ttouch.com

Liz Graves
Gathering Gaits
Spring Valley, Minnesota
www.lizgraves.com

Pat Parelli
Natural Horse Training Method
Pagosa Springs, Colorado
www.parellinaturalhorsetraining.com

Peter Campbell
Wheatland, Wyoming
www.petercampbellhorsemanship.com

WEBSITES & BLOGS

Equine-Assisted Therapy & Learning

Equest Therapeutic Horsemanship
www.equest.org

Equine Assisted Learning and Growth Association (EAGALA)
www.eagala.org

HerdWise, LLC
www.herdwise.com

North American Riding for the Handicapped Association (NARHA)
www.narha.org

R.E.A.C.H. (Riding Equines to Achieve Confidence and Health) Therapeutic Riding Center
http://reachtrc.org

Fitness & Health

Bikram Yoga
www.bikramyoga.com

Fitness High
www.fitnesshigh.com

Women & Horses™ Fitness and Performance Program
www.womenandhorses.com

Horse Rescue & Adoption

CANTER (The Communication Alliance to Network Thoroughbred Ex-Racehorses)
www.canterusa.org

Equine Adoption Center
www.thehorse.com

Ever After Mustang Rescue
www.mustangrescue.org

Habitat for Horses
www.habitatforhorses.org

Kindred Spirits Animal Sanctuary
www.kindredspiritsnm.org

LOPE (LoneStar Outreach to Place Ex-Racers)
www.lopetx.org

Lifesavers Wild Horse Rescue
www.wildhorserescue.org

New Vocations Racehorse Adoption
www.horseadoption.com

Unwanted Horse Coalition
www.unwantedhorsecoalition.org

Camping & Tours

Camping and Horses
www.campingandhorses.com

Equitours
www.ridingtours.com

Hidden Trails Equestrian Holidays
www.hiddentrails.com

High Pointe International Equestrian Tours
www.equestrian-vacations.com

Horse Trail Directory
www.horsetraildirectory.com

Horseback Riding and Ranch Vacations
www.riding-vacations.info

Horseback Riding Vacations Worldwide
www.ridingworld.com

Real Adventures
www.realadventures.com

Horse Activities & Disciplines

American Competitive Trail Riders Association (ACTHA)
www.actha.us

American Cutting Horse Association (ACHA)
www.achacutting.org

American Driving Society
www.americandrivingsociety.org

American Endurance Riding Conference (AERC)
www.aerc.org

Cowboy Mounted Shooting Association (CMSA)
www.cowboymountedshooting.com

Fox Hunt Virginia
www.foxhuntva.com

Masters of Foxhounds Association of America (MFHA)
www.mfha.org

National Barrel Horse Association (NBHA)
www.nbha.com

National Cutting Horse Association (NCHA)
www.nchacutting.com

National Pole Bending Association (NPBA)
www.polebending.org

National Reined Cow Horse Association (NRCHA)
www.nrcha.com

National Reining Horse Association (NRHA)
www.nrha.com

National Saddle Club Association (NSCA) O-Mok-See Competition
www.omoksee.com

North American Trail Ride Conference (NATRC)
www.natrc.org

Ranch Sorting National Championships (RSNC)
www.rsnc.us

United States Dressage Federation (USDF)
www.usdf.org

United States Equestrian Federation (USEF)
www.usef.org

United States Team Penning Association (USTPA)
www.ustpa.com

United States Team Roping Championships (USTRC)
www.ustrc.com

Horse Care & Management

AgriLife Extension Disaster Resources Database
http://texaseden.org/disaster-resources/category/preparedness-and-mitigation-information/for-animals/

American Association of Equine Practitioners (AAEP)
www.aaep.org

American Association of Natural Hoof Care Practitioners (AANHCP)
www.aanhcp.net

American Farrier's Association
www.americanfarriers.org

American Hoof Association (AHA)
http://americanhoofassociation.org

EasyCare, Inc.
www.easycareinc.com

Equine Podiatry Association (UK
www.epauk.org

eZall® Bio-Based Horse Care Products
www.ezall.com

The Horse's Hoof
www.thehorseshoof.com

How to Go Organic
www.howtogoorganic.com/index.php?page=pasture-management

La Pierre Performance Hoof Care and the International Institute of Equine Podiatry
www.equinepodiatry.net

Matt Taimuty, CJF
www.fairhillforge.com

Natural Balance Hoofcare
www.hopeforsoundness.com

Pasture Place
www.pastureplace.com

Tribe Equus
www.tribeequus.com

Tack & Equipment

David Genadek, Master Saddle Maker
www.aboutthehorse.com

McDaniel Custom Saddles
www.mcdanielsaddles.com

Myler Bits
www.mylerbitsusa.com

US Rider
www.usrider.org

Trainers & Instructors

American Association of Horsemanship Safety (AAHS)
www.horsemanshipsafety.com

American Riding Instructor Association (ARIA)
www.riding-instructor.com

Certified Horsemanship Association (CHA)
www.cha-ahse.org

Equine Studies Institute
www.equinestudiesinstitute.com

General Information & Good Reading

All About Horses
www.allabouthorses.com

Elizabeth Graves' Blog
http://elizabethgraves.blogspot.com

Free Equestrian Classifieds Worldwide
www.equineonline.net

O Horse! International Horse Directory
www.ohorse.com

The Stories, Challenges, and Adventures of a 50+ Rider
www.50plushorses.blogspot.com

ARTICLES

"Choose the Right Truck" by Neva Kittrell Scheve, online article, http://horses.about.com/od/basiccare/a/towingvehicles.htm

"Dressage Saddle Fit Importance" by Heather Smith Thomas, online article, http://www.equisearch.com/horses_riding_training/english/dressage/saddlefit_081904

"Equestrian Weight Lifting and Strength Training" by Linda Leistman, President of the North American Horseman's Association (NAHA), online article, www.fitnesshigh.com

"Equine Economics: Optimizing Horse Health and Management on a Budget," by Julie Wilson, DVM, and Krishona Martinson, PhD, University of Minnesota, downloadable PDF http://www.extension.umn.edu/distribution/livestocksystems/DI8645.pdf

"Get Going Showing" by Jennifer Forsberg Meyer, *Horse&Rider*, January 2010

"Hay and Pasture Management" by the United States Department of Agriculture Natural Resources Conservation Service, Columbia, Missori, downloadable PDF, http://plant-materials.nrcs.usda.gov/pubs/mopmcarestwsgrs.pdf

"Horse Trailer Safety Information" by EquiSpirit, online article, http://www.equispirit.com/info/faq.htm

"How to Safely Pull a Horse Trailer" by Kimberly Sharp, online article, http://www.ehow.com/how_5764514_safely-pull-horse-trailer.html

"Learn How to Do the Emergency Dismount" by Stacy Westfall with Jennifer Forsberg-Meyer, online article, http://www.equisearch.com/horses_riding_training/training/beginning_rider/learn_emergency_dismount_070910

"Minutes to a Fitter You" by Helen Peppe, *Practical Horseman*, March 2010

"Online Budget Tools for Horse Owners Offered by UK College of Agriculture" by Jill Stowe, PhD, University of Kentucky, online article, www.bloodhorse.com/horse-racing/articles/60363/online-budget-tools-for-horse-owners-offered-by-uk-college-of-agricultureine.net/

"Ring of Muscles Revisited" by Deb Bennett, PhD downloadable PDF, http://www.equinestudies.org/ring_revisited_2008/ring_of_muscles_2008_pdf.pdf

"Stacy Westfall on Saddle Fit" by Stacy Westfall, *Horse&Rider*, January 2010

"Truckin' and Trailerin'" by Gavin Ehringer, *Horse&Rider*, July 2010

"Who's Built Best to Ride" by Deb Bennett, PhD downloadable PDF, http://www.equinestudies.org/whos_built_best_2008/whos_built_best_2008_pdf1.pdf

Index

Acepromazine (Ace), 188
Acid detergent fiber (ADF), 172
Activities. *See* Riding activities
Aerobics, 62–63
Age. *See also* Midlife
*Age Is Just a Number: Achieve
    Your Dreams at Any Stage in Life*
    (Torres and Weil), 9
*The Age of Miracles: Embracing the
    New Midlife* (Williamson), 3
Alfalfa, 172
All Horse Systems Go (Loving), 179
Allen, David, 47, 49
Allen, J.A., 57
American Association of Equine
    Practitioners (AAEP), 105–106,
    182–183
American Association of
    Horsemanship Safety (AAHS),
    255
American Competitive Trail Riders
    Association (ACTHA), 86–87
American Farriers Association
    (AFA), 193
American Riding Instructor
    Association (ARIA), 255
Anderson, Clinton
    Clinton Anderson Signature
        Horse, 18
    on deworming, 186–187
    on grooming, 162
    groundwork and, 73–74
    Horsemanship 101 DVD series,
        114–115
    as instructor, 240
    Lessons Well Learned, 304–305
    loading horse into trailer,
        235–238
    on natural hoof care, 195–196
    on purchasing horse, 122
    on rescue horses, 102–103
    on riding/training time,
        164–165
    safety tips of, 280–281
    on time committment for horse
        ownership, 118
    training DVDs of, 248–249
    and wheelchair-bound
        horsewomen, 22–23
Anger, Survey Your Relationship
    Patterns (exercise), 21
Aron, Elaine, 16
Authenticity
    decision-making and, 40
    and moving to the country,
        161–162

need for, 3
personal inauthenticity and, 21
and successful horsemanship,
    308–309
Autism, 24

Balance. *See* Conditioning exercises
    (for rider)
Banamine®, 188
Barnett, Andrea, 215
Barns. *See also* Facilities
    building considerations,
        146–149
    fencing and, 149–150
    pens/paddocks and, 150–151
    scheduling of cleaning, 163
Barrel racing, 90–91
Barrows, Denise, 303, 305–308
Beck, Martha, 2, 6–7, 133
Bedding, 137
Benedik, Linda, 73
Bennett, Deb, 209
Bento, Amy, 75–76
Beyond a Whisper (Gingerich), 295
Bits, 222–224
Bittel, Ella, 104
Blackmon, Tom, 136–140
Blanketing, 138–139
Boarding horses. *See also* Facilities
    away versus home, 126–129
    bedding and, 137
    blanketing, 138–139
    body condition of other horses,
        137
    community and, 139
    feeding, 138
    insect control, 138
    manure management and,
        137–138, 141
    references for, 139–140
    riding arenas at, 139
    safety and, 136–137
    structural material of facilities,
        137
    tack storage, 139
    tips for successful, 141
    turnout/exercise at, 139
    ventilation, 138
    water, 138
Body condition scoring (BCS),
    178–179
Boundaries, 21, 33
Bowker, Robert, 196
Breathnach, Sarah Ban, 3
Breeds
    breeding/bloodline interest,

106–107
    personalities of, 121
    saddle fit and conformation,
        208–209
    for saddle seat, 99
Bridles, 224–225
Brown, Rita Mae, 89
Business world
    EAL and, 29–32
    horses and CEOs, 33
    team-building and horses,
        30–31
Bute, 188

Calcium/magnesium balance and
    calcium/phosphorus balance, 173
Calf roping, 100
Campbell, Peter, 262–263
Carriage driving, 93
Castillo, Jolene, 102–104
Catastrophe theory, 270
Cattle, working, 80–81, 100–101
Cerebral palsy, 24–26
Certified Horsemanship Association
    (CHA), 24–26, 87–88, 255, 257
Certified Journeyman Farrier (CJF),
    192
Chisholm Trail Challenge, 23
Clinics, 249–255
Clinton Anderson Signature Horse,
    18
Cole, Mark, 233
Communication
    barn notice boards for, 161
    directory of contacts, 159–161
    with farrier, 194–195
    horse communicators, 288–295
    Taylor, Kathy on, 31
    and tips for successful
        boarding, 141
    with veterinarians, 191
Competitions. *See* Horse shows
Competitive Trail Challenge (CTC),
    86–87
Concentrates, 173–174
Conditioning exercises (for rider)
    alignment and, 72
    barn chores as, 74–75
    benefits, 75–76
    cross-training, 58–59, 71–74
    *Fitness, Performance, and the
        Female Equestrian* (Midkiff),
        58, 69–70
    importance of, 55–56, 77
    lower back/pelvic, 69–70
    nutrition and, 76

pelvic circles, 70
pelvic tilts, 70–71
personal programs for, 60–61
personal trainers for, 59–60
riding as fitness, 58
for seat, 67–68
side to side, 71
swinging circles for shoulders/
elbows/wrists, 69
targeting muscle groups,
63–64
for thoracic girdle, 68–69
Conformation
bars/palate/tongue of mouth,
222–223
halter class, 94
saddle fit and, 208–209
Connected Riding®/Connected
Groundwork®, 264
Control, 21
Costs
farrier, 193
feed/vet care/boarding,
131–132
methods for budgeting,
132–133
purchase price, 130–131
veterinary, 182
Country life
directory of contacts, 159–161
examples, 140, 142–144
farm/ranch equipment,
158–159
pasture management and,
151–156
Cowboy mounted shooting, 94–96
Cowboy Mounted Shooting
Association®, 94
Cross-training, 58–59, 71–74. *See
also* Conditioning exercises (for
rider)
Crude protein (CP), 172, 174
Crunches, 65–66
Cummings, Peggy, 264
Curb bits, 223–224
Cutting/penning, 80–81, 96

Dante, 2
A Day with Tom Dorrance DVD
(Maravilla Productions), 297–298
Decision-making, 35–36, 38–40, 51
Delgado, Magali, 293
Deworming, 184–187
Dial, Greg, 73
Dicker, Julie, 292, 296
Disabled riders
autism, 24
cerebral palsy, 24–26
non-mounted activities, 50
wheelchair-bound, 22–23
"Discovering That Journey Called
Horsemanship" (Graves), 267
Divine force, 43–44
Dorrance, Tom, 243, 262, 296–301

Downunder Horsemanship Method,
18. *See also* Anderson, Clinton
Dreams, into reality, 1–2
Dressage, 77, 96, 282
Drugs, 188
Dyer, Lucinda, 154

Eastern encephalitis (EE), 184
Eco-Horsekeeping (Dyer), 154
Education. *See also* Anderson,
Clinton
becoming student of the
horse, 50
choice of method for rider,
242–244
choosing instructors/trainers,
255–260
clinics, 249–255
EAL and, 27–29
importance of lucidity/
consistency/control, 306–308
knowledge types and horses,
261
lessons, 50
reading horse expressions,
300–301
self-paced study, 244–249
therapeutic riding and teaching,
24–25
trainer agreements, 260–261
TV/websites for, 107
Ehringer, Gavin, 229
Electric fences, 150
Emotional intelligence (EQ), EAL
and, 29–30
Encephalitis (sleeping sickness),
183–184
Endurance/competitive trail riding,
97
Equest, 25
"Equestrian Weight Lifting and
Strength Training" (Leistman), 63
Equine-assisted activities and
therapies (EAAT), 20, 22
Equine Assisted Growth and
Learning Association (EAG-ALA),
28
Equine-assisted learning (EAL),
27–29, 29–32
Equine-assisted psychotherapy
(EAP), 27–29
"Equine Experience" (Hacienda Tres
Aguilas), 12–13
Equine massage therapy, 41
Eventing, 97
Exercises. *See also* Conditioning
exercises (for rider)
Awaken Your Horse Sense, 15
Create An Action Plan of
Small, Accomplishable Steps,
277–278
Create Your Saddle Wish List,
219
Factor Your (Horse) Joy

Dividend, 133
Find Your "Dream Clinic", 251
Find Your Soul Values, 41
How to Get the Most from a
Training Book, Article, or
DVD, 245–248
Locate Your "Joy", 5
Processing New Information
in a Learning-Intensive
Environment, 254
Recapture Your Day, 48
Start Clearing Your Own Trail,
45
Survey Your Relationship
Patterns, 21
Tracking the Causes of Pain and
the Harbingers of Joy, 46
Visualize Success-With All Your
Senses, 277–278
What Are You Afraid Of?,
276–277
What Are Your Goals?,
274–275
What Can You Do" How Well
Can You Do It?, 275–276
What You Really, **Really**
Want, 5
"Who's Your Horsie?", 121
Why Do You Ride?, 274

Facilities
amount of land, 144–145
bedding and, 137
blanketing, 138–139
boarding, 126–128
community and, 139
decisions regarding, 124–126
feeding, 138
home/"hands-on", 128–129
human housing, 145–146
insect control, 138
manure management and,
137–138, 141
references for, 139–140
riding arenas at, 139
scheduling of cleaning, 163
shelters/barns, 146–148
structural material of, 137
tack storage, 139
turnout/exercise at, 139
ventilation, 138, 147–148
water, 138
Farrier. *See* Hoof care
Fear
catastrophe theory, 271
overcoming, 35–36
safe habits, 279–284
Survey Your Relationship
Patterns (exercise), 21
understanding, 271–279
Fédération Equestre Internationale
(FEI), 99
Feed Your Horse Like a Horse
(Getty), 170, 174, 177, 179

Feeding. *See also* Nutrition
  boarding horses, 138
  horse treats (Ice Pops), 157
  scheduling of, 162
Fencing, 149–150
Ferress, Timothy, 45–46
Finch, Jerry, 103
Finding Your Own North Star
  (Beck), 2
First aid. *See* Injuries
*Fitness, Performance, and the
  Female Equestrian* (Midkiff), 58,
  69–70
The 5 Dysfunctions of a Team
  (Lencioni), 30
Flare, 211
Flexibility and Fitness for Riders
  (Allen), 57
Flunixin meglumine, 188
Focusing, 10, 119
Forages. *See* Nutrition
Forsberg, Jennifer, 92
Fort Worth Horseshoe club, 136
The 4-Hour Workweek (Ferress),
  45–46
Foxhunting, 89–90
Foxhunting Mystery Series (Brown), 89
Francis, Ian, 223, 284
Full lease, 114

Gallop to Freedom (Delgado and
  Pignon), 293
Genadek, David, 208–211
"Get Going Showing" (Forsberg),
  92
Getty, Juliet, 169–171, 174, 177, 179
Getting in TTouch with Your Horse
  (Tellington-Jones), 294
Gingerich, Ryan, 295
For the Good of the Rider
  (Wanless), 270
Grass hay, 172
Graves, Liz, 83–85, 156–157,
  263–267
Grooming
  safety and, 281
  scheduling of, 162
  teeth/sheaths and, 189
Groundwork, 116, 119
Gullet, 211
Gymkhanas, 90–92

Habitat for Horses, 102–104
Hacienda Tres Aguilas (San Antonio,
  Texas), 12–13
Hardin, Jackie, 102
Hatha yoga, 62
Hatley, George, 88
Healing, 19–20, 33
Health. *See also* Veterinarians
  deworming, 184–187
  first aid, 185, 187–188
  teeth/sheaths and, 189
  vaccinations, 183–184

Helmets, 282
Henneke Body Condition Scoring
  System, 178–179
HerdWise, LLC, 27, 29, 33
The Highly Sensitive Person (Aron),
  16
Hippotherapy, 20, 24–26
Hoof care
  choosing a farrier, 190–194
  cleaning/inspecting hooves,
  200–201
  scheduling of, 162
Horse camping, 87–88
Horse Camping (Hatley), 88
Horse care, basic ownership skills
  for, 116–117
Horse Economics (O'Brien), 132
Horse Housekeeping (Korda and
  Korda), 144–145, 148, 152, 225
Horse shows
  attending, 50
  carriage driving, 93
  choice of discipline for, 92–93
  conformation (halter), 94
  cowboy mounted shooting,
  94–96
  cutting, 96
  dressage, 96
  endurance/competitive trail
  riding, 97
  eventing, 97
  hunt seat equitation (on flat/
  over fences), 97–98
  hunter (under saddle/over
  fences), 98
  jumpers, 98
  ranch sorting, 98
  reining, 98–99
  saddle seat, 99
  showmanship, 99
  team penning, 99
  team roping/calf roping, 100
  trail, 100
  western horsemanship, 100
  western pleasure, 100
  working cowhorse, 100–101
Horse treats, 157
Horsemanship 101 DVD series
  (Anderson), 114–115, 120
Hunt, Ray, 262
Hunt seat equitation (on flat/over
  fences), 97–98
Hunter (under saddle/over fences),
  98
Hunting, 52

Ingram, Katherine, 16
Injuries
  basic ownership skills and, 117
  first aid, 185, 187–188
Inner strength, beginning questions
  for, 34
Insect control, 138, 154

Jackson, Kelly, 18
Johnson, Matt, 271–279
Joy, 5–7, 46
Jumpers, 98

Keyhole race, 91
Kidd, Sue Monk, 16–17
Kindred Spirits Animal Sanctuary,
  104
Kohanov, Linda, 14–16, 120, 243
Korda, Margaret, 144–145, 148,
  152, 225
Korda, Michael, 144–145, 148,
  152, 225
Kutz, Emily, 41–42

Lamb, Rick, 196, 222, 241
Laminitis, 201
The Language of Emotions
  (McLaren), 16
Lead mare
  "inner lead mare mentality", 14
  Xenophon on, 17
Learning to Ride as an Adult
  (Prockl), 67–68
Leasing horses, 112–114
Legged up, 55
Legume hay, 172
Leistman, Linda, 63
Lencioni, Patrick, 30
Lessons. *See also* Education
  costs of, 132
  importance of, 111–112
  Lead Mare Lesson, 14
  minimal, 50
Lessons Well Learned (Anderson),
  304–305
Levine, Peter, 16
Lighting/electricity in barns, 148
Loading horse into trailer, 235–238
Logan, Jill, 216
LOPE (LoneStar Outreach to Place
  Ex-Racers), 53
Loving, Nancy, 179
Lunges, 66
Lunging, 239–240
Lyons, John, 281

Making Choices (Stoddard), 42–43
Making It All Work (Allen), 47, 49
*Making Natural Hoof Care Work for
  You* (Ramey), 196
Manure, 137–138, 141, 154–155
Massage, 41
McCormick, Adele von Rust, 12
McCormick, Deborah
  on becoming student of the
  horse, 50, 243, 262
  on horses and honesty, 17
  horses as healers, 19–20
  "inner lead mare" and, 12-14
McCormick, Tom, 12
McDaniel, Ron/McDaniel Saddlery,
  210, 218

McLaren, Karla, 16
Mews, Anna Clemence, 292
Meyer, Forsberg, 92
Midkiff, Mary, 58, 69–70, 72
Midlife
    determination of wants, 4
    dreams into reality, 1–2
    stories, 18, 22–23
    traditional thoughts as
        outdated, 7
Miller, Robert, 196, 208, 222, 241
Minerals, 174–175
"Minutes to a Fitter You" (Peppe),
    74
Mirroring
    example of, 18
    fear and, 286
    human characteristics in horses,
        15–17
    Survey Your Relationship
        Patterns (exercise), 21
    Taylor, Kathy on, 29
    Thigpen, Carol on, 32–34
Molds, 175
Mountain Horse Incorporated, 88
Mrakava, Everett, 262–263,
    288–289
Multitasking, 48
Mycotoxins, 175
Myler Bits, 222

Neil, Buck, 181–187
Neutral detergent fiber (NDF), 173
Nin, Anaïs, 16
"No", how to say, 42–44, 48
Non-fibrous carbohydrates (NFC),
    173
Non-mounted activities, 22,
    106–108
Non-steroidal anti-inflammatory
    drugs (NSAIDS), 188
Non-structural carbohydrates (NSC),
    173
North American Horseman's
    Association (NAHA), 63
North American Riding for the
    Handicapped Association
    (NARHA), 20
Nutrition
    and activity level of horse,
        179–181
    amount of feed necessary,
        176–178
    concentrates and, 173–174
    feed labels, 174
    feeding "easy keeper", 179
    feeding "hard keeper", 180
    forages, 171–173
    hay value, 172–173
    and hoof care, 202–203
    and horse digestive system,
        170–171
    horse treats, 157
    minerals/salt and, 175

toxic molds, 175
types of feed, 171–172

O'Brien, Catherine, 132
Olympics, 96–98
Online horse communities,
    106–108
Online horse/tack/trailer deals, 107
Ownership
    horses without, 110–111
    leasing horses, 112–114
    necessary skills for, 116–117
    time committment for, 117–119

Paddocks, 150, 163
Parelli, Pat, 28–29
Parkinson's Law, 46–47
Pasture management
    foul weather and, 155–156
    grasses/grazing, 151–152
    maintenance, 151–153
    manure management and,
        154–155
    water and, 153
Pat Parelli Natural Horse Training
    Method, 28–29
Peppe, Helen, 74
Phenylbutazone, 188
Physical fitness. *See* Conditioning
    exercises (for rider)
Pignon, Frédéric, 293
Pilates, 59, 62
Pole bending, 91
Pony Club, 51–53
Positive attitude, 9
Power via inner strength, 13–14
Practical Equine Solutions, 305
Problems
    digestive, 170
    encephalitis, 183–184
    habits of safety to alleviate,
        280–281
    hoof care, 200–201
    poor saddle fit, 216–218,
        220–221
    rabies, 183
    shoeing, 197–199
    tetanus toxoid, 183
    West Nile Virus, 184
Prockl, Erika, 67–68
Professional Bull Riding Association
    (PBR), 23
Proust, Marcel, 41
Proust Questionnaire, 41
Psychology, mirroring and, 15–17
Psychotherapy, McCormicks and,
    12–14
Purchasing a horse
    first horse, 119–124
    importance of being true to
        oneself in, 52–53
    impulsiveness and, 35–36
    qualities of leased horse,
        113–114

Pushups, 65

Rabies, 183
Ramey, Pete, 195–196
Ramsey, Lisa, 22–23
Ranch sorting, 98
Rashid, Mark, 30
REACH (Riding Equines to Achieve
    Confidence and Health)
    Therapeutic Riding Center, 26
Reining, 98–99, 100–101
Relationships. *See also*
    Communication
    horse communicators and,
        292–296
    importance of, 243
    importance of horses for,
        27–29, 33
    women and horses, 11, 69–72
Relative feed value (RFV), 173
Rescue horses, 101–104
The Revolution in Horsemanship
    (Miller and Lamb), 196–197
RFD-TV, 102–103
Richardson, Cheryl, 43
Riding activities
    barrel racing, 90–91
    as basic ownership skill, 116
    cutting/penning, 80–81
    for disabled riders, 22–26, 50
    foxhunting, 89–90
    gymkhanas, 90–92
    horse camping, 87–88
    horse shows. *See* Horse shows
    keyhole race, 91
    and need for conditioning
        exercises for rider. *See*
        Conditioning exercises (for
        rider)
    pole bending, 91
    stake race, 91–92
    trail riding, 83–87
    without having horses,
        106–108
Riding arenas, 139
Riding Between the Worlds
    (Kohanov), 14–16, 120
Riding lessons. *See* Education
"Ring of Muscles" (Bennett), 209
Rock(er), 211
Roping, 100

Saddle seat, 99
Saddles. *See also* Tack
    bars/panels of, 210–211
    choice of, 82–83, 206-208
    Create Your Saddle Wish List
        (exercise), 219
    English fit, 214–216
    rigging/billet system of,
        211–212
    seating system of, 212–213
    skirting system/sweat flap
        of, 213

tree of, 209–210
    Western fit, 213–214
Safety. *See also* Fear
    of barns, 147
    helmets, 282
    practices of, 282
    for veterinarians, 189–190
Salt, 175
Scheduling
    barn/horsekeeping routines,
        162–165
    for conditioning exercises for
        rider, 56, 64–66
    horse dates, 50
    how to make time/room for
        horses, 45–47, 109
    methods for, 47, 49
    personal fitness, 60–63
    Recapture Your Day, 48
    riding/training time, 164–165
    time committment for horse
        ownership, 117–119
Scrima, Carrie, 86
Self-management
    and art of saying "no", 42–44,
        48
    control and, 21
    giving up something for horse
        purchase, 41–42
    how to make time/room for
        horses, 42–45
    inner strength, 35–36
    soul values of, 41
Septic tanks, 153–154
Share lease, 114
Sheath health, 189
Shoeing. *See* Hoof care
Shooting, cowboy mounted, 94–96
Show jumpers, 98
Showmanship, 99
*Simple Abundance: A Daybook of
    Comfort and Joy* (Breathnach), 3
Smith, Gina, 77
Snaffle bits, 223
Snipe, Melisa, 88
Spirituality, 32–34, 43–44
Squats, 66
Stake race, 91–92
Stalls. *See* Facilities
Stand Up for Your Life (Richardson),
    43
Stock horse, 100–101
Stoddard, Alexandra, 42–43
Student of the horse, 50, 261–262.
    See also Communication

Tack
    boarding facilities and storage
        for, 139
    bridles/bits, 221–225
    care of, 225
    protective helmet/riding gear,
        282, 285
    saddle, 82–83

saddle fit, 208–209, 213–216
saddle pads, 217–218, 220
saddle parts, 209–213
safety and, 281
scheduling and care of, 165
Taimuty, Matt, 192, 200–201
Taylor, Kathy, 27–33
Teaching. *See also* Anderson,
    Clinton; Education
    choosing instructors/trainers,
        255–260
    Dorrance, Tom on, 296–300
    honesty/ethics in, 265–266
    NARHA Instructor Certification
        Course of Equest, 25
    of rider by horse, 124
    therapeutic riding and, 24–25
    trainer agreements, 260–261
Team penning, 99
Team roping/calf roping, 100
Teamwork, EAL and, 30
Technology and horse
    opportunities, 106–108
Teeth health, 189
Tellington-Jones, Linda, 104, 294
Tellington Method®, 104
10-10-10: A Life Transforming Idea,
    38–41, 111
Teskeys Saddle Shop, 215–216
Tetanus toxoid, 183
"The Joy Dividend" (Beck), 133–134
thehorse.com, 106
Therapeutic riding
    autism, 24
    cerebral palsy, 24–26
    EAAT and, 20
    hippotherapy and, 20
    NARHA and, 20, 25
    non-mounted activities, 22, 50
    REACH Therapeutic Riding
        Center, 26
    and wheelchair-bound
        horsewomen, 22–23
Thigpen, Carol, 32–34, 51
"Top 5 Ways that Horses Can Bring
    Teams Together" (Taylor), 33
Torres, Dara, 8–10, 76–77
Trail riding, 83–87, 100
Trailer. *See* Transportation
Training. *See also* Anderson,
    Clinton; Education
    to avoid shoeing problems,
        197–199
    horse communicators and,
        290–296
    re-training, 304–306
Transportation
    backing up trailer, 232
    breakdown tips, 233
    choice of truck/trailer, 229–230
    loading horse into trailer,
        235–238
    safety and, 230–234
    trailer maintenance, 234–235

True Unity (Dorrance), 297
Trust, 30–31, 33
Twist, 211

Unwanted Horse Coalition,
    105–106

Vaccinations, 183–184
VanGetson, Karen, 86
Venezuelan encephalitis (VEE), 184
Ventilation, 138, 147–148
Veterinarians. *See also* Health
    choosing, 181–183
    communication with, 191
    hoof problems, 200–201
    safety and, 189–190

Waking the Tiger (Levine), 16
Wanless, Mary, 270
Water, 138, 148, 153, 162
Weight training, 62
Weil, Elizabeth, 9
Welch, Suzy, 38–41
West Nile Virus, 184
Western encephalitis (WE), 184
Western horsemanship, 100
Western pleasure, 100
Westfall, Stacy, 213, 283
Wheelchair-bound horsewomen,
    22–23
When the Heart Waits (Kidd), 16
Williamson, Marianne, 3, 17
Wirth, Veronica, 73
Women & Horses™, 69–70, 72
Working cowhorse, 80–81,
    100–101
World Equestrian Games, 99

Xenophon, 17

Yoga, 59, 62, 72–74, 279
Yoga for Equestrians (Benedik and
    Wirth), 73